DIRECT ELECTIONS TO THE EUROPEAN PARLIAMENT 1984

DIRECT ELECTIONS TO THE EUROPEAN PARLIAMENT 1984

Edited by

Juliet Lodge
Senior Lecturer in Politics, University of Hull

MACMILLAN

First published 1986

Published by
THE MACMILLAN PRESS LTD
Houndmills, Basingstoke, Hampshire RG21 2XS
and London
Companies and representatives
throughout the world

Printed in Hong Kong

Filmset by Latimer Trend & Company Ltd, Plymouth

British Library Cataloguing in Publication Data
Direct Elections to the European parliament 1984.
1. European Parliament—Elections, 1984
I. Lodge, Juliet
324.94′0558   JN36
ISBN 0–333–34527–4

306311

To David and to Keri-Michèle

Contents

Contents

Preface

The prospect of the second direct elections to the European Parliament (EP) in 1984 generated a host of optimistic and pessimistic expectations about what they would show about the EP's evolution since the first direct elections to the EP in 1979, and about the EP's impact upon the public and the European Community (EC) between 1979 and 1984. From the outset, contrary to the hopes of many Members of the European Parliament (MEPs), there were fears that turnout in 1984 would be less than in 1979 and that, as a result, the EP's less than glowing image would be so damaged as to impair if not negate its quest for greater powers in EC decision-making. Moreover, strenuous efforts had been made – partly through the use of the European Elections Information Programmes – on the eve of the first Euro-elections to inform the voters about the EP's role in the EC. The aim was to persuade them that, notwithstanding the EP's rather limited formal powers, it would nevertheless be worthwhile turning out to vote (if only so one could claim at least to have voted in the first Euro-elections). On the eve of the second Euro-elections, similar efforts had been made though they were less extensive but not necessarily less effective. The presuppositions and hopes attending the second Euro-elections are addressed in the introduction to this book, and the elections are put into the context of the EP's own record which is summarised briefly. This is followed by a chapter that examines the various electoral procedures used in each of the EC's ten member states for the Euro-elections in default of an agreement on a uniform electoral procedure as provided for by Article 138 of the Rome Treaty.

How the Euro-election campaign unfurled is explored through case studies of the elections in each of the Ten. The contributors try to cover, as relevant, a common range of questions. All start, therefore, with a succinct survey of the background to the 1984 EP elections and isolate issues and problems peculiar to a given member state or common to several member states. Where pertinent they take up controversial electoral law issues. However, they focus on the Euro-campaign with reference to the role of the national, supranational and transnational parties and organisations, sitting-MEPs, the media and public opinion before analysing the results. All highlight the problems of mobilising electorates and portraying the EP elections as elections of a different order to general or local elections in the member states. Differences and similarities became apparent in the campaign dynamics. They differed in scale and scope but all member states found it hard to mount sustained campaigns that made clear the EC dimension to the elections. Thus, the case studies highlight the problems deriving from the election of an EP that is not associated, for a number of reasons explored in the introduction and conclusion, with achievement in the EC. It becomes clear that it was not just a matter of the level of information people possessed about the EP, or whether voting was compulsory that determined turnout at the election. In some member states, the public may be relatively ill-informed about the EP, the EC and the elections. In other member states, they have a sophisticated understanding of how the EC works. However, the point of the EP elections was often lost as national parties interpreted the Euro-election as simply another occasion for political jousting. Indeed, this seemed to be the case even in member states seen as among the most pro-EC of the Ten, as the case studies make clear. The conclusion takes up this theme and looks at the results from the EP's standpoint, its composition, preoccupations and future prospects.

All the contributors have tried to ensure that their chapters are intelligible to non-specialists and can be understood by those unfamiliar with the member state in question, the EC itself or the previous EP election. While a comprehensive bibliography has been omitted for space reasons, some books containing useful bibliographies on the EP and Euro-elections are referred to in a bibliographical note at the end of the book. It should be noted also that a lot of material, particularly on the 1979 EP elections, exists in all EC languages and students should consult foreign as well as English language sources. Much but by no means all of the most useful recent literature is cited in notes and references at the end of each chapter.

We thank the Press and Information Offices of the EP throughout the EC, the EP party groups, the transnational federations, MEPs and national parties for providing us with information, election material and manifestos. We are grateful to the numerous officials, sitting-MEPs and prospective MEPs who withstood questioning with good humour.

Additionally, the editor wishes to acknowledge the support of the Nuffield Foundation. Thanks are due also to Ken Newton and the

European Consortium for Political Research for help to convene a Euro-election planning session at the Consortium's Joint Sessions at Salzburg in April 1984, where some chapters were discussed in draft form.

Editing the volume has been a mammoth task partly because few contributors proved either able or willing to follow simple house-style rules, and partly because two of the original contributors had not delivered by September. 'The two Neils' are to be thanked for joining the project in the final phase. Finally, the editor wishes to thank Peter Lodge without whose unfailing support the task could not have been accomplished.

Our experience of the second direct elections to the EP has not robbed us of the belief that a democratically elected EP does have a place in the EC and has an important role to fulfil in the future not least in stimulating debate about the proper compass and purpose of the EC, integration and European Union. We look forward to the third direct elections to the EP in 1989 in a possibly enlarged EC of Twelve. It is to be hoped that by that time some progress will have been made on the outstanding issues of the first direct elections to the EP, such as a uniform electoral procedure, a single EP seat and the EP's role in EC decision-making.

Hull, October 1984   JULIET LODGE

List of Abbreviations

AGALEV	Anders Gaan Leven
CAP	Common Agricultural Policy
CD	Centrum-Demokraterne
CDA	Christen Demokratisch Appèl
CDS	Centre des Démocrates Sociaux
CDU	Christlich-Demokratische Union
CDU	Communistes Démocrates Unitaires
CERES	Centre d'Études de Recherches et d'Éducation Socialistes
CFM	Conference of Foreign Ministers
COM	Communist and Allies Group
CONS	Conservative and Unionist Party
CP	Centrum Partij
CPAS	Centre Public d'Aide Sociale
CPN	Communistische Partij Nederland
CSCE	Conference on Security and Co-operation in Europe
CSP	Confederation of Socialist Parties of the EC
CSU	Christlich-Soziale Union
CSV	Chreschtlech Sozial Vollekspartei
CVP	Christelijke Volkspartij
DC	Democrazia Cristiana
DIFE	Défense des Intérêts de la France en Europe
DM	Deutsch Mark
DP	Demokratesch Partei
DP	Democrazia Proletaria
DR	Danmarks Retsforbundet
DR	Drachma
D'66	Demokraten 66
DUP	Democratic Unionist Party
EBU	European Broadcasting Union
EC	European Community
ECJ	European Court of Justice

xiii

ECOLO – V	Mouvement 'Ecolo' – 'Les Verts'
ECSC	European Coal and Steel Community
ECU	European Currency Unit
ED	European Democratic Group
EDC	European Defence Community
EDF	European Development Fund
EDIK	Union of the Democratic Centre
EDU	European Democratic Union
EEC	European Economic Community
EEIP	European Elections Information Programme
EIB	European Investment Bank
ELD	European Liberals and Democrats
EMS	European Monetary System
EMU	Economic and Monetary Union
EP	European Parliament
EPC	European Political Co-operation
EPD	European Progressive Democrats Group
EPEN	National Political Union
EPP	European People's Party
ERDF	European Regional Development Fund
ERE	Entente Radicale Écologiste pour les États-Unis de l'Europe
ESC	Economic and Social Committee of the EC
ESF	European Social Fund
ESPRIT	European Strategic Programme of Research and Development in Information Technology
ETUC	European Trade Union Confederation
EUA	European Unit of Account
EUCD	European Union of Christian Democratic Parties
EUE	Liste pour les États-Unis d'Europe
EURATOM	European Atomic Energy Community
EUT	European Union Treaty
EVP	Europese Volkspartij
EVP	Evangelische Volks Partij
FB	Folkebevaegelsen mod EF
FDF	Front Démocratique des Francophones
FDF – CFE	Front Démocratique des Federalistes pour la Communauté Française et l'Europe
FDP	Freie Demokratische Partei Deutschlands
FF	Fianna Fail
FG	Fine Gael
FN	Front Nationale

FRG	Federal Republic of Germany
FRP	Fremskridtspartiet
GMO	God Met Ons
GPV	Gereformeerd Politiek Verbond
I'84	Initiative 84
IND	Independent
IRA	Irish Republican Army
KF	Det Konservative Folkeparti
KKE	Kommounistiko Komma Hellados (Communist Party – 'exterior')
KKE – es	Kommounistiko Komma Hellados-Essoterikou (Communist Party – 'interior')
KODISO	Komma Dimokratikou Socialismou (Social Democrats)
KP	Komma Proodevtikon (Progressive Party)
KPB	Kommunistische Partij van België
KRF	Kristeligt Folkeparti
KVP	Katholieke Volkspartij
LAB	Labour Party
LDE	Libéraux Démocrates Européens
LI	Liberal Group
LIB	Liberal Party
LO	Lutte Ouvrière
LSAP	Letzeburger Sozialistich Arbechterpartei
MdB	Member of the Bundestag
MEP	Member of the European Parliament
MF	Member of the Folketing
MRG	Mouvement des Radicaux de Gauche
MSI – DN	Movimento Sociale Italiano – Destra Nazionale
NA	'Non-attached' Member of the European Parliament
NATO	North Atlantic Treaty Organisation
ND	Nea Dimokratia (New Democracy)
NEC	National Executive Committee
NOP	National Opinion Poll
NPD	Nationaldemokratische Partei Deutschlands
OJ	Official Journal
OUP	Official Unionist Party
PAC	Political Affairs Committee in the European Parliament
PASOK	Panellinio Socialistiko Kinima (Panhellenic Socialist Movement)
PCB	Parti Communiste de Belgique

PCF	Parti Communiste Français
PCI	Parti Communiste Indépendant
PCI	Partito Communista Italiano
PCL	Parti Communiste Luxembourgeois
PCS	Parti Chrétien Sociale
PD	Parti Démocratique
PDUP	Partito Democratico di Unità Proletaria
PFN	Parti des Forces Nouvelles
PLI	Partito Liberale Italiano
POE	Parti Ouvrier Européen
POSL	Parti Ouvrier Socialiste Luxembourgeois
PPR	Politieke Partij Radikalen
PR	Parti Républicain
PR	Partito Radical
PR	Proportional Representation
PRI	Partito Repubblicano Italiano
PRL	Parti Réformateur Libéral
PRS	Parti Radical Socialiste
PS	Parti Socialiste
PSC	Parti Social Chrétien
PSD	Parti Social-Démocrate
PSDI	Partito Socialista Democratico Italiano
PSI	Partito Socialista Italiano
PSP	Pacifistisch Socialistische Partij
PSU	Parti Socialiste Unifié
PVDA	Partij van de Arbeid (formerly the Social Democratic Labour Party (SDAP))
PVV	Partij voor Vrijheid en Vooruitgang
PWE	Présence Wallonne en Europe
RPF	Reformatorisch Politieke Federatie
RPR	Rassemblement pour la République
RV	Radikale Venstre
RW	Rassemblement Wallon
S	Socialdemokratiet
SCANFIT	Social Consequences and Need-Oriented Aspects of New Information Technologies
SDLP	Social Democratic and Labour Party
SDP	Social Democratic Party
SF	Socialistisk Folkeparti
SGP	Staatkundig Gereformeerde Partij
SNP	Scottish National Party

SOC	Socialist Group
SOFRES	Société Française d'Enquêtes par Sondages
SP	Socialistische Partij
SPD	Sozialdemokratische Partei Deutschlands
STV	Single Transferable Vote
SVP	Südtiroler Volkspartei
TCG	Group for the Technical Co-ordination and Defence of Independent Groups and Members
TD	Teachta Dala
The Nine	Members of the EC after the first enlargement (Six plus Denmark, Ireland and the United Kingdom)
The Six	Members of the EC before enlargement (France, Italy, the Federal Republic of Germany, Belgium, Luxembourg and the Netherlands)
The Ten	Members of the EC after the second enlargement (Nine plus Greece)
UA	Unit of Account
UCR	Union Centriste et Radicale
UDCA	Union de Défense des Commercants et Artisans
UDF	Union pour la Démocratie Française
UDL	United Democratic Left
UDRT-RAD	Union Démocratique pour la Respect du Travail-Respekt voor Arbeid en Demokratie
UFE	Union pour la France en Europe
UK	United Kingdom
USA	United States of America
USSR	Union of Soviet Socialist Republics
UTILE	Union des Travailleurs Indépendants pour la Liberté d'Entreprendre
V	Venstre, Danmarks Liberale Parti
VS	Venstre Socialisterne
VU	Volksunie
VVD	Volkspartij voor Vrijheid en Democratie
WEU	Western European Union

Notes on the Contributors

Simon Bulmer is a Lecturer in European Studies at the University of Manchester Institute of Science and Technology (UMIST). His main research interest is the role of national politics in the EC. He is currently writing a book on West Germany and the EC and completing a project on the European Council for publication.

Paul-H. Claeys is Chargé de Cours at the Université Libre de Bruxelles. He teaches internal political sociology, social stratification and bargaining theory. His research work and main publications are about interest groups, political parties and more generally about sociopolitical pluralism.

Neil Collins is the Irish Director of the European Election Study based at the University of Mannheim and a Lecturer in Irish Politics and Public Policy at the University of Liverpool.

Neil Elder is a Reader in Politics at the University of Hull. He is the author of *Government in Sweden*, co-author of *The Consensual Democracies: Government and Politics in the Scandinavian States* and he has written numerous articles on Scandinavian politics. He is Chairman of the Scandinavian government and politics sub-group of the Political Studies Association of the United Kingdom.

Kevin Featherstone is a Lecturer in Political Studies at the University of Stirling. He has written various articles and papers on West European politics, particularly on issues related to the EC. He was formerly a Schuman scholar at the European Parliament and a Visiting Professor in International Relations at the University of Minnesota. He is currently writing a history of socialist parties and their attitudes towards European integration.

John Fitzmaurice works in Brussels for the Commission of the European Communities. He is the author of *The Party Groups in the European Parliament, The European Parliament, Politics in Denmark* and *Politics in Belgium*, co-author of *The European Parliament: a Guide to Direct Elections* and he has written numerous articles on Danish and European politics.

Derek Hearl is a Research Associate at the University of Essex. He has been working for the last three years on the European Consortium for Political Research manifestos project. His research interests include Benelux politics, parties and party systems, and the EC.

Isaac Lipschits is Professor in Contemporary History at the University of Groningen, the Netherlands, where he founded the Study and Documentation Centre on Political Parties. Formerly he lectured on national politics and international relations at the Universities of Amsterdam, Haifa, Jerusalem, Leyden and Rotterdam, at the Netherlands Society for International Relations and at the Dutch Air Force Academy. He is the author of books and articles on Dutch political parties, the 1979 direct elections to the European Parliament and on simulation techniques in international relations. He has translated Karl Marx's *Das Kapital* into Dutch.

Juliet Lodge is a Senior Lecturer in Politics at the University of Hull. She was formerly a Lecturer in Political Studies at the University of Auckland, New Zealand, Visiting Fellow in the Centre for International Studies at The London School of Economics and Political Science and a Leverhulme Research Fellow. She is the author of *The European Policy of the SPD* and *The European Community and New Zealand*, co-author of *The New Zealand General Election of 1975, The European Parliament and the European Community* and *Direct Elections to the European Parliament: a Community Perspective* and editor of *Terrorism: a Challenge to the State, The European Community: Bibliographical Excursions* and *Institutions and Policies of the European Community*. She is a frequent contributor to leading journals of political science, international affairs and European Community law.

Nicole Loeb-Mayer is Chef de Travaux at the Institut de Sociologie at the Université Libre de Bruxelles. She specialises in political science and in the sociology of European integration. She is the author of numerous publications on the Belgian political system, on Belgian parties and groups and their attitudes towards European integration, and on transnational party co-operation.

David Millar is Head of the Political Affairs Division in the Directorate General for Research and Documentation, European Parliament. He was formerly a Clerk in the House of Commons. His work is concerned principally with assisting rapporteurs with reports on direct elections to the EP, the uniform electoral procedure, inter-institutional relations, Southern Africa and the Middle East. He is the author of papers and articles on parliamentary procedure.

William E. Paterson is a Reader in Politics at the University of Warwick. He is the author of *The SPD and European Integration*, co-editor of *Social Democratic Parties in Western Europe*, and author of numerous articles on West German politics.

Geoffrey Pridham is a Reader in European Politics at the University of Bristol. He is the author of *Christian Democracy in Western Germany* and *The Nature of the Italian Party System: a Regional Case-study*, co-author of *Transnational Party Co-operation and European Integration: the Process Towards Direct Elections*, and editor of *The New Mediterranean Democracies: Regime Transition in Spain, Greece and Portugal*. He is currently doing comparative research on coalition studies, and is writing a book on *Political Parties and Coalition Behaviour in Italy: an Interpretative Study*.

Anne Stevens is a Lecturer in Politics and presently Sub-Dean (Academic Affairs) of the School of European Studies at the University of Sussex. Formerly she was a civil servant, serving in both London and Malaysia. She is the author of a number of articles on the EC and on French government and administration.

Guido van den Berghe is Head of the European Secretariat of the Socialistische Partij. He was formerly a member of the Cabinet of Mr H. Simonet, Vice-President of the European Commission. He is the author of *Political Rights for European Citizens*, co-editor of *The European Parliament: Towards a Uniform Procedure for Direct Elections*, and author of a number of articles on European integration.

Introduction

JULIET LODGE

BACKGROUND TO THE 1984 EP ELECTIONS

The elections to the European Parliament (EP) on 14–17 June 1984 provided electors in all European Community (EC) member states with the opportunity, for only the second time in the history of the EC, to directly elect representatives to serve in a common parliament. Although the treaties establishing the EC provide for the election of the assembly (as it is termed) by direct universal suffrage, such was the political controversy surrounding the election of a common institution purporting to be a 'parliament' and having, despite its formally limited supervisory and advisory powers, clear legislative pretensions, that successive EC member governments managed to postpone the first EP elections until 1979. Even then, the elections took place not only some twelve months later than scheduled originally (after the then nine EC member governments had agreed in 1976 that such elections should indeed take place) but several years after the Six had committed themselves at the Hague summit of 1969 to democratising the EC and to direct elections within the next few years.

That the member governments should have agreed at all to EP elections was in itself remarkable. This was the first sign that the traditional deadlock would be broken over whether it would be proper to elect a parliament lacking, supposedly, many of the legislative powers and attributes of the national parliaments (with which, inevitably, it was compared) before it had acquired the sort of authority and power that would allow it to perform functions and roles akin to those of the national parliaments (or, more specifically, lower chambers of parliaments where bicameral legislatures existed). A common fear voiced at this time was that unless the EP had an effective role and some real legislative power (as opposed merely to influence) in EC decision-making, it would be unreasonable to expect people to turn out and vote.[1] The cliché of the EP being a powerless assembly unworthy of attention and votes, coupled with a less than flattering image of it portrayed in the media (notably of the reluctant EC member states)[2] in turn affected the whole conduct of the first elections to the EP in 1979.[3]

The chief, though not sole, worry centred upon what might loosely be termed enhancing and making credible the EP's democratic legitimacy. Subsumed under this heading were four key questions. First, would it be possible to mobilise the electorate to vote? Second, how was one to explain and justify the EP's role in the EC to an electorate largely ignorant of its existence? That is, would it be possible to make the EP visible and intelligible to the electorate?[4] Third, how was the uniqueness of the common elections to be impressed on the electorate in the absence of understood, tangible features of those elections (such as a common electoral system, common political parties, common manifestos, common candidates, common election-night results programmes, and a common polling day)?[5] Was the first EP election to be seen as a European election or as a series of nine more or less simultaneous elections to a common parliament?[6] Fourth, would eventual turnout throughout the EC be sufficiently high as to allow the newly elected Members of the European Parliament (MEPs) to justify claims for an increased role and powers for the EP in the EC with reference to their enhanced democratic legitimacy? After all, unlike their predecessors (who had been nominated members from the national parliaments and who, therefore, held dual mandates in two parliamentary chambers as several new MEPs did also),[7] they could at least claim to have been elected by the voters as their representatives in the EP. Moreover, the EP alone among EC institutions could claim to have been directly and democratically legitimated by virtue of having been elected. The Council of Ministers, while able to insist that most of its members had been elected at a national election, could not make quite the same claim. Some MEPs and observers, therefore, were quick to contest the Council's moral right to thwart the EP's aspirations.

The linkage of the question of electoral turnout with the EP's traditional quest for greater powers revived earlier fears that direct elections would herald the transformation of the EC into a federal super-state. This argument derived from over-simplified interpretations of both federalism and the EP's ambitions. Nevertheless, the argument that the EP by virtue of its direct election would become the repository of supranational sovereignty (that, therefore, the sovereignty of the member states would be weakened) fanned fears over the sensitive issue of national sovereignty. This term itself was ill-understood. For space reasons, the whole contentious matter of whether or not sovereignty is indivisible, and is meaningful outside legal, diplomatic and international fields in an age of state permeability and economic interpenetration, cannot be discussed here. But, in the context of the debate over sovereignty in the EC, the term seems to have become shorthand for and synonymous with the assertion and preservation of national over supranational *qua* EC interests.

It is in this respect that member governments' concern over an elected EP's aspirations can best be appreciated. Anxiety was voiced (notably in the United Kingdom (UK), France and Denmark) lest the EP usurp and rival member governments and national parliaments. This anxiety bore striking resemblance to fears articulated during the early 1970s when President Pompidou revived the idea of all EC member states having ministers responsible for EC affairs in order to inject greater continuity into the work of the Council whose sometimes disparate composition appeared to suggest a lack of coherence in its work. It was argued that the effect of this was to deprive member governments of an overall picture of inter-linkages between issue-areas discussed by different ministers according to the items on the agenda. However, the main fear was that an elected EP would seek to extend its powers at the expense of the dominant Council. Any encroachment by the EP on the Council's pre-eminence as, for example, by way of power-sharing through powers of co-decision – as in the budgetary field – was to be resisted.

For their part, MEPs had, during their campaign to secure the member governments' agreement to direct elections, strongly denied any suggestion that elected MEPs would indeed seek an extension of the EP's powers.[8] Clearly, it was politically expedient to adopt such a line. Thus, MEPs noted that the EP's formal powers could only be extended if the member governments agreed to amend the EEC treaty. However, under Article 236, Treaty amendments can only come into effect if ratified by *all* the member states in accordance with their respective constitutional requirements. It was felt, therefore, that increasing the EP's powers by treaty amendment would be doomed to fail.

Furthermore, it was asserted that the EP could increase its *influence* in EC decision-making by simply exploiting those powers that it possessed. Yet, MEPs must have been aware that they could not bind their elected successors to remain content with a limited role in decision-making. It is, after all, striking that in English the reference is to decision-making rather than to a legislative process. Indeed, if the EP was to assert itself as a parliament of a type recognisable as such in the member states then not only was a quest for greater legislative powers, as opposed to influence, inevitable but justified, especially if the democratic legitimacy argument meant anything at all beyond a simple 'democratisation' of the EC by the expedient of electing by universal suffrage that institution purporting to be a parliament.

On the eve of the first elections, then, candidates seeking election to the EP were preoccupied with two linked questions: first, securing as high a turnout as possible; and second, using that turnout subsequently to vindicate their claim to a right to exercise effectively a representative function on behalf of the electorate. This claim not only derived from a more or less shared view of the function of an MEP in an elected legislative body but implied a right to be afforded the means to exercise that role effectively – that is, greater powers both to influence and determine legislative outputs and to hold the Commission and, more especially, the Council accountable for their actions and inactions.

It was somewhat surprising, perhaps, that on the eve of the end of the elected EP's first five-year term of office (a fixed term that member governments had attempted unsuccessfully to curtail by one month in first advocating 17–20 May 1984 as the date for the second EP elections) there appeared to be a number of parallels to the situation on the eve of the first EP elections. For example, as in 1979, elections were to be held over several days (from 14–17 June 1984) rather than on either one day or on two consecutive days (Sunday and Monday having been advanced but predictably rejected by some member states, notably the UK). There was no common electoral procedure so, as in 1979, the 1984 elections were to be conducted in accordance with national provisions drafted in response to the Council Decision and Act of 20 September 1976. Notwithstanding its direct election, the EP had continued to receive an often poor press – if it gained media attention at all. Its work continued to be vilified as irrelevant; and the media (particularly but not only in anti-EC member states like Denmark and the UK) perpetuated the EP's 'gravy-train' image. As in 1979, so in 1984, the visibility and intelligibility of the EP to the electorate remained problematic. *Eurobarometer* polls showed public awareness of the EP to be rather low and months before the election concern was expressed by MEPs, including EP President Pieter Dankert, over the problems of mobilising the electorate to turn out and vote. This time the issue was not so much one of enhancing the EP's democratic legitimacy as ensuring that its credibility should not be eroded by a low turnout. Equally importantly, it was felt that as a low turnout would reflect badly on the EP and its record (to the extent that its record was at all apparent and/or relevant to voters). Hence, the EP's quest for greater influence and powers would be dealt a severe blow.

Moreover, the turnout-powers argument remained as potent in 1984 as it had been in 1979 for as then MEPs' ability to 'deliver the goods' and to fulfil electoral promises hinged upon the EP's ability to determine financial and legislative priorities. While the EP's demonstrable capacity to influence decision-making had enabled it to advance its wishes to some degree, it had not acquired (as of right) codified powers to determine legislative programmes and spending priorities. For example, it had not been able to do anything to redress unemployment. Nor had it sought a reform of the Rome Treaty to ensure the accretion of its powers. This was recognised as a *non sequitur*. Thus, as in 1979, it was still the case that the MEPs would only be able to represent effectively their constituents if the EP's powers were increased. In 1984, MEPs faced the same dilemma as their predecessors of how to mobilise the electorate without generating unrealistically high expectations concerning their ability to 'deliver the goods'.

However, it would be misleading to take the parallels between the 1979 and 1984 eve of the election scenarios too far. Whatever the different situations in the Ten, and no matter the extent to which it seemed that the elections would again be a series of loosely co-ordinated national elections to a common parliament rather than a genuine Euro-election (complete with common parties, common voting rights, common electoral procedure, and so on), the situation had changed in one crucial respect. Namely, there was an acceptance, notably on the part of member governments, that the EP did have a legitimate right to seek an increase in its powers to enhance its ability to perform legislative functions. This implied not simply an accretion of the EP's powers and influence but some reform of the EC's inter-institutional balance.

By no means all member governments or all MEPs acquiesced in the EP's claim for greater powers. Nor were MEPs sanguine about their chances of success: they remained as concerned about ensuring a high turnout as ever. However, electoral rhetoric aside, by 1984 in the wake of the EP's initiative on European Union, several member governments accepted not only the gist of the draft treaty establishing the European Union (EUT) passed by the EP in February 1984 (which proposed, in effect, the transformation of the Council and the EP into a bicameral legislature)[9] but prepared to scrutinise it. It would be wrong to infer from this that member states such as Italy, Belgium and the Federal Republic of Germany (FRG) had endorsed, without reservation, the logic of the EUT and unquestioningly accepted that the EP should realise its legislative ambitions. However, there was a good deal of genuine support for the accretion of the EP's powers. This was couched often in terms of the enhanced democratic legitimacy accruing to the EP from its direct election.

At the same time, the EUT and the second EP elections must be seen within the context of the failure of successive EC summits – in the shape of meetings of the European Council – to meet pressing problems effectively. By the time of the 1984 EP elections, the first inadequate steps were being taken towards reforming the Common Agricultural Policy (CAP) while member governments still prevaricated over the vital linked issue of budgetary reform. Moreover, the member governments' own efforts to improve, expedite and rationalise EC decision-making by way of the July 1983 'Solemn Declaration on European Union' (known also as the Stuttgart Declaration) had been emasculated systematically from the time they had surfaced first as a proposal for the Draft European Act (the Genscher–Colombo initiative).[10] In other words, the member governments had proved incapable or unwilling to confront, in an innovative and realistic manner, the need to build on the EC and to take new steps to facilitate integration and to enhance their joint capacity to meet the challenges of the 1990s. This is not to say that they did not recognise the problems arising from the now inappropriate decision-making procedures. Rather that they refused to advance changes in inter-institutional relations necessary to attain policy goals, both old and new.

The Spinelli initiative on the EUT was, thus, welcome *per se*, if not in all its details, because it represented an innovative but pragmatic approach to opening a far-reaching debate on the EC's future that successive reports from Vedel to Tindemans to the Three Wise Men and Genscher–Colombo had failed to do. Furthermore, the EP's adoption of the EUT shortly before the elections added an air of legitimacy to the enterprise as it became enmeshed in the election campaigns. While not a prominent campaign issue, it was one of several issues. As a legacy to the second elected EP, the EUT could not simply be forgotten by the new MEPs. Moreover, the demonstrable inability of the EC, and especially of member governments, to address swiftly and effectively the growing budgetary, financial and agricultural problems highlighted the need for some re-arrangement of decision-making to facilitate the adoption of much needed reforms. Consequently, whereas several government members, national MPs and observers questioned the right of the EP, in effect unilaterally to expand its powers by adopting a 'constituent' role,[11] prevailing circumstances deterred them from rejecting outright consideration of the EUT. On the contrary, some had come to accept publicly, and more so privately, the legitimacy of a range of arguments that MEPs had advanced since the first EP elections and before.

Such acceptance was neither unanimous nor unequivocal. But it marked an important shift in attitude. That the EP should have more influence and power was no longer unthinkable. It was recognised that if it were more effective in influencing legislative outputs, it might be able to command more media attention and recommend itself to voters. For their part, MEPs hoped that as a result electoral turnout in 1984 would be boosted above the 1979 level (and so be higher than the average turnout for US presidential elections with which Euro-election turnout had been compared) and vindicate an increase in the EP's powers possibly as foreseen in the EUT. More ambitiously, it was hoped that this would so democratise and reform the EC as to realise principles of representative democratic government; improve and, if appropriate, re-define and expand the EC's decision-making capacity, competence and jurisdiction: the aim being to enable it to take common action if likely to be more effective and successful than haphazard national action.

It is striking that even when leading politicians spoke about the EC's future, and intimated expanding its activities in telematics, space and so on (as did President Mitterrand,[12] for example), they alluded not always directly to the EUT but to its spirit and to the implicit possibility of permitting goal attainment on a two- or three-speed basis. Thus, instead of member states halting integration by blocking it, there was a return to the idea of the multi-speed EC that Brandt and Tindemans had advocated – possibly by exploiting provisions of the Rome Treaty. The idea was revived when the prospect of the EC's further enlargement, coupled with rifts between pro and anti-integrationist member states, made it seem logical.[13] Moreover, expectations of the EC exceeded, for want of resources and jurisdiction, the EC's capacity to act. ESPRIT, SCANFIT and the EUT thus spurred governments into considering what structures would be needed to facilitate change. Yet the degree to which this apparent change of attitude can be solely attributed to the EP should not be exaggerated. But neither should it be ignored.

There is an important sense in which the EP helps shape political opinion, notably among elites. The Council, Commission and EP are not quite the self-contained, impenetrable institutions they are often portrayed as being. While 'engrenage' and the oversimplified Commission–Council dialogue are seen as important parts of EC decision-making, the degree of interaction between officials from the EP, the Court, the Council and the Commission provides scope for mutual influence and the shaping of opinion. This sort of interpenetration cannot be readily and accurately quantified[14] but it is one element in the process of effecting attitude change in the EC.[15] It is also a more subtle notion than crisis as the catalyst for reform. Clearly, the two co-exist. In the context of the 1984 EP elections, another important element in persuading at least some member governments of the need for institutional changes (if only in a marginal way) was the coincidence of government initiatives – notably the Genscher–Colombo plans – with MEPs' deliberations on a range of institutional matters, including the Genscher–Colombo initiative.[16] These developments indirectly primed opinion to make it receptive at least to the idea of institutional reform, if not to the EUT itself, both inside and outside the EP. It is worth outlining briefly the most significant EP developments in this respect.

MEPs pursued simultaneously a 'minimalist' and a 'maximalist' strategy to secure greater powers for the EP. But the minimalists and the maximalists shared a conviction that institutional reform was needed. They were united in their realistic appreciation of the impossibility of reforming the EEC treaties. However, they deviated over tactics. Whereas the maximalists, led by Altiero Spinelli, were to pursue a strategy to devise a treaty to supersede the EEC treaties – a strategy that culminated in the EUT[17] – minimalists opted for a strategy least likely to antagonise member governments. Thus, the minimalists' approach was based upon exploiting existing treaty provisions (such as Articles 149 and 175)[18] and upon reforming the EP's own Rules of Procedure.[19] This enabled MEPs to improve the EP's capacity for influence within the confines of its powers. There can be little doubt that the minimalists' approach met with some success.

MEPs proved adept at both exhausting treaty provisions, notably in respect of the EP's budgetary authority, and seeking alternative means of enhancing their chances of influencing EC decision-making. This went beyond exploiting the 1981 Rules of Procedure and Court of Justice's ruling striking down in the isoglucose case a piece of legislation on which the EP had not been consulted properly. It went beyond invoking Article 175 against the Council for failure to act on transport. It extended to tactics involving co-operation between the national parliaments and the EP. Thus, some attempt was made by EP committees to persuade representatives from counterpart national committees to advance the EP's ideas to the member governments on proposed legislative items. Some headway was made at the national level where (as, for example, in the Bundestag) MPs instituted a regular discussion of forthcoming EC business with MEPs.[20] The relevant committees of the House of Lords not only made their expert reports available to UK MEPs and other MEPs but also to the relevant EP committees in the hope of influencing their deliberations.[21] The House of Lords' committees also invited evidence from MEPs on specific issues. In 1982 all members of the EP's Economic and Monetary Committee met a committee from each of the House of Lords and House of Commons. The EP's Transport Committee adopted a quasi-educative role *vis-à-vis* chairmen of the national parliaments' transport committees. While the latter were invited to send one or more representatives to joint-meetings, some demurred.[22] Yet joint-committee meetings were the exception rather than the norm. Nevertheless, links between the EP and national parliaments' committees grew. This was an important development as hitherto the EP's links with the national parliaments had been presumed to have existed by virtue of dual-mandated MEPs. After the first EP elections, some institutionalisation of such exchanges was deemed necessary. (The EP, of course, continues to exchange delegations with many extra-EC parliaments.)

Linked to the tactic of institutionalising contacts between national parliamentary bodies and the EP to augment the EP's capacity for influence was a strategy based on increasing the EP's ability to influence deliberations within the Council and the Commission at the pre-decisional stage. It had been axiomatic to assert that the EP's influence would increase if its peripatetic existence were ended and if it shared a common site with (or were to be located in the same city as) the Commission and the Council. However, while it is the member governments' prerogative to fix the EP's seat, their failure to do so led the EP to press for a decision. Yet, MEPs were unable to resolve the question of the seat among themselves.[23] Highly controversial steps were taken to move some EP personnel from Luxembourg to Brussels and to cease meetings of the EP in Luxembourg. On 7 July 1981, the EP decided to hold plenary meetings in Strasbourg and, as a normal rule, committee meetings in Brussels. But such moves did nothing to solve the basic problem of the EP's three work places. Rather, the EP quickly became embroiled in a legal dispute with the Luxembourg government over its apparent desire to leave Luxembourg, the seat of its Secretariat and the place where the Luxembourg government had built a new conference centre to house the expanded and elected EP. The Luxembourg government took the EP to the Court of Justice on the grounds that the matter of the EP's seat fell within member states' competence. The details of this dispute need not detain us, but they revealed how politically sensitive the question of the EP's seat remained. Thus, on the eve of the second EP elections, the Parliament's position in this respect was little better than that of its predecessor.

More significantly, the minimalist approach had by then run its course and demonstrated the limits of gradualism. There was a point beyond which the EP could not go in exploiting treaty provisions to assert its views in EC decision-making. The point had been reached. But this did not mean that the maximalist approach supported by many minimalists would succeed automatically. However, following the EP's adoption of the EUT, maximalists hoped that the EUT would be a unifying and stimulating theme in the 1984 EP election. To this end, instead of directing the EUT to the member governments, it was lodged with the national parliaments. Various bodies like the European Movement and university academics began to lobby for the EUT to be considered seriously.[24] It was hoped thus to deter member governments from despatching the EUT to bureaucratic committees from which it would never surface again. This strategy was based on the assumption that if the EUT became an election issue, its legitimacy would be enhanced to such an extent that the member governments would feel obliged to heed it. It was recognised certainly that a low turnout might have the opposite effect. Nevertheless, it was hoped that the EUT's prescriptions – oriented as they were to critical policy matters as well as institutional problems – would prove sufficiently relevant as to add to and stimulate debate over the EC's future.

There was another reason for hoping that this EP initiative would be well-received. This relates to the nature of the EP's powers. Except in the matter of proposing a common electoral procedure for elections to the EP under Article 138 of the Rome Treaty, arguably the EP has no formal powers of legislative initiative under the terms of the Rome Treaty (though, as indicated above,[25] it has taken steps under its own Rules to assert a legislative initiating role that could be legitimately derived from the Rome Treaty's provisions). The member governments had refused to countenance the EP's 1982 proposals on a common electoral procedure.[26] Their continued prevarication over one key aspect of the EP elections that would be highly visible to the electorate, robbed MEPs and candidates of a chance to assert the uniqueness and transnational character of the Euro-elections. While the EUT's strategists saw the EP elections in an instrumental sense as a means of encouraging the adoption of the EUT, they hoped also that the EUT would be both a key election issue throughout the Ten and show that the EP could take the initiative to propose a relevant reform of the EC to enable it to meet the challenges of the 1990s. All this presupposed that the EUT would receive the requisite media exposure and public discussion, and that people would be interested in the EP.

As was to become clear during the election campaign, public interest in the EP was low. The EP's record was modest and not well-known. The EUT's import, therefore, could not easily be set against or alongside it. It could not emerge as the apex of the EP's achievements. Furthermore, discussion of the EUT was to vary widely from member state to member state with only Italy supporting it unequivocally. Additionally, for many MEPs seeking re-election, this supremely Community issue was one that they subsumed for national or national party reasons in a campaign that focussed mainly on parochial national or local issues. That the campaigns should have been denuded of much Europeanism was due to a number of factors that are explored in subsequent chapters. However, if national issues dominated the election campaign, did this imply that the EP itself and its record were either irrelevant or ignored in favour of national politics?

THE EP'S RECORD

In surveying briefly the EP's record, it is pertinent to recall that the first elected EP regarded itself first and foremost as the spokesman of the EC's publics with a duty to voice their view, protests and worries.[27] As awareness of the EP grew, an increasing number of letters and petitions[28] were sent to MEPs irrespective of whether their subject-matter fell within the EC's competence. Interest groups belonging to national and European associations lobbied the EP increasingly. The EP's stature grew within the international community. It was addressed by Heads of State (for example, President Sadat and King Hussein). The EP's workload grew: the duration of plenary sessions rose from 58 days and 376 hours in 1978 to 64 days and 439 hours in 1983. The number of committee meetings rose from 225 meetings in 378 days in 1979 to 336 meetings in 611 days in 1983.[29]

The growth in the EP's workload does not necessarily mean that MEPs became commensurately more effective than their non-elected predecessors. It must be remembered that whereas the members of previous parliaments largely held dual mandates, the proportion of dual-mandated MEPs in the elected EP fell from over 30% in 1979 to 11% in 1984. In theory, at least, elected MEPs should have been able to concentrate more on their EP work than their predecessors. But the greater amount of time spent formally on EP business could be, at least partly, a function of the EP's size having risen from 196 members in 1978 to 434 members in 1984. Similar caution is needed in interpreting statistics regarding MEPs' outputs. Tables I.1 and I.2 show that between 1978 and 1983 the number of working documents tripled and the number of resolutions adopted doubled. The number of 'own

TABLE I.1   *European Parliament working documents* (1978–83)

	1978	1979	1980	1981	1982	1983
Reports	213	188	244	243	261	227
Consultations	248	222	241	270	235	256
Motions for resolutions	76	218	464	550	676	885
Miscellaneous	2	15	3	–	–	–
Total	539	643	952	1063	1172	1418

SOURCE   EP General Secretariat, *On the Right Road* (Luxembourg: EP, 1984) p. 15.

TABLE I.2   *European Parliament texts adopted* (1978–83)

	1978	1979 (from 7/79)	1980	1981	1982	1983
Resolutions adopted including:	233	250 (105)	306	342	392	467
consultations	131	102 (50)	127	147	146	157
on urgent questions with early vote in combination with an oral question		(29)	72	62	91	128
(Rule 47(5))	108	148 (10)	17	10	13	16
under written procedure		(–)	–	–	14	4
own-initiative reports		(16)	90	123	128	162

SOURCE   EP General Secretariat, *On the Right Road* (Luxembourg: EP, 1984) p. 15.

initiative' reports rose fom 90 in 1980 to 162 in 1983. However, the higher output could be partly attributed to the greater number of MEPs, party groups and committees, and not all of it was welcome. There continued to be criticism of the presentation and nature of many reports and EP documents. Yet, these qualifications should not detract from the EP's record: it had instigated reports and adopted resolutions on a wide range of important issues. These related to the contentious matter of the EC's role in security matters[30] which seemed outside the EC's competence if the Rome Treaty was interpreted narrowly. They extended over EC finances – own resources, lending and borrowing activities, convergence and budgetary matters,[31] competition policy and the customs union – to the creation of a European legal area, combatting terrorism, and related institutional questions. They covered also human and civil rights as they affected both EC citizens (for example, the recognition of special rights of EC citizens, including voting rights and the protection of individuals' rights in data processing) and people elsewhere (for example, resolutions on human rights in the world were adopted, as were several on such issues as Afghanistan, Poland and South Africa). Additionally, numerous resolutions were adopted over the spectrum of EC policies from the CAP, Lomé, energy, research, environment and information policies to unemployment. The resolutions indicated key areas of concern to the EP. However, MEPs faced the problem of how such concern could be translated into action.

The EP's restricted powers, of course, posed a limit. MEPs did try, with some success, to shape opinion. The EP committees' specialist expertise in some areas came to be acknowledged and valued, but this was not tantamount to a major increase in the EP's ability to determine EC policy and spending priorities. While the EP committees were primarily engaged in scrutinising Commission proposals, there was a sense in which they developed a modest 'think-tank' capacity, though this was scarcely recognised by other EC bodies or member governments and bureaucracies. Nevertheless, MEPs were able to influence policy outputs in a limited way. Why was it that this was not clear to the electorate? The answer lies partly with the sporadic and often unflattering media coverage of the EP, partly with the nature of the EC's decision-making process, and partly with the difficulty of disentangling from it the EP's own record. This was singularly hard to do. Yet, a record does exist. The first elected EP did have an impact on organisational, decision-making matters, and on international and internal affairs. Briefly, one may cite the following examples of how, through organisational changes and by capitalising on treaty provisions, the elected EP tried to show that it was more effective, influential and ultimately more powerful than its predecessors.

First, the elected EP made fuller use of its budgetary powers[32] and in December 1979 for the first time ever vetoed the draft budget for 1980. This was coupled with attempts to change expenditure priorities. For example, the EP tried somewhat inconsistently to curtail CAP spending. The Parliament had endorsed in 1981 both a plan to reform the CAP based on a quota system and cuts in subsidies and a switch in EC spending. In principle, MEPs supported – following the 30 May 1980 mandate[33] – reports on future financing and the UK contribution to the budget by the Commission and the EP. Yet, in spring 1980 and 1982, MEPs had supported the Council against the Commission for higher farm prices. In 1982, a majority of MEPs supported a 14% rise in farm prices against the Commission's 9% price rise proposal. Moreover, following the protracted Council dispute in spring 1982 about farm prices for 1982–83, the EP adopted a resolution calling on the Council to take a majority decision (and so defy the UK veto). The Council's President-in-Office, Mr Leo Tindemans, argued subsequently that the Council had been influenced by the EP's view to adopt majority voting.[34] In 1983, the farming lobby pressed for a seven per cent price rise against the Commission's proposed price rise of 4.4%. The Council agreed on 6.9% but as funds were exhausted, and the payment of certain subsidies and refunds to farmers was suspended, needed to raise extra money.

Throughout the EP's five year term of office and with bankruptcy looming, budgetary problems exacerbated EP-Council relations and led to the Council threatening Court action against the EP.[35] For its part, the EP was anxious both to flex its muscles in an area where as part of the EC's budgetary authority it had codified rights, and it tried to prevent the Council from eroding them.[36] Indeed, acrimonious exchanges between the Council and the EP on budgetary issues preceded and succeeded even the second EP elections. Attempts to improve relations in this sphere too often were to little avail despite the signing in June 1982 of a Joint Declaration[37] by the EP, the Council and the Commission on the introduction of measures to improve the operation of the budgetary procedure and to clarify the distinction between 'obligatory' and 'non-obligatory' expenditure over which disputes persist.[38]

The EP has tried systematically to raise the amount of non-compulsory expenditure which is subject to the EP's decision. The UK budget rebates are a case in point. The Commission proved unable to solve the problem of UK and German budgetary contributions and proposed *ad hoc* arrangements in the supplementary budget that the EP rejected in December 1982. The Council, having been forced to amend it, then accommodated EP views in part: nearly half the expenditure relating to the UK contribution was classified as non-compulsory, and was thus to be monitored. Unused funds were to be reimbursed and the Commission undertook to submit radical proposals to expand policies and diversify own resources.[39] While successive European Councils (Stuttgart, June 1983, Athens, December 1983 and Fontainebleau, July 1984) discussed the problems also, solutions have yet to be found as budgetary and CAP issues are intertwined and linked to the decision on EC enlargement and the launching of new policies. However, the EP has had some impact in the budgetary sector even if its behaviour has often been contradictory when pressed by the farm lobby. It has influenced the Council and the Commission. The Commission took up some of the EP's May 1983 guidelines on the EC's own resources. Having set up a committee on the budget and a committee on budgetary control, the EP scrutinised spending more closely, in conjunction with the Court of Auditors. Thus the EP deferred the discharge to the Commission for the implementation of the 1980 budget until January 1983.

Going on to extend its influence over other policy sector deliberations, the EP asserted its scrutiny powers over the Council and Commission. It established its right to intervene in legislative proceedings. In a contentious ruling in the so-called 1980 isoglucose case, the Council's failure to await the EP's Opinion led to the draft legislation being struck down. At issue here was not so much the content of the legislation as the EP's role in the legislative process. While the Council cannot be bound to heed or incorporate any amendments that the EP may propose to draft legislation, it must be in receipt of the EP's formal Opinion on it where the treaty so provides. In effect, as the EP recognised, this gave it a delaying power that could be politically useful if deployed circumspectly. However, to underpin its consultative rights in decision-making and to streamline its own work, the EP reformed its own Rules of Procedure. Exploiting its power of delay, the EP introduced a new procedure of committee scrutiny, notably under Rules 33 and 35. These permitted re-referral back to committee of a proposal where important differences persisted over the proposal's content between the Commission and the EP. In this respect, the EP tried with some success to capitalise on the Commission's right, under Article 149 of the Rome Treaty, to amend a proposal at any stage

before the Council had acted. Its aim was to persuade the Commission
to adopt EP amendments, and so make the emission of the EP's
Opinion possible.[40]

Procedural reforms were introduced also to enable the EP to devolve
responsibility for technical matters and the more esoteric proposals to
committees: the aim being to free plenary time for discussion of topical,
political issues that, it was hoped, would be relevant to the public and
prove that the EP was not a mere talking-shop immersed in the
minutiae of technical proposals with no understanding of vital topical
political issues. Thus, a register procedure was introduced to allow
motions to be adopted not only in plenary sittings but through the issue
of written declarations of the EP's position. The EP derived a right of
initiative from treaty provisions and, as noted above, duly increased its
output of 'own initiative' reports. It was hoped that the Commission
would then transform these into formal proposals for consideration by
the Council. On a more modest, less public level, EP initiatives
stimulated Commission and Council action. In 1981, during the
International Year of the Disabled, the EP prompted the Commission
to submit a communication to the Council on the social integration of
the disabled. In December 1981, the Council agreed a Resolution that
incorporated many EP proposals. Similarly, in 1979, the EP's *ad hoc*
Committee on Women's Rights drafted a report on the position of
women in the EC that the EP adopted in February 1981. The
Commission then set up a Special Consultative Committee on
Women's Rights and in 1982 advanced a new EC action programme to
promote equal opportunities for women. The Council adopted it in
July 1982 in the shape of a resolution. While the EP can, in these
instances, claim to have influenced decision-making, its impact was
limited not least because a Council resolution lacks the binding effect of
a Regulation or Directive.

However, one of the most publicised and successful outcomes of the
'own initiative' procedure was the initiative of the EP Committee on the
Environment, Public Health and Consumer Protection that in 1982
proposed an EC-wide ban on imports of baby-seal products. Lobbyists
won over five million signatures for the ban and after several EP
debates the EP's resolution for a ban was passed to the Council. By a
Regulation, the ban came into force in 1983–84. The same committee
prompted action on the introduction of lead-free petrol in the EC.

To underline its ability to play an effective grand forum role and to
publicise its scrutiny function, the EP held a number of committee

meetings in public and made increasing use of hearings with experts and, more significantly perhaps, with various Council Ministers. Between January 1980 and April 1982, there were 56 such meetings.

The EP also set a precedent by establishing committees of enquiry on the situation of women in Europe (which subsequently became one of the 20 standing committees), on the transportation of dangerous substances (dioxin), and on economic recovery in Europe. The EP underlined its refusal to exercise no more than an advisory and supervisory function by initiating debate on issues instead of simply reacting to steps taken elsewhere, notably by the Commission and by the Council. Thus, in a debate on arms procurement, the EP in September 1979 asserted its right to discuss all matters of concern to the EC. Since then, it has increasingly asserted a right to be consulted about international political issues. Gradually, the member governments have accepted, if grudgingly, the EP's demand for greater involvement, not least in the ratification of treaties with non-EC states. (In this respect, it is interesting to compare the EP's proposals with those originally proposed for the Genscher–Colombo initiative, and those of the 1983 Stuttgart 'Solemn Declaration'.)[41] Indeed, following the EP's adoption in 1981 of the first five of several reports on future inter-institutional relations,[42] the Ten's Foreign Ministers agreed for the first time to meet the EP's Enlarged Bureau in November 1981. This was followed in December 1981 by the first report to the EP by the then Council President-in-Office, Mrs Margaret Thatcher. The member governments tacitly gave qualified acceptance to the idea of the EP having some right to be informed of the progress of deliberations within the context of European Political Co-operation (EPC) that formally lies outside the ambit of the Rome Treaty. There was some recognition of the way in which the member governments and the EP could reinforce each other's public pronouncements, for example in condemning Soviet intervention in Afghanistan and Poland, and in respect of the Conference on Security and Co-operation in Europe (CSCE), Lomé III, the Lebanon, the Korean airline disaster and the Falklands crisis. But this should not be overstated for the UK government graphically highlighted that there were clear limits to government tolerance of the EP's investigative activities when it deplored the Parliament's decision to make a report on the situation in Northern Ireland. By contrast, tempers flared in September 1983 when some MEPs felt that the Greek Council President failed to distinguish adequately between national and EC positions. Yet, by the closing stages of the legislature, the EP had had some impact on the governments in international matters and had begun to grasp the highly divisive issue of the deployment of missiles in Western Europe.

While the EP clearly developed a comparatively high profile in international affairs, this should not mask its continued attempts to exert itself *vis-à-vis* the Commission and especially the Council in order to hold them accountable to EC publics' elected representatives. Thus, the EP did not eschew direct confrontation with the Council when it initiated legal proceedings, under Article 175 of the Rome Treaty, against the Council for failure to act in the field of transport policy. In January 1983, the Court of Justice was seized of the case. The EP gave vent also to dissatisfaction with the Commission but, while threatening to censure it on a number of occasions, did not use this power. Steps were taken to ensure that even if the EP were not consulted on the composition of the Commission, it should hold a vote of confidence and invest it on the basis of the new Commission's programme. Even though this proved problematic in 1980,[43] the second elected EP prosecuted the issue from the outset. Thus, even though MEPs' pressure for a woman to be appointed as one of the new Commissioners seemed to be in vain and the member governments soon overlooked their undertaking to consult the EP on the appointment of the new Commission President, the eventual Commission President-elect himself undertook to submit in early 1985 the Commission to an EP vote of investiture even though the Rome Treaty does not require this.

Apposite though many of the EP's actions during 1979–84 may have been, they often seemed esoteric and lacked impact. For instance, the special EP session held in Brussels in April 1983 to debate measures to combat unemployment received relatively little media coverage. The EP's special session in June 1983 in Strasbourg on the outcome of the Stuttgart summit fared only slightly better. Thus, it is clear that much of the EP's most important work was not conveyed to the public which was to remain largely ignorant of the ways in which, and the policies over which, MEPs had put pressure on the member governments.

POPULAR AWARENESS OF THE EP ON THE EVE OF THE 1984 ELECTIONS

In 1977–79, European Election Information Programmes (EEIPs) had been launched by the relevant sections of the Commission and the EP in conjunction with their national press and information offices.[44]

These had been designed to make people – and notably 'opinion-leaders' who could act as 'multipliers' by disseminating information to others with whom they would be in contact – aware of the EP's existence, organisation, composition and functions. Whatever the strengths and weaknesses of the various EEIPs, they were originally seen almost as a one-off exercise for the first EP elections. It was expected that, thereafter, while the institutions would continue their usual information activities, they would have less of, if any, such role in the second EP elections. This was because it was assumed that the political parties contesting the elections would be the chief actors in the second EP elections and that they would assume the voter mobilisation roles associated with parties in elections. Moreover, the party groups in the EP had insisted that they would assume these functions and sought finance accordingly. Nevertheless, in 1984, there were limited EEIPs based largely on a set of common publications prepared in Luxembourg in the EC's official languages, and on a short-film about the EP (which was censured and adapted for use in the television advertisement seen in the UK). Press and television advertising was undertaken by the national EP offices where appropriate. Yet, as before, this was not sufficient to counteract negative press and television coverage and commentary, such as it was, about the EP in the pre-campaign and campaign periods. Nor was it enough to make those unaware of the EP and MEPs conscious of them, their record, performance, manifestos and aspirations. *Eurobarometer* findings in 1983–84 on the level of public awareness of the EP and impending elections were, therefore, as in 1978–79, good indicators of the level of awareness and the state of play.

Eight months before the EP elections, *Eurobarometer* found that on average only 14% of those interviewed (that is, 29% of those respondents who claimed to have seen or heard something about the EP) mentioned the elections spontaneously. This compares poorly with the situation in October 1978 when twice as many people seemed aware of the impending elections. Awareness of the elections ranged from 62% in Belgium to 44% in Denmark; 40% in the FRG and Ireland; and 32% in France. It was under 22% in Italy, Luxembourg, the Netherlands, Greece and the UK, even though awareness of the EP itself was over 50% everywhere except in Belgium (32%), Ireland and the FRG (47%) and the UK (48%). The discrepancy between awareness of the EP itself and awareness of the elections could be due to a number of factors.

The September 1983 plenary meeting of the EP had received extensive media coverage in most EC member states: the vote on the EUT was widely reported as an historic event, and the plenary itself, both in terms of topics covered (Christmas butter, the presentation of the draft 1984 budget and nuclear disarmament) and the conduct of the session (notably Questions to the Council and Questions to the Conference of Foreign Ministers (CFM)), proved highly controversial. Heated exchanges took place between the Greek Foreign Minister and MEPs. It may be, therefore, that reports of these events were recalled vaguely by *Eurobarometer*'s respondents whereas the association between the elections and the EP was not.

Yet the decline, relative to 1978, in awareness of the elections was somewhat surprising not least because an elected EP had existed for over four years. The findings contradicted hopes expressed on the eve of the first elections that public awareness of the EP would rise and be reinforced during the first elected EP's lifetime. But the fall in awareness of the elections can perhaps partly be explained by the context of the 1979 and 1984 elections. Eight months before the 1979 elections the EP had been mentioned generally in terms of the impending (but postponed from 1978) first elections and there had been a good deal of public and sometimes heated party political debates in the member states about proposed electoral provisions governing those elections. Contrastingly, in 1984 the absence of a common electoral procedure had been taken for granted given both general and member governments' neglect of the EP's draft proposals for one.[45] The EP and the elections were not issues even in those member states that altered the detail of their Euro-electoral laws amidst some local protest (see Chapter 1).

The extent of the controversy over electoral procedures alone cannot explain the widespread ignorance about the elections. As in 1979, so in 1984, the context of the run-up to the elections was crucial. Whereas in 1978–79 knowledge about the EP was presumed to be low, in 1983–84 not only had public knowledge about the EP to be reinforced selectively or generated but the predominantly negative image of the EP had to be counteracted at a time when the EC itself had proved incapable of responding to pressing crises. The problems, then, of improving interest in and dispelling myths about the EP and mobilising the electorate proved formidable. Further factors that help to account for relatively low awareness levels of the elections in autumn 1983 concern individuals' perceptions of MEPs, the EP's powers and the EP's role in the EC. *Eurobarometer* found that in the Ten, a majority regarded MEPs as too remote from the electors. Somewhat paradoxically perhaps in view of Britain's repeated claims that even the mega-Euro-constituencies provided a better link between MEPs and voters than any system of proportional representation could do, more respondents from the UK (78%) than elsewhere felt that MEPs were too remote.[46] Whether or not this perception of remoteness would be mitigated were there to be a common system of electing MEPs or were the EP to be given a single seat remains to be seen. However, the psychological impact of a common seat and other symbols of identification with the EC were accepted by member governments at the Fontainebleau summit shortly after the 1984 EP elections when they set up committees to look at the EUT and the means of creating a sense of popular identity with the EC.

Symbols of attachment to the EC whether they take the form of the Euro-stamp marking the EP elections, a Euro-passport, anthem, flag, or a common parliament, common political rights and obligations have an importance beyond the provisions of a tangible means by which individuals can identify themselves as being part of the EC. They form a frame of reference for organising latent knowledge about the EC. The absence of such a frame of reference was apparent well before the second EP elections took place. A poll commissioned by the EP's information and documentation services in April 1983 revealed a gap between respondents' level of knowledge about the EP and related matters, suggesting that knowledge about the EP, unless ordered in some way within a comprehensible frame of knowledge, was virtually useless or irrelevant. Thus whereas 57% of respondents recalled voting in the first EP elections, they failed to equate this act with electing MEPs.[47] They failed also to link related information to the EP and the elections. Across the EC, 55% were aware that the EP was the Ten's parliament, and among the Nine awareness of MEPs being elected ranged from 56% in Belgium to 36% in France.[48] These findings show a basic disjunction between awareness of isolated facts about the EP and recognition of their actual relevance. The suspicion is that the 1984 EP election took place in a contextual vacuum: it lacked meaning before polling day and, unless things change – unless, that is, the newly-elected MEPs can supply voters with a frame of reference to order their knowledge of the EP and the EC – the EP election will remain generally meaningless. Without this, awareness of and interest in the EP and/or the elections may increase sporadically without any internalisation taking place. Thus, the elections may continue to be ill-understood and castigated as irrelevant.

However, working on the premise that knowledge about the EP and of the ability of MEPs' to 'deliver the goods' might be expected in part to affect voters' propensity to turn out, *Eurobarometer* asked limited and possibly too abstract questions to probe public awareness, under-standing and expectations of the EP. Taking awareness first, what is striking was the very low percentage (39%) of respondents who in March–April 1984 had heard recently about the EP and spontaneously mentioned the elections. This compares poorly with the 67% awareness level of the electorate in April 1979. In the case of the latter, EEIPs had been running for the preceding four months, whereas the more limited EEIPs for 1984 had only been scheduled for March and April, the time when the poll was taken, and some of the more eye-catching of these, such as television advertising, occurred later. Once again there was disjunction between awareness of the EP and the associated elections. Thus, a simple linear relationship between awareness levels and pro-pensity to vote does not necessarily hold.

Given general disenchantment with the EC, it is unlikely that a positive press for the EP would have been enough alone to cause a higher turnout.[49] Yet, if voters had felt that the EP could do something to redress the situation, it may be that turnout would have been higher. The utilitarian argument can be deduced from *Eurobarometer* which has elicited views repeatedly on the EP's powers. Findings about public understanding and, more importantly, expectations of the EP are instructive and corroborate this. Thus, it was clear that voters' assess-ment of the utility of voting, of what was at stake and the EP's image might affect turnout.

While parties might be better able to mobilise voters if the electorate is aware of the EP and the elections, it does not follow that awareness alone will cause voters either to notice and relate party campaigns to that knowledge, or to vote. Indeed, party campaigns might have a dissuasive effect and obscure the linkage between electing MEPs and the EP itself. Given the national biases of the ten election campaigns, there is a suspicion that party campaigns negated rather than rein-forced awareness of a relationship between electing MEPs and the EP, and undermined any views as to the utility of voting. Why? The reasons for this lie both with the EP's poor image and with the campaigns' natures and content, and will be examined in more detail in Chapter 12. However, here, a few brief remarks are in order.

THE PARTY DIMENSIONS TO THE EP ELECTION CAMPAIGN

Party Euro-election campaign activity took effect at the national, supranational (that is, EP) and transnational levels. At the national level, national party bodies were responsible for mobilising the electorate. At the supranational level, the major national parties supported their own candidates seeking election or re-election to the EP; and at the transnational level, the three major ideological groupings (Christian Democrat, Socialist and Liberal) linked sister parties from the member states together in the European People's Party (EPP), the Confederation of Socialist Parties of the EC (CSP) and the Federation of European Liberals and Democrats (ELD).[50] Smaller parties, like the Greens and the Ecologists were also to develop transnational links of a more rudimentary kind.

It is important to note that neither the supranational, EP party groups nor the transnational party bodies are strictly analogous to national parties. Ideological and policy cleavages are more acute and sometimes aggravated by national differences. Experience of working together in the EP may on occasion mitigate division but it has not resulted in the creation of parties as cohesive as those in national politics are presumed to be. Furthermore, a number of EP groups are outside the three major ideological groupings and exhibit either even greater polarities (as in the case of the Communists, and the former Group for the Technical Co-ordination and Defence of Independent Groups and Members (TCG) formed principally by MEPs keen to acquire the advantages enjoyed by the EP's formal party groups) or a more limited national make-up (for example, the European Democratic Group (mainly UK and a few Danish MEPs), and the former Group of European Progressive Democrats (mainly French and Irish MEPs)). It is hardly surprising then that within the looser transnational federations, even more pronounced divisions and hence less cohesion are found.

As in 1979, so in 1984 the EP party groups received funds from the EP.[51] They were earmarked strictly for campaign expenditure.[52] The EP funds were divided between the EP party groups, their member parties and the transnational federations.[53] Other arrangements were made for parties not in the EP (see Chapter 1). Thus, the UK Social Democratic Party (SDP) benefitted through their links in the Alliance but whereas the Liberals (UK) got funds before the election, the SDP did so afterwards. The EP party groups once again spent their funds on various pamphlets outlining both their work since 1979, and their policy priorities and views. They funded also limited advertisements, briefed journalists, and tried to attract media attention. The Socialists and the Liberals also made films shown in the member states. However, whereas the EP party groups' activities were primarily 'educative', their respective transnational federations were to undertake the task of helping their national parties to mobilise the electorate. Apart from their publicity-stunt type activities, the transnational parties engaged in the more serious task of preparing and adopting common election programmes/manifestos. As will become clear from the survey of their content, all covered a wide range of issues.

THE MANIFESTOS

For the first EP election, the CSP had been able to agree on an 'Appeal to the Electorate' rather than on a manifesto comparable to those of the EPP and the ELD. But for the 1984 elections, the CSP was able to adopt a manifesto at its 13th Congress in Munich in March 1984. Its chief themes were jobs, peace and freedom. The preamble of the manifesto stated that the EC was a supplementary instrument for the realisation of European Socialists' goals: social justice, solidarity and freedom: 'We need a European Community which is not a commercial and technocratic Europe, but a fraternal Europe of the people. The 1984 elections can contribute to this transformation.'[54] The five chapters of the manifesto built on this, stressing the need for co-ordination rather than integrated common policies – an approach necessitated by internal rifts (mainly along national lines). The first chapter, 'A European way out of the crisis', insisted 'that competitive austerity must be replaced by co-operation for social progress'.[55]

As in national politics, so at the European level, Socialists proclaimed their absolute priority to be 'the fight for jobs' based on a three-pronged economic strategy of recovery, re-structuring and re-distribution of work and, wealth. This was to be supported by 'co-ordinated action on a European level', a common policy in the shape of a European employment plan, supplemented by co-ordinated major public investment programmes, more funds for research, and an industrial programme elaborated by the Commission and the EP. The proposals in the manifesto also covered consumer and energy policies, reform of the Regional Fund, EC support for co-operatives, industrial democracy, work sharing, a 35-hour week, more jobs and training for the under-25s, the elimination of discrimination against women and immigrant workers, justice and social security improvements, rejection of monetarism, environmental protection and a strengthened European Monetary System (EMS). Other proposals dealt with the need for a renovated CAP to be responsive to consumer needs, and to take account of Mediterranean enlargement and the need for food aid to the Third World to be replaced by food production.

The EC was portrayed as a factor for peace, justice and freedom in the world. The CSP called on the EC to act as a 'civilian power' and to speak with one voice on major international issues. Oppression in Turkey and the division of Cyprus was condemned, and solidarity with the peoples of Europe (including Poland) was advocated along with solutions to problems in the Middle East, Asia, Latin America and Africa. On security, the CSP again stressed the need for the EC to expand and develop an independent, influential role. Human rights and Northern Ireland were also broached. The final chapter dealt with the highly controversial issue of more democratic and efficient institutions as the prerequisite for desired policy advances.

The British Labour Party and the Danish Social Democrats dissociated themselves from calls to augment the EP's influence. The Labour Party also dissociated itself from the section in the manifesto condemning the concept of a 'juste retour' and called for a better financial system. For their part the Italians (PSI and PSDI) added an annex confirming their support for the EUT and declaring their intention to organise their activities and campaign in its support.[56] While the CSP manifesto was clearly a minimal document, it was an advance on the situation in 1979. Moreover, though a slim document compared to that of the ELD, it was supplemented by a dense pamphlet – 'A European Way Out of the Crisis'[57] – drafted and adopted unanimously by a CSP working group, formed by the CSP manifesto committee, and including Portuguese and Spanish representatives.[58] This expanded upon the manifesto.

The CSP chose to give special prominence to jobs as a detailed analysis of issue areas had found this to be the issue on which Socialists could win votes. However, the recession meant that none of the parties could afford to ignore unemployment. Not surprisingly, it featured prominently too in the ELD and EPP manifestos.

The ELD's manifesto – 'Pour une Europe libérale et démocratique' – was adopted by eleven parties from nine member states (excluding Ireland) in December 1983 in Munich. Over twice the length of the CSP manifesto, it was divided into five broad chapters that subsumed a number of themes, many of which (especially the CAP, energy, security, and the economy) had been debated heatedly, not least in Munich. The ELD's first priority was progress towards a European Union based on democracy, human rights and the rule of law.

Accordingly, it called for majority voting in the Council, co-decision between the Council and the EP, a role for the EP in the nomination of the Commission and in ratifying EC treaties with third states, and the extension of budgetary control to income as well as expenditure. These all mirrored successive EP demands made both before and especially since the first EP elections,[59] and confirmed the need for institutional and procedural changes (including a common seat for key institutions) in the EC to enable it to meet future challenges. The sentiments expressed echoed those of the EUT. The issue of a uniform electoral procedure based on proportional representation and less restrictive rules governing eligibility to vote in EP elections (especially regarding residence and nationality qualifications) was also advocated. The first section of the manifesto also dealt with another pressing issue: the EC budget and the UK's contribution to it. It was noted that the budget was unfair to the UK whose income was below the EC average but which had to make the largest budgetary contribution. This led the ELD to insist that the gravity of the problems facing the EC – decision-making paralysis, the financial crisis, the need to increase substantially the EC's competence *vis-à-vis* foreign affairs and economic policy – demanded urgently a new initiative in integration and the EUT's adoption. The ELD manifesto thus opened with references to both topical debates (for example, the budget crisis) and the one issue that was supposed to be the major, common election issue throughout the EC: European Union.[60]

Concerning human rights, the ELD called on the EP to draft charters to outline and defend human rights for EC citizens; and to affirm social rights based on equal pay for work of equal value, collective bargaining, social security, free and equal access to education and training.

Chapter two of the manifesto dealt with the economic crisis. The ELD called for an integrated social market economy to make the EC competitive internationally without resorting to self-destructive protectionism and inappropriate interventionism;[61] for free trade, increased worker participation, limiting the public sector expenditure, increased investment, greater employment opportunites (including more vocational training and part-time work) bolstered by a vast research and development programme exploiting information technology and new industries, and a system of life-long education supported by the Social Fund.[62] To guarantee economic recovery, the manifesto called for the mobilisation of latent and under-used human resources, especially the young. To set up a stable monetary system within EMS, co-operation with the USA and Japan and the accession of all EC member states to the EMS were advocated along with support for the European Currency Unit (ECU) as a convertible currency. The social policy section called for a uniform approach in the EC to combatting drug abuse and poverty. Further sections dealt with the environment and pollution, consumer protection and EC action to eliminate artificial and traditional barriers to women fulfilling their potential.[63]

The ELD advocated also CAP reform and a more rigorous fisheries conservation policy.[64] Mention was made of small and medium size businesses, energy, communications and transport, regional development, and protecting and developing Europe's cultural heritage. Finally, a chapter on Europe's role in the world portrayed the EC as a force for peace, progress and stability with the potential to become a Union with a common foreign and security policy, determining its future while acknowledging the importance of Atlantic co-operation. One specific recommendation, calling for the establishment of a permanent EPC secretariat, took up past arguments voiced in the EP (not only by Liberal MEPs) and in the European Council not least in respect of the Genscher–Colombo initiative. Similarly, on development policy, past themes were revived, including the call to stop aid to Third World countries that persistently violated human rights.[65]

From this brief survey of the ELD manifesto, it is clear that the member parties' concerns were akin to those contained in the first manifesto. However, since 1979, the EC's economic fortunes had vastly deteriorated, budgetary and agricultural problems had become more acute, and some progress had been made on the institutional front. Though European Union featured prominently, the ELD could not claim it uniquely as their achievement. Indeed, the EPP's claim – despite the EUT's submission by Spinelli, an Independent MEP standing on a Communist (PCI) list – was greater, and not just because of a Christian Democrat (Colombo) and a Liberal (Genscher) initiative on European Union.

Like the Liberals, Christian Democrats claim a strong pro-integrationist heritage that they tried to exploit in the election campaign. Indeed, the EPP group in the EP published a special edition of its magazine (with a centre-fold depicting EPP candidates for specific member states)[66] in February 1984 that not only stressed 'what you should know' and gave facts and figures about the EPP's record, but highlighted the need for European Union. EPP President Tindemans wrote:

[It] is both possible and indispensable and represents our only chance to prevent Europe falling further into economic decline.[67]

The magazine was dotted with quotations from eminent Europeans like Adenauer, Monnet, de Gasperi, as well as figures and cartoons supporting the EC's maintenance. National egoism was depicted as the greatest threat to European Union. The issue concluded with a picture of the EPP logo, and a list of EPP member parties 'working towards the same objective: European Union for peace, liberty and justice'.[68]

European Union was at the forefront of the EPP campaign that was launched in Rome from 2–4 April 1984 when the EPP Congress adopted an 'Action Programme' for the elected EP's second term of office. Indeed, one of the only *demands* in the Action Programme comes in Chapter five on 'Greater Democracy in Europe' where the extension of the EP's powers as 'a dynamic process and a step on the road towards European Union' is firmly advocated; and where the EPP (that in the first elected EP presented a draft constitution for the EC on the same day as the Spinelli initiative)[69] asserts its first political aim to be the EC's transformation into a European federation, the United States of Europe.[70] The EPP's institutional and policy recommendations parallel both the EUT (as, for example, in the espousal of subsidiarity) and important resolutions of the first elected EP. The EPP committed itself to securing the EUT's ratification by the Ten's national parliaments.

While the introduction to the Action Programme notes the need for a European Union and united action in a wide variety of areas, like the CSP and ELD manifestos, subsequent chapters focus on the general themes of jobs, justice, civil rights, peace and democracy. These again stress the importance of co-ordination by the Ten to preclude national policy initiatives, notably in the economic sector, from being negated. Improved job prospects for the under-25s were seen as a priority in an economic recovery policy based 'on the principle of a socially and ecologically responsible market economy',[71] on a strengthened EMS and the ECU's use as a reserve currency. The EPP promoted the ECU as a means of payment, it having a stronger role in the international monetary system, and its use for deposit accounts and travellers cheques to stabilise the world money market. The section on social policy, as in the CSP and ELD manifestos, highlighted the consequences of micro- and information-technology, advocated more worker co-determination as called for in the Vredeling–Davignon directives, strengthening the Social Fund and, *inter alia*, EC labour legislation, and measures to prevent the creation of jobs having an adverse effect on the environment, the Third World and underprivileged or minority groups.

Turning to the CAP and fisheries, problems were ascribed essentially to the failure to set up Economic and Monetary Union (EMU). The EPP also addressed the question of the development of the individual in a section that was as ambitious as the section on economic and social policies in its advocacy of a code of conduct for the use of computer records, data protection, co-ordinated action against terrorism and drug traffic, and the protection of citizens' privacy and security. The value of the family and of equal rights for women were also espoused. Education was described as a 'fundamental social right' that must have a European dimension if people are to feel European. The EPP called for a European educational passport to allow people to train in any member state, co-ordination of vocational training, the mutual recognition of diplomas, more European news in the media, and a literacy programme. Various integrative measures for public health, combatting trans-frontier pollution and consumer protection were advocated.

Concerning international affairs, a section of the manifesto headed 'Towards peace with greater security through justice and solidarity' not only indicated the EPP's 'theory of peace' and commitment to a strong Atlantic Alliance and arms reductions, in particular in nuclear armaments as a priority goal but called for the solution to the German question (central to East-West relations) within the framework of a global European Peace Treaty. It was noted that West Berlin was a part of the EC and the cornerstone of genuine *détente* in Europe. This was clearly dear to the hearts of German EPP members. The most important recommendation concerned the creation of a European (EC) Security Council by the European Council. In the first instance, security policy would become part of EPC and subsequently become an EC responsibility in a European Union. The development of a Community concept of security was seen as of prime significance. It is noteworthy that the recommendation mirrors some Genscher–Colombo, Spinelli and EP proposals.[72] Policy towards developing countries was outlined also and treaties akin to Lomé were advocated for South and Central America.

From the foregoing it is clear that the manifestos broached similar topics, most of which had been raised in the EP though this was not always usefully made clear. Not only was a hierarchy of issues hard to discern, but the CSP, ELD and EPP were basically agreed on the key issues facing the EC and there was little to differentiate sharply their various policy recommendations. The electoral programmes among member parties mirrored national preoccupations and frustrated efforts to develop clear-cut common policy recommendations for all issues raised in the electoral programmes. This was to undermine their usefulness in the campaign. The electoral programmes were not really designed for public so much as for national party elite consumption. As noted already, it fell to national parties to conduct the campaigns in the member states. How they fared and the extent to which the 1984 EP election was to be a *Euro*-election are the subjects of the following chapters.

NOTES AND REFERENCES

1. See V. Herman and J. Lodge, *The European Parliament and the European Community* (London: Macmillan, 1978).
2. See J. G. Blumler (ed.), *Communicating to Voters: Television in the First European Parliamentary Elections* (London: Sage, 1983).
3. See J. Lodge and V. Herman, *Direct Elections to the European Parliament: a Community Perspective* (London: Macmillan, 1982).
4. See J. Lodge, 'Citizens and the EEC: the Role of the European Parliament', *The Parliamentarian*, 58 (1977) 176–81.
5. See Lodge and Herman, op. cit.
6. *European Journal of Political Research,* Special Issue: The First European Elections, 8 (1980)
7. On the dual mandate, see J. Lodge, 'Members of the House of Commons and the European Parliament', *The Parliamentarian*, 59 (1978) 239–45, and J. Lodge, 'MP–MEP Links: Members of the House of Commons and the Dual Mandate' in V. Herman and R. van Schendelen (eds), *The European Parliament and the National Parliaments* (Farnborough: Saxon House, 1979) pp. 219–37.
8. See *Report drawn up on behalf of the Political Affairs Committee on the Adoption of a Draft Convention Introducing Elections to the European Parliament by Direct Universal Suffrage* (Patijn Report) (Luxembourg: European Parliament, Doc. 368/74).
9. See *Draft Treaty establishing the European Union* (hereinafter EUT) (Luxembourg: European Parliament, Feb. 1984). Also see, J. Lodge, 'European Union and the First Elected European Parliament: The Spinelli Initiative', *Journal of Common Market Studies*, 22 (1984) 377–402, and J. Lodge (ed.), *European Union* (London: Macmillan, 1986).
10. See J. H. H. Weiler, 'The Genscher–Colombo Draft European Act: The Politics of Indecision', *Journal of European Integration,* 6 (1983) 129–53.
11. See A. Spinelli, 'Das Verfassungsprojekt des Europäischen Parlaments', and chapters by J-P. Jacqué and C-D. Ehlermann, in J. Schwarze and R. Bieber (eds), *Eine Verfassung für Europa* (Baden-Baden: Nomos, 1984). Also see J. Lodge (ed.), *European Union*, op. cit.
12. See report of his speech in The Hague in *Le Monde*, 9 Feb. 1984.
13. See C-D. Ehlermann, 'Mitgliedschaft in der EG-Rechtsprobleme der Erweiterung, der Mitgliedschaft und der Verkleinerung', *Europarecht*, 19 (1984) 113–25.

14. See, for example, W. J. Feld and J. K. Wildgen, 'National Administrative Elites and European Integration: Saboteurs at Work?', *Journal of Common Market Studies*, 13 (1975) 244–65.
15. On the legal side to this, see B. Beutler, 'Mehr Macht durch Recht? Das Europäische Parlament vor dem Europäischen Gerichtshof', *Europarecht*, 19 (1984) 145–54.
16. See J. H. H. Weiler, in *Journal of European Integration*, op. cit.
17. See *Crocodile* (Letters to the Members of the European Parliament, edited by Altiero Spinelli and Felice Ippolito and published since October 1980); J. Lodge, in *Journal of Common Market Studies*, op. cit; and J. Lodge (ed.), *European Union*, op. cit.
18. See M. Palmer, 'The Development of the European Parliament's Institutional Role within the European Community, 1974–1983', *Journal of European Integration*, 6 (1983) 183–202.
19. See J. Lodge, 'The European Parliament after Direct Elections: Talking-Shop or Putative Legislature?', *Journal of European Integration*, 5 (1982) 259–84.
20. See E. Schoof, 'Bundestag und Europäisches Parlament. Zur Neugestaltung der Beziehungen seit der Direktwahl', *Zeitschrift für Parlamentsfragen*, 13 (1982) 199–203; and U. Raderschall, 'Bundesrat und Europäisches Parlament', ibid., pp. 204–8.
21. See J. Lodge, 'The United Kingdom Parliament and the European Parliament', *The Parliamentarian*, 62 (1981) 119–23.
22. For example, Denmark and Ireland allegedly for want of funds.
23. See J. Lodge, 'The European Parliament: in search of institutional change', *The World Today*, 38 (1982) 365.
24. See J. Lodge, 'European Union and Direct Elections 1984', *The Round Table*, 289 (1984) 57–68; and J. Lodge, D. Freestone and S. Davidson, 'Some Problems of the Draft Treaty on European Union', *European Law Review*, 9 (1984) 387–400.
25. See J. Lodge, in *Journal of European Integration*, op. cit; and M. Palmer, in *Journal of European Integration*, op. cit.
26. *Report drawn up on behalf of the Political Affairs Committee on a draft uniform electoral procedure for the elections of Members of the European Parliament* (Seitlinger Report) (Luxembourg: European Parliament, Doc. 1-988/81/A and Doc. 1-988/81/B–C).
27. EP General Secretariat, *On the Right Road* (Luxembourg: European Parliament, 1984) p. 1.
28. The number of petitions rose from 16 in 1975 to 31 in 1978, and from 57 in 1979 to 81 in both 1981 and 1983. These figures include only those submissions complying with the provisions of the Rules of Procedure regarding the form and content of petitions.
29. EP General Secretariat, *On the Right Road*, op. cit., pp. 9–11.
30. See *OJ* C327, 14 Dec. 1981; *OJ* C42, 13 Jan. 1983; *OJ* C322, 26 Oct. 1983; and *European Parliament Working Documents (EPWD)*, 1-80/84.
31. See *OJ* C101, 9 Apr. 1981; *OJ* C125, 20 Apr. 1982; and *OJ* C342, 16 Nov. 1983.
32. See F. Wooldridge and M. Sassella, 'Some recent legal provisions increasing the power of the European Parliament, and establishing a Euro-

32   Introduction

pean Court of Auditors', *Legal Issues of European Integration*, 2 (1976) 14–52.

33. See M. van den Abeele, 'The Mandate of 30 May 1980, Budget financing and the revitalisation of the EC: An Unfinished Journey', *Common Market Law Review*, 19 (1982) 501–19.

34. See *Bull. EC* 5–1982 and D. Strasser, 'La décharge donnée par le parlement européen pour les exercices 1979 et 1980', *Revue du Marché Commun.*, no. 265, 3/1983, 124–67.

35. See C-D. Ehlermann, *Europarecht*, op. cit.

36. See, for example, the EP's guidelines for the 1983 budget and related reports: *EPWD*, 1-97/82; *EPWD*, 1-778/82; *EPWD*, 1-779/82; *EPWD*, 1-777/82; *EPWD*, 1-777/82/B; and *EPWD*, 1-777/82/Annex.

37. See Joint Declaration of 30 June 1982, *OJ* C194, 28 July 1982.

38. It cut the EP's margin for manoeuvre and in certain circumstances the Council may completely eliminate the possibility of increasing the overall amount of the budget. Small wonder that antagonism persists. Though the EP's right of budgetary amendment is still substantial compared to many national parliaments' rights to amend national budgets. The EP was also vigilant of the Commission over the collection of own resources. See *EPWD*, 1-695/80; and C-D. Ehlermann, 'The Financing of the Community: the distinction between financial contributions and own resources', *Common Market Law Review*, 19 (1982) 571–89.

39. Commission of the European Communities, 'The Future Financing of the Community', Communication from the Commission to the Council and the EP, COM (83) 10 fin, Brussels, 10 February 1983. See also, Commission of the European Communities, 'The Draft Decision on new own resources', COM (83) 270 fin, Brussels, 6 May 1983. On UK contributions, see C. Cova, 'La contribution britannique: un dossier toujours plus complexe', *Revue du Marché Commun.*, no. 265, 3/1983, pp. 117–19.

40. See J. Lodge, *Journal of European Integration,* op. cit.

41. See ibid., and J. H. H. Weiler, *Journal of European Integration*, op. cit.

42. See *EPWD*, 1-207/81 (Van Miert Report); *EPWD*, 1-216/81 (Hänsch Report); *EPWD*, 1-206/81 (Diligent Report); *EPWD*, 1-335/81 (Elles Report); and *EPWD*, 1-226/81 (Baduel Glorioso Report).

43. See *Bull. EC* 1 and 2-1980.

44. See J. Lodge and V. Herman, *Direct Elections to the European Parliament: A Community Perspective*, op. cit.

45. See Seitlinger Report, op. cit. Also see, J. Lodge, 'The 1984 Euro-Election Tour: The Quest for Uniformity?', *The Parliamentarian*, 64 (1983) 204–12.

46. *Eurobarometer*, no. 20, Dec. 1983, p. 72.

47. 'Le parlement européen et l'élection de 1984', *Faits et Opinions*, Paris, August 1983, p. 49.

48. Ibid., pp. 47–8.

49. See J. G. Blumler (ed.), *Communicating to Voters: Television in the First European Parliamentary Elections*, op. cit.

50. For details on their origins, see J. Lodge and V. Herman, *Direct Elections to the European Parliament: A Community Perspective*, op. cit.; and G. Pridham and P. Pridham, *Transnational Party Co-operation and European*

Integration: The Process Towards Direct Elections (London: Allen & Unwin, 1981).

51. The chairmen of the EP party groups were responsible for how the funds were used and the Court of Auditors monitored them.
52. See *EPWD*, 1-777/82/B and *EPWD*, 1-185/82/Annex.
53. O. Niedermayer, 'The Transnational Dimension of the Election', draft of an article to be published in *Electoral Studies* (1984).
54. *Manifesto* (Luxembourg: CSP, 1984) p. 5.
55. Ibid., p. 9.
56. Ibid., p. 32.
57. CSP, *A European Way Out of the Crisis* (Luxembourg: CSP, 1984).
58. Marques for the Partido Socialista and Calvet for the Partido Socialista Obrero Español.
59. See J. Lodge, *Journal of European Integration*, op. cit.
60. See *The New Federalist*, 2, 1984. See also, J. Lodge, *Journal of Common Market Studies*, op. cit. and J. Lodge, *The Round Table*, op. cit.
61. ELD, *Pour Une Europe Libérale et Démocratique* (Brussels: ELD, 1984) p. 22.
62. Ibid., pp. 25–30.
63. Ibid., pp. 35–7.
64. See D. Freestone with A. Fleisch, 'The Common Fisheries Policy' in J. Lodge (ed.), *Institutions and Policies of the European Community* (London: Frances Pinter, 1983) pp. 77–84.
65. See J. Lodge (ed.), *Terrorism: a Challenge to the State* (Oxford: Martin Robertson, 1981).
66. For example, 'Election 84 Ireland'.
67. *DC-Europe*, 2/84 Brussels.
68. Ibid.
69. See J. Lodge, *Journal of Common Market Studies*, op. cit.
70. EPP, *Action Programme* (Rome: EPP, 1984) points 5.1.1–5.7.3.
71. Ibid., point 1.7.
72. For example, *EPWD*, 1-946/82 (Haagerup Report).

1 European Election Procedures

DAVID MILLAR

INTRODUCTION

In drawing up their national legislation to enable the first direct elections to the European Parliament to be held in 1979, the Governments and Parliaments of Belgium and the Federal Republic limited its scope to cover only these elections. No clearer indication could have been given that they expected that a uniform electoral procedure would have been introduced for the 1984 elections, for which new national electoral laws would have been necessary.

This paper will examine the proposal for a uniform procedure made by the European Parliament; the reasons for which it was not adopted by the Council of Ministers; the subsequent reversion to national electoral systems and changes in them; and their possible effects on the composition of the European Parliament.

PROPOSAL FOR A UNIFORM ELECTORAL PROCEDURE

Article 138, paragraph 3, of the EEC Treaty lays upon the European Parliament the obligation to:

> draw up proposals for elections by direct universal suffrage in accordance with a uniform procedure in all Member States.

In partial execution of this obligation, the Parliament had in January 1975 adopted a draft Convention on its direct election,[1] on which the

Council founded its Act of 20 September 1976, which itself provided the framework for the first direct elections in 1979.[2] The draft Convention deliberately comprised only those provisions absolutely essential to the holding of the first elections, as the EP envisaged making further proposals to provide for the adoption of a uniform electoral procedure.

Immediately after the first elections, the EP's Political Affairs Committee set up a Sub-Committee with the object of drafting a proposal on the uniform procedure. Following two-and-a-half years of discussion, the Political Committee reported to the EP, which in March 1982 adopted a Proposal for a Decision, incorporating a draft Act on a uniform electoral procedure by 158 votes to 77, with 27 abstentions.[3]

During its discussions, the Political Committee had considered alternative proposals for a uniform procedure put forward by the rapporteur, M. Jean Seitlinger (EPP – France), and had rejected a proposal based on the system of election to the Bundestag, by which a number of candidates would be elected from constituencies by simple majority, and a number from national lists by proportional representation.

OUTLINE OF THE DRAFT ACT

The proposal adopted by the House comprised a uniform procedure by which candidates would be elected by proportional representation from lists in multi-member constituencies (Article 2). This system was akin to that adopted by the Italian Parliament for the 1979 election to the EP. A minimum of three and a maximum of 15 candidates were to be elected in each constituency. Member States were to decide:

how their territory was to be divided into constituencies,
how to combine at national level the lists submitted in the various constituencies,
what conditions to lay down for the submission of lists,
whether to permit preferential voting within a list (Article 2), and
whether to introduce a threshold below which a list would obtain no seats (Article 4).

The draft Act went on to propose in Article 3 that seats should be allocated to each list or combination of lists in accordance with the d'Hondt system, taking account of the total number of votes secured at national level by such lists. The seats so allocated nationally should then be distributed between the lists in each constituency on the basis of the number of votes secured by each and within the number of seats fixed for that constituency. Vacant seats would be filled by the first non-elected candidate from the list of the party to which the retiring Member had belonged (Article 3).

The draft Act laid much emphasis on the right of nationals of the Member States to vote and to be a candidate. It proposed in Article 5 that all such nationals resident in the European Community should have the right to vote, no matter in what Member State they resided. They should be enabled to cast their votes in the elections in their country of origin. The right to stand for election was to be granted irrespective of the place of residence, and extended by Member States to nationals of another Member State who had been resident in their territory for at least five years (Article 6).

In order to take account of special geographical or ethnic factors recognised by the constitution, written or unwritten, of a Member State, the latter was permitted to adopt measures deviating from the provisions of Articles 2 and 3. This was to provide, for example, for the existence of ethnic minorities, e.g. in Northern Italy, and for the situation of West Berlin, and of Scotland, Wales and Northern Ireland within the United Kingdom (Article 4).

The Rapporteur, Mr Seitlinger, undertook a round of visits to the ten capitals during autumn 1982, to explain the draft Act and seek support for it. In almost all the capitals, both Government and Parliamentary leaders pledged their political support; the Rapporteur was also able to allay misgivings expressed in several quarters about the compatibility of the draft Act with existing electoral systems.

COUNCIL ACTIVITY ON THE DRAFT ACT

In May 1982 the Council set up a working group to consider the draft Act, composed usually of one official from the Ministry of the Interior, and one from the Ministry of Foreign Affairs of each Member State. The working group reported to the Council in December 1982, but was unable to reach consensus on the main provisions of the draft Act. The Council considered the group's first and subsequent reports on several occasions between December 1982 and May 1983, but were themselves unable to achieve consensus.

It became known that the two Member States which did not use a Continental-style proportional system were opposed to Article 2 of the draft Act, while other Member States found difficulty in accepting certain of the detailed proposals on the uniform procedure made by the EP.

A conciliation meeting between Parliament and the Council, held on 25 April 1983, did no more than to indicate the depth of disagreement in the Council on the uniform procedure.[4] Finally on 24–25 May, the Council stated that:

the task ... of laying down a uniform electoral procedure applicable in all the Member States, remains essential.

It undertook to:

pursue its work on introducing a uniform electoral procedure for the elections which will take place in 1989.[5]

The Council included the following passage in its statement:

5. Within the framework of the construction of Europe the Council appeals to the Member States to make every effort, as far as possible, to fulfil the objective that all nationals of Member States should have the right to vote in the election of members of the European Parliament, either in their country of origin or in their country of residence.

EFFECTS OF THE COUNCIL'S FAILURE

The failure of the Council to reach agreement on a uniform electoral procedure was a blow to the legitimacy and representative capacity of the EP. Without the same proportional electoral procedure in all Member States, the shortcomings of the electoral systems used in 1979 will be perpetuated for another five years. Of these, the principal was the consequence of simple majority voting in single-member constituencies in Great Britain, where 6.5 million votes returned 60 Conservative Members, 4.3 million votes returned 17 Labour Members and 1.7 million votes won no Liberal seats. Votes amounting to 40 000 were sufficient to return the only Scottish National Party Member elected (the Party's total vote being 248 000).

The consequent distortion of British representation in the European Parliament has been criticised in the EP[6] and elsewhere. It also affected the relative strength of the political groups and was clearly resented by the Socialist and Liberal and Democratic Groups, who would have gained British Members under a proportional system.

The disagreement on the uniform procedure marked a further blow to the process of European integration and created the danger of national governments and Parliaments introducing national measures to the detriment of the Council Act of 1976 (see below: Belgian electoral law). Finally, the momentum towards a uniform procedure created by Parliament's draft Act, the initiative of the rapporteur, Mr Seitlinger, and the efforts of the political parties has been lost and will be difficult to recreate.

THE 1979 ELECTORAL SYSTEMS

Of the electoral systems adopted in 1977–79 by the Member States (and in 1981 by Greece) to elect their representatives to the EP, eight out of the (then) nine were proportional and one (Great Britain) a plurality system. The electoral formula used was that of d'Hondt, except as follows:[7]

Greenland – first-past-the-post
Ireland and Northern Ireland – single transferable vote
Italy – highest remainder and national quota (Hare)
Luxembourg – (Hagenbach–Bischoff)
Great Britain – first-past-the-post

Preference voting was used in all Member States except the Federal Republic, France, Great Britain and Greenland. 'Panachage' (vote splitting) was also permitted in Luxembourg.

In Belgium, Ireland and Great Britain, this represented no change from the traditional system, but in the other seven countries and in Northern Ireland changes in the electoral formula were made. This can be taken as a useful precedent for the eventual introduction of a uniform procedure.

National lists were used in Denmark (except Greenland), the FRG, France, Greece, Luxembourg and the Netherlands. There was an option in the FRG to use Land lists. Regional lists or constituencies were used in Belgium, Ireland, Italy, Great Britain and Northern Ireland. These arrangements represented a change from the national electoral system in all countries except Ireland and Great Britain. Once again, this augurs well for the introduction of a uniform procedure.

An electoral threshold was used in the FRG and France (5%), and thresholds existed in practice also in Denmark, Luxembourg (14.3%) and the Netherlands (3.9%). Party bans operated in the FRG and Italy. Deposits were required in France, Ireland, Netherlands and the United Kingdom and signatures in support of nominations, under certain conditions, everywhere except in France and Ireland. Special regulations were made for minorities by Denmark (electoral alliances and Greenland), Italy (electoral alliances: linguistic minorities) and United Kingdom (Northern Ireland).

Apart from the distortions already noticed caused by the plurality systems in Great Britain, the ten electoral systems suffered from certain other shortcomings. In the Federal Republic, although the 'Greens' won 3.2% of the vote, and in France the Ecologists won 4.4%, the threshold prevented them from winning seats. By contrast, in Italy three parties, each with less than 3.2% of the vote, won seats. The deposit called for in France (Fr. 100 000) caused difficulties to the smaller parties and was considerably higher than the deposit required in any other country.

British and Irish nationals resident in other Member States were disenfranchised, except for Irish resident in the United Kingdom, Britons in Ireland, and Irish and British nationals resident in the Netherlands.

A unique consequence of the use of a national list in France was the introduction of the so-called 'tourniquet' system by the Party for the Defence of the interests of France in Europe (DIFE), the title adopted by the Gaullist RPR party in the European elections. Candidates were asked to sign an undertaking that, after serving one year in the European Parliament, they would resign their seat in favour of the non-elected candidates in the 81-strong DIFE list. A few leading candidates were excepted from this rule.

In the event, several candidates who won seats in the election, or who subsequently took the places of Members who had resigned, refused to retire after one year, causing some controversy. The object of the system was to ensure the widest representation possible of DIFE voters, but against this must be set the disruption caused to the work of the European Progressive Democratic Group in the Parliament (which also included Irish, one Danish and one Scottish member).

The Credentials Committee eventually made a report to the EP in which it concluded that the tourniquet system was in conformity with the Rules of Procedure but against their spirit.[8] A resolution contained in the report was adopted in February 1983.[9] The system is not to apply in the 1984 elections to RPR candidates.

CHANGES IN ELECTORAL SYSTEMS FOR 1984 ELECTIONS

As has been seen, it was not until late May 1983 that the Council admitted its inability to agree upon a uniform electoral procedure. This reduced the time available to national governments to bring forward proposals to alter the electoral systems used in the 1979 elections. Briefly, the situation was as follows:

A. Member States which retained existing electoral laws:
    France, Federal Republic, Netherlands and the United Kingdom
B. Member States which amended their electoral laws:
    Belgium, Denmark, Greece, Ireland, Italy and Luxembourg.

Of category A, the United Kingdom altered the boundaries of European election constituencies to align them with the new boundaries adopted in 1983 for national elections. This was done without amendment of the electoral law (the European Assembly Elections Act 1978).

MEMBER STATES WHICH HAVE AMENDED THEIR LAWS

Belgium

The principal amendments made to the Belgian electoral law are as follows:[10]

1. New incompatibilities have been introduced to bar the holders of the following posts from sitting in the European Parliament:

    Members of the Chamber of Representatives or of the Senate
    Members of the executive body of a Community or region
    Members of the Flemish Council, or of the Council of the French Community
    Members of a regional council, of a permanent deputation and of the council of a conurbation (collège d'agglomération/ agglomeratie – college)

The legality of this prohibition of the 'dual mandate' has been questioned by the Commission and is under consideration by a committee of the European Parliament as possibly being contrary to Article 5 of the 1976 Council Act. The Act stated that membership of the European Parliament shall be compatible with membership of a national Parliament.

On the other hand the extensions of the right to vote are both welcome and place Belgium in the same position in this regard as the Netherlands. For example, United Kingdom and Irish citizens resident in these two countries, who had no right to vote for candidates in their own country, were able to vote for Belgian and Dutch candidates.

Denmark

Amendments have made technical changes in the following fields:[11]

  the right to vote and to be elected; lists of candidates; voting procedures; and the count.

The Danish Parliament adopted a second law in April 1984 amending the European elections law in order to take account of the withdrawal of Greenland from the EEC, due to take place on 1 January 1985. The main points of the law are:

  from 1 January 1985 the single seat allocated to Greenland will be incorporated with the 15 seats from Denmark; the country will then form a national constituency,

  from 1 January 1985 the 16th seat will be filled from the list of the party which, following the elections on 14 June 1984, is due to provide under the proportional system the next candidate for election to the EP,

  no further elections to the EP will be held in Greenland or the Faroe Isles, to whom the electoral law will no longer apply,

  from 1 January 1985 electors resident in Greenland and the Faroe Islands will have no right to vote in European elections.[12]

Greece

One month before the elections, the Greek Parliament amended the 1981 European elections law to provide that the first and second candidates on every party list could hold a mandate in both the national and the European Parliament. This was done to permit prominent national politicians to retain their seats in the Greek Parliament if elected to the EP. Thus only in Belgium is the dual mandate now completely prohibited.[13]

Ireland

The Irish Parliament adopted a Bill to provide for lists of 'replacement candidates' for the European elections. This move followed criticism by the EP that the method of filling vacancies in Irish seats in the Parliament was not in accordance with the Council Act of 1976, which required that Members of the European Parliament should be elected by direct universal suffrage. Vacancies have since 1979 been filled by election by the Dail of a candidate proposed by the party of the Member who had previously held the seat.

The scheme is that parties, or independent non-party candidates, deposit with the returning office a list of replacement candidates, which is published at the time of the nomination of candidates. Each party may propose replacement candidates to the number of the principal candidates proposed plus four; each independent candidate should be able to nominate three replacement candidates. Lists of replacement candidates may be withdrawn. In the event of no such candidate being available to fill a seat which has fallen vacant, the Dail may select a person from any replacement candidates list to fill the vacant seat.[14]

Luxembourg

The Chamber of Deputies adopted two main amendments to the 1979 electoral law. The first gives the right to vote by post to all Luxembourgers living outside the Grand Duchy. The effect of the second is that a Luxembourg MEP who is appointed a Minister in the Luxembourg Government and resigns his European seat can, if he subsequently leaves ministerial office, be reinstated in the first place on the party's list of non-elected candidates. Equally, a substitute Member who has succeeded to a seat in the EP and is then appointed a Minister can, on leaving ministerial office, be reinstated as first of his party's non-elected candidates.[15]

Italy

Article 1 of the Italian law contained one change which is of importance here. It amended Article 2 of Law No. 18 of 24 January 1979 so that, instead of a fixed number of seats being allocated to each of the five regional constituencies, the allocation of seats is determined on the basis of the results of the last general population census. This is done by dividing the number of inhabitants of the Republic by 81 (being the number of Italian MEPs), and distributing the seats in proportion to the population of each constituency, according to the rule of quotients and highest remainders.[16]

SUMMARY OF ELECTORAL LEGISLATION 1984

It will be seen that only in Belgium and Luxembourg has progress been made towards the introduction of a uniform electoral procedure. The enfranchisement of Belgian nationals resident in other Member States, and of nationals of other Member States resident in Belgium who have no right to vote in their country of nationality respond both to the EP's proposal of March 1982 and the Council's appeal of May 1983. Against this advance must be set the prohibition of a dual mandate in the Belgian and European Parliament, which would appear to conflict with the Council Act of 1976, and the introduction of particular national incompatibilities in respect only of MEPs, which could be held to be discriminatory in effect.

In Luxembourg the franchise has been extended, but not to Community nationals resident there. The United Kingdom Government published in January 1984 a White Paper which proposed the enfranchisement for both national and European elections of British nationals resident outside the United Kingdom. These proposals are to be the subject of legislation in 1985, and, although a major step forward, include a suggested bar on the granting of voting rights to British nationals who have been resident abroad for more than seven years. This would be a unique feature in the electoral legislation of the Member States and may be contrary to Community law on the ground of discrimination against a group of Community citizens.

FINANCING THE CAMPAIGN

In three Member States – Denmark, the Federal Republic of Germany and Italy – financial assistance is granted to the political parties from public funds to cover the parties' general and electoral expenses. In these three countries, the sums made available to the parties and the rules governing their use vary considerably. In three other Member States – France, Ireland and the United Kingdom – government assistance is provided in various ways for electoral purposes only. In

Ireland and the United Kingdom, public buildings are made available for meetings and one leaflet per elector may be sent free of postal charges. In France, the cost of paper, electoral posters and leaflets is refunded to candidates who gain at least 5% of the votes.

The decision of the European Parliament of 5 November 1981 forms the legal basis for the introduction of Item 3708 (contribution to preparations for the forthcoming elections to the European Parliament[17]). The appropriations entered under this item are to be used 'to cover a contribution to the cost of preparations for the information campaign leading up to the second direct elections in 1984. The Bureau of the European Parliament will lay down the conditions governing this expenditure'.

In the event 17.4 million ECU were made available to the groups for the preparation of the information campaign from the 1982 Budget, about 7 million ECU from the 1983 Budget and 18.6 million ECU[18] from the 1984 Budget of Parliament – a total of 43 million ECUs (about 51 m $US). In each year, 1% of the total available was allotted to each political group = 7%. Of the 93% remaining of the annual total, two-thirds were allocated to the political groups and independent members in relation to the number of seats won in 1979.

In October 1983 the Enlarged Bureau of Parliament published in the Official Journal the rules it had adopted for reimbursement of expenditure incurred by political groupings which had taken part in the 1984 elections.[19] Only Rules 1 to 3 need be quoted here, and read as follows:

RULE 1

31% of the total appropriations adopted by the budgetary authority from 1982 to 1984 and entered in Item 3708 of the budget of the European Parliament shall be used to reimburse expenditure incurred by political groupings taking part in the 1984 European elections.

RULE 2

The following shall be entitled to such reimbursement:

members elected or re-elected in 1984,
political groupings which, while failing to obtain a seat, have secured:
(a) either 5% of the votes cast in the Member State in which they participated in the 1984 European elections;
(b) or more than 1% in each of at least three Member States in which they so participated.

RULE 3

Any party, list or alliance of parties putting up candidates for the European elections in accordance with national regulations shall be entitled to reimbursement on the terms laid down in Article 2.

ANNEX
FORMULA FOR ALLOCATION

One-third of election funds $= x$

Grand total of valid votes cast* $= y$

Funding factor per vote $= \dfrac{x}{y}$

Votes obtained by each grouping $= z$

Quota of funds for each grouping $= \dfrac{x}{y} \times z$

* Only votes cast for political groupings with more than 5% in one country or associated groupings securing more than 1% in each of at least three countries shall be taken into account.

Thus 31% of 43 m ECU = 13.3 m ECU will be available to reimburse expenditure by the groups, and by the members elected or re-elected in 1984. It will be noted that only political groupings which have failed to win a seat and which fulfil the conditions in paragraphs (a) and (b) of Rule 2 will qualify for reimbursement. Those groupings from which members are elected to the European Parliament will receive reimbursement related to the number of such members.

THE FRENCH ECOLOGISTS' CASE

The French Ecologist Party has introduced three cases in the EC Court of Justice in relation to the arrangements made by Parliament to fund the information campaign and to reimburse election expenses. The cases are:

1. *Against the Decision of the Bureau of Parliament*
The Party objects to the decisions of the Bureau of 12 October 1982 and of the enlarged Bureau of 29 September 1983 on payments to be made to the EP political groups for their campaigns for the 1984 elections. The Party contests the right of the EC to finance the political groups from the EC's Budget, on the ground that, under Article 13 of the Council Act of September 1976 on direct elections,

the EP is empowered only to make proposals for the adoption of measures to implement the Act, while the right of decision rests with the Council, after having consulted the Commission.[20]

2. *Against Decisions of Parliament on the Budget*
The French Ecologist Party contests decisions taken by the EP on the draft Budget for 1984 in November and December 1983, on the ground of discrimination in the funds voted for the electoral campaign in this Budget, of which 69% is allocated to political groups and 31% to other candidates and parties.

3. *Against Decisions taken by the President of Parliament*
The Party contests the definitive adoption of the 1984 Budget in December 1983 by the President, on the ground that the discriminatory measures contained therein are contrary to the internal rules of French law.

ELECTORAL ALLIANCES

The papers covering each Member State will cover the selection of candidates by political groupings, and also independent candidatures. It is interesting to note on a Community basis however that the 'Green' parties agreed in October 1983 to create a European ecology alliance for the European elections. The parties involved were 'Les Verts' and 'Les Verts-Parti écologiste (France), the Ecology Party (UK), Comhaontas Glas (Green Alliance) (Ireland), AGALEV and ECOLO (Belgium), 'Die Grünen' (Federal Republic); the Groene Progressief Akkord and the Europese Groenen (Netherlands) and Di Greng Alternativ (Luxembourg) joined later. Thus 'Green' parties from seven Member States entered into an electoral alliance, motivated, in part at least, by the possibility of obtaining some repayment of the cost of fighting the elections. In the event Die Grünen won 7 seats, ECOLO/AGALEV 2 seats and the Akkord 2 seats, and received payments for electoral expenses on this basis. The French and Luxembourg 'Greens' and the Europese Groenen, although winning no seats, obtained more than 1% of the votes and, having in advance formed a valid electoral alliance under the rules, received payments corresponding to the votes obtained by each.

Electoral alliances were also formed, pursuant to the rules laid down by the EP's enlarged Bureau, between the Communist parties of France, Italy, Belgium and Luxembourg, of whom the first two won seats; between the Rassemblement pour la République, Fianna Fail and the Scottish National Party, all of whom won seats; and between the ERE, D'66 and Radikale Venstre parties, none of whom won seats. The Liberal parties of Belgium, Denmark, Federal Republic, France, Italy, Luxembourg, Netherlands and the United Kingdom (including an independent candidate from Ireland) were also affiliated and all won seats save the FDP in the Federal Republic and the Alliance in the United Kingdom (Alliance of the Liberal with the Social Democratic Party).

EFFECT OF PROCEDURES ON THE CAMPAIGNS

The new procedures introduced in six of the Member States did little to 'prepare the way for the introduction of a uniform electoral procedure'. Although in Belgium, voting rights were extended, the dual mandate, probably contrary to the Council Act of 1976, was prohibited and restrictions placed on other offices to be held by MEPs.

Although there had been an inter-party agreement in Greenland that the mandate of the sitting Member should be prolonged for six months before being transferred to the mainland, an election was held. The result was simply to confirm that Member, Mr Finn Lynge, in office. In Greece, the full vigour of the abolition of the dual mandate was abated by the exception arranged for the leaders of each list. In Ireland, the system of replacement candidates' lists was a step towards the direct election of all MEPs, but remained flawed by the possibility of such a list being withdrawn thus leading to a recourse to the system used since 1979 of election by the Dail. Neither in Greece nor in Ireland, then, was notable progress made towards a uniform procedure. The Irish problem indeed forces one to the conclusion that the single transferable vote system is unusable for Euro-elections for this reason alone. The procedural changes in Italy were mainly technical, whereas in Luxembourg, the extension of voting rights was welcome, but the system for filling vacant seats was a step backward from the 1979 procedures.

CONCLUSION

The Euro-elections were held in unfavourable circumstances. The only major decision taken by the Council or the European Council from the 'package' of proposals under discussion since 1981 was that on agricultural prices in March 1984. This, by its nature, was unpopular with dairy farmers, who are an important group in the electorate in many of the Member States. But it was principally the obvious disarray of the Community and the breakdown of its decision-making process that led to abstention from voting and probably to voting against candidates representing parties in government. Thus Parliament suffered from the failures of the Council, as the President-in-Office of the European Council, Mr Garret FitzGerald, told Parliment in July 1984.[21]

This situation serves to highlight the need for a uniform electoral procedure in order to help make the elections a European event and not a series of national polls. Another factor militating towards a uniform procedure is the distortion caused by the system of voting used in Great Britain, which has resulted in the disfranchisement of the 2.6 million voters who voted for the Alliance in that country. As in 1979, this has weakened the Liberal and Democratic Group in the EP to the advantage of the European Democratic (Conservative) and Socialist Groups.

Important as the electoral procedures were in 1979 and 1984, it was the notable absence of commitment by the national parties to the European electoral campaign of 1984 which resulted in the predominance of national issues, the weakness of Community themes and the disappointingly low turnout.

NOTES AND REFERENCES

1. Official Journal (OJ), C. series No. 32, 11.2.75. Resolution of 14 Jan. 197 .
2. OJ, L series, no. 278, 8 Oct. 1976.
3. OJ C 87, 5 Apr. 1982, p. 60 ff. Proposal and Resolution of 10 Mar. 1982.
4. *Bulletin of the European Communities*, no. 4-1983, point 2.4.9.
5. Op. cit., no. 5-1983, point 2.4.7.
6. *Debates of the European Parliament*, 10 Mar. 1982. Annex no. 1-282 to the OJ.
7. C. Sasse *et al.*, *The European Parliament: Towards a Uniform Electoral Procedure*. European University Institute, Florence, 1981, p. 169 ff. (Publications Office of European Communities.)
8. Second Report by the Credentials Committee. Doc. 1-1078/82.
9. OJ C 68, 14.3.83.
10. Loi relatif à l'élection du Parlement européen, 27 Feb. 1984: *Moniteur belge*, 6.3.84, p. 2914 ff.
11. Law on the election of Danish representatives to the European Parliament. Law No. 204, 25 May, 1983. Codified with Law No. 609 of 14 Dec. 1977 as Law No. 309, 22 June 1983. See Official Gazette A, 1983, No. 47.

12. Draft Law No. L 115, passed by the Folketing, 6 Apr. 1984, amending Law No. 309 of 22 June 1983 (see note 11 above).
13. Official Journal of Greek Government, vol. one, 22 May 1984, no. 73. Law no. 1443, Article 13.
14. European Assembly Elections Bill 1984, adopted 11 Apr. 1984.
15. Memorial, A, no. 24, 21 Mar. 1984, p. 319.
16. Technical provisions concerning the election of Italian representatives to the European Parliament. Law no. 61 of 9 Apr. 1984.
17. OJ C 311, 30.11.81, pages 58.59, Amendments adopted to 1982 Budget.
18. Rounded figures.
19. OJ C 293, 29.10.83.
20. OJ L 278, 8.10.76.
21. *Verbatim report of proceedings of European Parliament*, 25 July 1984, pp. 36–9.

2 Belgium

PAUL-H. CLAEYS, NICOLE LOEB-MAYER AND GUIDO VAN DEN BERGHE

BACKGROUND

In 1979 13 parties competed for the French-speaking area's 11 seats, and 9 parties for the Dutch-speaking area's 13 seats. Only well-established parties in the national parliament won any EP seats: the Christian Democrats gained 10 seats (Parti social chrétien (PSC) 3 seats and Christelijke Volkspartij (CVP) 7 seats); the Socialists won 7 seats (Parti socialiste (PS) 4 seats and Socialistiche Partij (SP) 3 seats); the Liberals took 4 seats (2 each for the Parti réformateur libéral (PRL) and Partij voor Vrijheid en Vooruitgang (PVV); and the Regionalists gained 3 seats (1 each for the Rassemblement wallon (RW), Front démocratique des francophones (FDF) and Volksunie (VU). The Communists with 4 of the Chamber of Deputies' 212 seats were outranked for the first time by the Ecologists who led the smaller parties but did not win any seats.[1] Of the 24 MEPs 19 held a dual mandate: 8 were senators and 11 members of the Chamber of Deputies. By 1984 only 3 MEPs held dual mandates. Soon after being elected MEPs, 2 gave up their national mandates (F. Herman (PSC) and E. Glinne (PS)). Several others did not stand for national election in 1981 or were not re-elected. Turnover in the first elected EP was particularly high. Of the original MEPs, only 12 completed the term. Seven left the EP for national life (five became ministers), two retired and three died. Each was replaced automatically by a substitute from a list of elected substitutes. For the CVP and for the PVV, even the fourth elected substitute proved to be useful. As there had been a genuine fear that the

51

list of substitutes would be exhausted, the number of substitutes was increased for the 1984 elections.

Christian Democrats, Socialists and Liberals have from the very start been members of both the corresponding EP party groups and the transnational federations. The Regionalists, who had not been in the non-elected EP, had to choose an affiliation. All three became founding members of the Group for the Technical Coordination and Defence of Independent Groups and Members (TCG) when the new directly elected EP first met. After only a few days, Spaak (FDF) and Gendebien (RW) left the TCG in protest against its obstructive tactics aimed at securing its recognition in the EP. Both became 'non-attached' members. Gendebien returned to the TCG in late 1981, after resigning from the RW where he belonged to the radical independent faction which opposed alliance with the FDF. Thus the Flemish and Walloon regionalist representatives sat in the same group, while the Brussels FDF member remained isolated.

The first EP election highlighted the difficulty of mobilising party activists and electors in a new and strange field that was exacerbated by the drafting of larger constituencies (preventing the usual local personalisation), by the lack of patronage rewards available at the European level, and also by the high degree of consensus for the construction of Europe among national politicians. Although the campaign was dominated by domestic concerns, turnout was relatively low despite obligatory voting, compared with that in national elections, and the number of blank and invalid votes was high.

The November 1981 parliamentary election was a turning-point in Belgian politics. The Liberals' rise, the collapse of Christian Democrats and the stagnation of Socialists, in both the Dutch- and French-speaking electorates, put the three traditional political families at national level more on a par than they had ever been. The distribution of seats between them in the Chamber of Deputies is now 61–61–52, as against 82–58–37 in 1978 (in 1965, when the previous Liberal breakthrough took place, the distribution had been 77–64–48). The similarities between the Flemish and the Francophone parties' results did not extend to the Regionalists: the Flemish nationalists (VU) made up for their 1978 losses and recovered the level of twenty seats which they had held since 1968, thereby keeping up the pressure on the CVP. The Walloon and Brussels federalist parties (RW and FDF) lost heavily, winning but eight of the 25 seats they had won in 1974. Two notable changes in 1981 were a breakthrough of Ecologists who won four seats and increases in votes (notably in Brussels) for 'other' lists, especially the Union démocratique pour le respect du travail-Respekt voor Arbeid en Demokratie (UDRT-RAD).

A centre-right coalition was formed after the 1981 election: instead of the Christian Democrat-Socialist-FDF centre-left coalition that was in office in 1979, there was a Christian Democrat–Liberal government. An important change took place in political dynamics: the Christian Democrats were on the defensive, while Liberals were no more the makeshift partners that merely allowed the Christian Democrats to do without the Socialists. A change occurred both in the balance of forces and in political will. Not only were the three political families more on a par but for the first time since the war the Liberal parties came second in all three regions. For years they had occupied third place and been of minor importance in a symmetrical system with the Christian Democrats as the first Flemish party and the Socialists coming second, and *vice versa* in Wallonia. The Francophone PRL was reorganised just after the first EP election under a new and dynamic leadership. The Flemish PVV had also recently turned over a new leaf. Both parties adopted a clear-cut neo-liberal line. With Socialist parties in opposition, ideological polarisation was more perceptible than in recent years and made the Christian Democratic parties uneasy given discontent in their left-wings. Yet, heightened left–right polarisation does not mean less language–community tension.

Shortly after the 1979 EP election, amendments to the Constitution and special laws of constitutional reform established the basic framework of new institutions for the Belgian State, except for the problem of Brussels that remains unsettled. The partitioning of the country into four 'linguistic territories' (French, Flemish, German and bi-lingual Brussels), three 'communities' (French, Flemish and German)[2] and three 'regions' (Wallonia, Flanders and Brussels); and the creation of autonomous legislative and executive bodies for the communities and regions (except Brussels) did not lessen conflicts. Resurgences of 'linguistic' tensions were acute in early 1984 both in the Brussels periphery and in the Fourons. This is a small territory with a French-speaking majority. Incorporated in the Flemish region, it has been the scene of numerous clashes between Flemish activists and advocates of a return to the French-speaking province of Liège. One episode involved a Flemish denial of the capacity of the elected 'bourgmestre' (mayor) Happart, also leader of the French-speakers' 'Action fouronnaise', to exercise his mandate unless he proved his proficiency in Dutch. Some elected French-speaking office-holders in the Brussels periphery faced similar denials. These details may appear trivial, but they had a considerable impact on party strategies for the EP elections and Happart's admission to the new EP Socialist Group proved problematic.

The obligation to hold an election a year before the next parliamentary election was due (the last took place in November 1981, followed by municipal elections in October 1982) hit the coalition government hard. In its efforts to cut the State deficit, it had tried to arbitrate between neo-liberal and socially-inspired Christian democratic theses. Comprising an equal number of Dutch- and French-speaking ministers, it was beset by conflicting and irreconcilable demands from both sides. It was liable to be divided on the delicate question of schools ('private' versus 'public'), one of the ancient controversial issues that had recently popped up again. Thus all the cleavages of Belgian society were reactivated. On not one were the parties in office agreed.

1979: A TEST RUN?

In order to assess the specificity of the European elections and their place in the national electoral cycle, we shall examine to what extent the 1979 results gave an early indication of impending changes, and whether they accorded with existing national trends. An examination of both the Flemish and the Francophone parties' results shows the inadequacy of a 'government parties win or lose' theory. Governing CVP and SP did well, while their government coalition partners in the French-speaking community – PSC, PS and FDF – lost votes. For the Francophone parties the 1979 results were consistent with the national trend: sharp decline of the PSC after a rise in the 1970s; aggravating losses for the Socialists; Liberal revival; and Ecologist breakthrough. The only deviating result was that of the FDF-RW in Wallonia. However, in their case, the European campaign was totally different from national ones: they presented a common list led by FDF leader A. Spaak, daughter of P.-H. Spaak, who proved to be a vote-catcher in Wallonia as well as in her Brussels constituency. But the Flemish parties' results ran against the trend: the big winner in 1979 was the CVP, although on the verge of demise, while the European score of the PVV contrasted with gains in both the 1978 and the 1981 elections. All parties except the SP lost votes to the CVP and Ecologists. The VU did worse than in 1978 and only recovered in 1981.

The difference between Flemish and Walloon Euro-results is instructive as the electoral rules were the same. Furthermore, similar developments were clear in the two regions in 1981. The difference corresponds to important dissimilarities in the types of candidates advanced and in the nature of the electoral campaigns. The candidature of Leo Tindemans for the CVP and the need for the other Flemish parties to compete with political heavyweights resulted in a very personalised and very boisterous campaign in the Northern part of the country where, as a result, the number of preferential votes for candidates of the three traditional parties was far more important than on national occasions. The Francophone parties' campaigns, especially those of the PS and the PSC, were more subdued, and preference voting for those two parties was less than in 1978 or 1981. The successes of the PRL in Brussels and of the FDF-RW in Wallonia, with an increased number of preference votes, were not of the same nature: for the PRL it was a sign of a renewal of Belgian liberalism, a first outcome of the reunification of Walloon and Brussels Liberals with the additional attraction of the Beyer candidature (a television personality). For the FDF-RW, the score of A. Spaak in Wallonia under a common number proved to be a one-off event.

THE STRESS OF EP ELECTIONS ON COALITION GOVERNMENTS

The stress on coalition governments caused by the prospect and by the aftermath of EP elections was noticeable in 1979 and again in 1984. Their effect is more far-reaching than ordinary second order elections having important local or regional stakes even if also deemed national tests. Things are further complicated by the fact that national parties no longer exist in Belgium[3] which is unique in having government coalitions formed by parties that are all regionally based. Each party elaborates its strategy in terms of power at three levels: centre, region and community – all crucial for its existence. The lack of stabilisation of the system allows a party to concentrate on one of the three levels and so to jeopardise the equilibrium of the system, if that level appears to offer better chances for the party or for the defence of its interests. No party has an absolute majority at any one of the three levels (see Table 2.1 and 2.2) so coalitions must be formed.

The proximity of the 1979 EP elections was much in the minds of politicians trying to form a government after the November 1978 elections. This was eventually formed in April 1979. In 1984 the Liberal–Social Christian coalition (113 seats of the 212 seats in the Chamber of Deputies), in office since December 1981, was determined to complete its four-year term, something unknown since 1965. The

TABLE 2.1   *European elections results per electoral college*
(per cent of voters)

	Flemish electoral college				French electoral college		
	1979	1984	seats		1979	1984	seats
CVP	48.09	32.53	4(−3)	PSC	21.26	19.47	2(−1)
SP	20.90	28.13	4(+1)	PS	27.45	34.04	5(+1)
PVV	15.33	14.19	2(=)	PRL	17.77	24.14	3(+1)
VU	9.71	13.91	2(+1)	FDF	19.77	6.38	−(−1)
				RW		2.32	−(−1)
KPB	1.19	0.74	−(=)	PCB	5.07	2.75	−(=)
PVDA	1.09	0.88	−(=)	PTB	0.44	0.58	−(=)
SAP–RAL	0.32	0.44	−(=)	POS–LRT	0.31	0.47	−(=)
AGALEV	2.33	7.08	1(+1)	ECOLO–V	5.15	9.85	1(+1)
VL.BLOK		2.10	−(=)				

four government parties (CVP, PSC, PVV and PRL) wanted both a
relatively low-key campaign which would not endanger their co-
operation, and a result that would leave the majority and the balance
between its member parties intact (with regard both to the Liberal–Social Christian and to the French-Flemish equilibrium).

The distribution of offices in the new executive bodies at regional and
community levels is at present proportional: in the Flemish executive
(region and community), four CVP, two SP, two PVV and one VU; in
the Francophone community executive, two PS and one PRL; and in
the Walloon regional executive, three PS, two PRL and one PSC. All
parties have an eye on 1985 when both the next parliamentary elections
will occur and regional and community executives will be nominated by
majorities in the corresponding assemblies. Here government coalition
parties' interests diverge: for example, on the basis of the 1981 results,
Christians and Liberals might have a majority in the Flemish region,
while in the Walloon region a coalition would have to include the
Socialists.

DIRECT ELECTIONS TO THE EP 1984

The Electoral Law

Belgium was, as in 1979, divided into three voting districts: a Walloon
constituency, comprising all voting *arrondissements* of the French- and

TABLE 2.2 *Elections results per region (per cent of voters)*

	National elections		European elections		Gains or losses	
	1978	1981	1979	1984	1984/81	1984/79
Flemish districts*						
CVP	43.5	32.0	47.6	32.3	+0.3	−15.3
SP	20.9	20.6	21.1	28.1	+7.5	+7.0
PVV	17.2	21.1	15.2	14.0	−7.1	−1.2
VU	11.5	16.0	9.5	13.7	−2.3	+4.2
KPB	1.9	1.3	1.2	0.7	−0.6	−0.5
AGALEV	0.3	3.9	2.3	7.2	+3.3	+4.9
Others	4.7	5.1	3.1	4.0	−1.1	+0.9
Walloon districts						
PSC	26.7	19.3	23.7	21.4	+2.1	−2.3
PS	37.1	36.7	31.0	38.5	+1.8	+7.5
PRL	16.7	21.7	17.0	21.3	−0.4	+4.3
FDF–RW	9.3	5.5	14.1	5.3	−0.2	−8.8
PCB	5.9	4.3	5.6	3.0	−1.3	−2.6
ECOLO	1.2	5.9	4.9	9.4	+3.5	+4.5
Others	3.1	6.6	3.7	1.0	−5.6	−2.7
Brussels**						
CVP	9.5	6.7	14.1	7.4	+0.7	−6.7
PSC	14.6	9.3	8.7	9.1	−0.2	+0.4
SP	2.9	3.5	3.8	5.4	+1.9	+1.6
PS	13.3	12.3	10.2	12.9	+0.6	+2.7
PVV	3.8	5.7	4.5	3.8	−1.9	−0.7
PRL	6.4	15.8	14.9	27.2	+11.4	+12.3
VU	3.6	4.4	3.3	4.1	−0.3	+0.8
FDF–RW	35.4	22.5	29.9	16.7	−5.8	−13.2
PCB–KPB	3.0	2.1	2.5	1.6	−0.5	−0.9
AGALEV–ECOLO	1.8	4.5	4.7	10.0	+5.5	+5.3
Others	5.8	13.2	3.4	2.0	−11.2	−1.4

*Including the five Dutch-speaking cantons in the arrondissement of Bruxelles–Halle–Vilvoorde.
**The eight bilingual cantons in the arrondissement of Bruxelles–Halle–Vilvoorde (Bruxelles-capitale).

German-speaking areas; a Flemish constituency, comprising all voting *arrondissements* within the Dutch linguistic areas; and a Brussels constituency, comprising the 19 bilingual municipalities which form the administrative unit of the capital, plus the Dutch-speaking districts of Halle and Vilvoorde. Electors in Dutch linguistic areas belonged to the

Flemish electoral college; electors in French- and German-speaking areas belonged to the French electoral college; and electors in Brussels were free to choose to which college they wanted to belong. As in 1979, the Dutch-speaking community was allocated 13 of the 24 Belgian EP seats; 11 went to the French-speaking community. The electoral system was one of proportional representation with loose party lists. Electors had one vote which could be given to a list or to a candidate on the list and/or to a substitute on the same list. Voting was obligatory. The minimum voting age was 18. The minimum age for eligibility was 25. The electoral law for the 1984 elections, adopted in the Chamber of Deputies on 2 February 1984 and on 16 February 1984 in the Senate makes some major changes to the 1979 law.

Belgians resident in another member state were entitled to vote for Belgian candidates by postal vote. An elaborate procedure had to be followed to exercise that right. A special office was set up in the Ministry of the Interior to deal with this. As one did not know to which electoral college those electors belonged, they were placed on the same footing as the electors from Brussels. Applications for postal votes had to be in by 19 March 1984. As a result, only 2154 people (of an estimated 116 000) were put on the electoral register. (Nine were rejected for not meeting the necessary requirements.) Voting was obligatory for them.

Citizens of another member state resident in Belgium were enfranchised if they had been resident in Belgium for a minimum of three uninterrupted years and if they could not vote (either by proxy, postal vote or at their embassy or consulate) for candidates of their country of origin. Thus only United Kingdom and Irish citizens benefitted. Only 337 of the 15 295 British and 739 Irish residents got themselves put on the electoral register.

Proxy voting was permitted in an attempt to maximise turnout. But to limit abuse, this was restricted to relatives up to the second degree; and a proxy holder was only allowed to hold one proxy. Beneficiaries were the sick, the disabled and people unable for specific reasons (occupation, religious observance, sailors, and so on) to go to the polls. Proxy voting was also allowed for people who, for professional or holiday reasons, were not in Belgium on polling day, provided they had made a request sixty days prior to the elections; and for armed forces based in the FRG, diplomatic, consular and development aid staff abroad.

Article 5 of the 1976 Council Act on direct elections states: 'Membership of the European Parliament shall be compatible with membership of a Parliament of a Member State.' However, the Belgian electoral law prohibits the dual mandate and extends the list of basic incompatibilities in Article 6.1 of the Council Act to membership of: an 'exécutif communautaire' or an 'exécutif regional', a 'conseil de communauté' or a 'conseil regional', a 'députation permanente' (province executive), a 'collège d'agglomération', and 'bourgmestre, échevin ou président de CPAS' (Centre public d'aide sociale) in a commune of more than 50 000 inhabitants.

Problems over the electoral law centred on enfranchising citizens of other member states and the dual mandate. In both cases, the Liberal coalition partner (PRL) objected. It feared that extending voting rights to EC 'foreigners', many of them Italians, would not benefit them, and secured the smallest possible field of application for the extension. As to the dual mandate, it wanted to keep the option open for Deputy Prime Minister Gol to be a candidate while in national politics. However, on this, the PRL was beaten in both the Chamber of Deputies and Senate. Outside Parliament, the allocation of seats to the linguistic communities was questioned by the VU as unfair to the Flemish both before and after the election.

The Candidates

Experience of 1979 and the new electoral rules significantly affected party strategies in 1984. The number of lists fell from 22 in 1979 to 18 (9 per electoral college) in 1984. Among the parties that stood no chance of winning an EP seat, only the Communists, the extreme-left and the Flemish ultra-nationalists still showed up. The others either neglected that inconspicuous platform or recommended abstention in the hope of being credited with the general lack of interest.

It proved hard to consolidate at national level the EP results thanks to an unusual personalisation and massive publicity. Political 'stars' chose to wait and see until the last minute, anxious to use their clout only in first order contests. Moreover, concern over an uneasy governmental cohesion induced the coalition partners to spare one another up to a certain point. Finally, the only leaders who took the challenge were van Miert and Deprez, respectively chairman of the SP and of the PSC (minority parties, each in its own region). Neither were MPs at home but had in some way to test their popularity. Yet, a series of vote-catchers stood in the election, either as last on the list of effective candidates or as substitutes to reinforce the lists.

A novelty was the nomination of independent candidates: on the SP

list the priest, Ulburghs, from the 'doorbraak' (break through) movement favourable to 'ontzuiling' (bridging cleavages); on the PRL list
'bourgmestre' Nols, well-known for his restrictive views on immigration; and on the PS list, Happart, 'bourgmestre' of the Fourons,
seen by many French-speakers as a symbol of resistance to the Flemish.
The latter's candidature gave rise to trouble in the Socialist family: the
Flemish saw it as provocative and some French-speakers regretted
political opportunism prevailing over ideological rigour. The results
showed that the public welcomed these nominations. Other attempts
made by outsiders failed: for example, the Flemish Communists' wish
to enter candidates on the SP list; this party refused to extend its
overture to members of other parties.

Unlike in 1979, in 1984 drafting the lists did not give rise to
procedural difficulties: usually technical efficiency was preferred to
internal democracy. MEPs seeking re-election got a (hopefully) safe
place on the list or at least the first uncertain place.[4] Those not re-
elected owed their failure only to their party's declining popularity. The
nomination of outgoing MEPs had an interesting side-effect: whereas
only two women won an EP mandate in 1979, four were elected in
1984. Among them were two former substitutes (Dury (PS) and van
Hemeldonck (SP)) who had become sitting-members during the legislature. Although the Dutch- and French-speakers elected two women
each in 1984, it is noteworthy that the number of female candidates in
safe or first uncertain places was only three (for 13 available seats) in
Flanders compared with five (for 11 seats) on the Francophone side.

Special care was taken in selecting substitutes. Past experience
showed that they had a good chance of becoming MEPs during the
EP's term of office. Furthermore, some candidates had other priorities.
For example, Nols was elected, although last on the list, thanks to the
number of preferential votes he attracted but preferred to keep his
position in the Brussels political arena and immediately resigned in
favour of the first substitute (Ducarme) on the PRL list. Yet another
effect of the prohibition of dual mandates was an *a posteriori* unexpected salience of the 'national' substitutes elected in 1981: some of the
elected or re-elected EP candidates resigned from their national responsibilities and were replaced in the Belgian Parliament. In some cases
this affected the impact of different trends within the parliamentary
parties. The reverse may occur when the next national ballot takes
place as some MEPs may opt for national mandates so giving chances
to EP substitutes.

THE CAMPAIGN

The campaign was dull. It had difficulty getting started. The public at electoral gatherings comprised mainly party activists and supporters of the home candidate. As in 1979, different organisations sponsored debates between party leaders and/or top candidates from different parties: the audience was discouragingly scarce. All that has been said about the reasons for reluctant mobilisation in 1979 remained true in 1984. Moreover, no funds had been made available this time for a large-scale EC 'multi-media' information campaign. The Commission's Press and Information Office in Belgium could only use its ordinary budget, and a reduced one at that. The EP Information Office in Brussels devoted a relatively small amount (a few hundred thousand Belgian francs) in support of such events as multi-party debates. Six million ECUs were spent by the EP on a neutral information campaign via the Publicis Intermarco-Farner Company: the Belgian share went mainly on television spots, plus a half-page advertisement in daily newspapers.

Knowledge about the EP was low. In October 1983 only 35% of Belgian respondents had recently read or heard something about the EP: this was less than in any other EC member state, and also considerably less than in October–November 1978 (49%). By March–April 1984, the figure had risen to 74% – the EC average.[5] Interest in the EP's activities was low, and its later prominence was probably due to a special effort, from February 1984 onwards, by radio and television networks: presentation of the EC countries and of the EP groups, description of the EC institutions, assessment of the EP's five-year term, reporting from the last EP sessions and from the ELD, CSP and EPP congresses and also from the Ecologists' congress in Liège. Yet, it is noteworthy that, in March–April 1984, only 39% said they would 'certainly' vote on 17 June even if voting were not obligatory, while 17% said they would 'probably' vote: a total likely turnout of 56%, the lowest of all the voting intentions expressed in the Ten at that time.

Flemish parties tried with some success to overcome public apathy by innovating a more attractive style of gathering, namely the 'politiek café' where small doses of electoral speeches were dispersed in a programme of popular or hit-parade music and songs. In the same spirit but on a much grander scale and at EC level, the Commission sponsored a Euro-show in Brussels' largest show hall on 5 May that was to be re-transmitted on television in eight or nine countries (except Denmark). From Adamo to Toto Cotugno and Sylvie Vartan, ballet dancers and folk singers were mobilised to offer a non-technocratic image of Europe and to illustrate the blessings of cultural co-operation. The affair gave PS candidate A. M. Lizin an occasion for an early campaign activity in denouncing the large amount of money spent on it.

Parties and Programmes

The Christian Democratic parties did not prepare their own programme as they both used the EPP's. Both presented Europe as the one and only issue at stake, and themselves as belonging to the only true European party with the only common programme. The CVP, whose first candidate Croux was not widely known outside his constituency, referred to the charismatic leader and European great man Tindemans: the slogan 'Lijst met Tindemans' (List with Tindemans) stood on the main party poster linking the CVP–EVP(EPP) together with the slogan ''t moet beter worden. Zekerheid in Vlaanderen. In Europa' (Things have to go better. Security in Flanders. In Europe). Moderate use was made of that poster. A more vigorous decentralised campaign was held around the first candidates in their own constituencies. Here again, the slogan 'list with Tindemans' was always used.

The PSC's campaign material gave prominence to its six acting national and regional ministers (five of them candidates: one in the first uncertain place, the others as last effective and last substitutes). This was vindicated by the need for a European commitment of personalities responsible at national level. While the party slogan was 'Peace, freedom, justice through European Union', the most widespread poster was that of Deprez with the slogan 'Centre forward' to show the PSC's will to overcome its 1981 setback and its rejection of left-right polarisation.

The Socialist parties both prepared their own detailed programme without waiting for the final CSP manifesto. Both treated the EP election as a national test of government policies. The SP's programme was entitled 'Together strong for peace and work'. Its campaign focused on leader van Miert who was seen on posters all over Flanders with slogans such as 'Yes, there is a future' and 'Things can be different'. There was also an advertising campaign for several weeks in the four main Flemish newspapers. In these advertisements van Miert presented the main points of the SP programme such as the fight against unemployment, peace and security, a healthy environment and an EC close to the people.

For the PS the campaign was a continuation of the 'opération riposte' launched in early April 1984 against the centre-right government's economic austerity plan. Advertisements in the main newspapers in mid-May quoted seven clauses of the 'Contrat socialiste', an economic and social alternative to government policies. The main party poster showed the first five candidates under the slogan 'Europe also means justice at home'. It was made clear that Socialist aims – economic recovery, social justice and peace – were the same everywhere. Socialists were up against right-wing policies in most EC member states, and in the EP. The EP Socialist Group record was used by the three outgoing MEPs to illustrate this with reference to debates about the Vredeling directive and cutting the working week.

The Liberal parties were not content with using only the ELD programme as they had done in 1979. Rather late in the campaign, the PVV prepared its own manifesto: 'The blue acceleration'. It stressed liberalising the internal market and the need for better EC institutions. A colourful national poster was much in evidence in Flanders. Besides de Gucht (first candidate) it showed de Clercq (Deputy Prime Minister and Minister of Finance) and Verhofstadt (party leader). Large advertisements appeared in Flemish newspapers outlining the main manifesto points.

The PRL campaign was symmetrical to that of the PS. It claimed 'the same will for Belgium and for Europe' and accepted the Socialist challenge of a national test. Twenty proposals for Europe and the same number for Belgium, Wallonia and Brussels were put foward. The PRL capitalised on its ELD membership and even more on its affinities with Mme. Veil's list in France. But unlike the PSC it stressed the defence of Europe against marxism more than the actual construction of Europe. 'Freedom' was at stake both at European and at national level. This allowed the PRL to use its record as dedicated champion of liberalism in the national coalition. Although not candidates, two top personalities – party leader Michel and Deputy Prime Minister Gol – played major roles in the campaign.

All three federalist parties presented complete manifestos. The Front démocratique des fédéralistes pour la Communauté française et l'Europe (FDF–CFE, the label adopted by the FDF for the EP campaign) stressed the complementarity of the struggle to unite Europe and to federalise Belgium as essential to economic, social and political recovery. The slogan 'Assemble, Resist, Re-build' expressed Brussels-

Wallonia solidarity, resistance to the Flemish majority, and the will to reform the State in a united and peaceful Europe. The FDF called for direct and permanent concertation between the EC and the regions, and for MEPs to oversee the Belgian government's protection of Brussels and Walloon interests in Europe.

The programme of Présence wallonne en Europe (PWE, the common label adopted by the Rassemblement wallon and several Walloon parties and movements) demanded a United States of Europe where Wallonia would be an independent entity. Brussels was to be given international status, guaranteed by treaty, as a free European district: a multi-lingual district, adjoining both Flanders and Wallonia and serving as a link between the 'Latin' and the 'Germanic' areas. The PWE stands for a Europe of autonomy and pluralism, where all regions pool assets to multiply efficiency. It said: live in Europe, live united though different, live free.

The VU programme argued that in the EP Belgium was the first regionally represented state (the organisation of two electoral colleges with the Flemish electoral college embracing Flemish people living in Brussels was a realisation of the VU), and that Flanders' representation in the EP would stay symbolic if denied direct representation in other EC institutions. The VU demanded the creation of a Senate of the regions and increased competences and responsibilities for the regions. Its manifesto and posters noted that the VU fought the election as a member of the European Free Alliance, a grouping of European regionalist parties[6] of which the VU claimed to be the motor. As an opposition party it also stressed the national dimension to the EP election.

The Ecologists ran a modest campaign given their scarce financial means and they protested against funding advantages enjoyed by parties already in the EP. However, they made a solidarity contribution to the French Greens' campaign. Both AGALEV ('Anders gaan leven' – for a new way of life) and ECOLO-V (Mouvement 'Ecolo' – 'les Verts': the Greens) went to the polls with pro-European programmes. Europe is needed, they said, to tackle environmental problems. But a Europe of merchants has to be transformed into a Europe of the people. They advocated treating problems on a smaller scale, more democracy, a drastic cut in the working week, redistribution of wealth, peace and a new conception of development aid. Their posters did not show their candidates but the tree of life stifling a missile (AGALEV) and a globe with the words 'there is only one' (ECOLO). For ECOLO, European Ecologists had to set up a green space between left and right.

The Regional Dimension

As expected a regional dimension appeared in a regionalised campaign, especially among Francophone parties with minority appeal. Institutionalising direct links between the regions and EC institutions was a corner-stone of regionalist parties' projects. They could present themselves as the only true European federalists, in so far as they saw a European federation as complementing their demands in the national system. The regional dimension was prominent in the PS campaign where it was underlined by Happart's place (fourth) on the list. The PS called for regions' direct representation in the EC and for a dialogue between them and EC institutions without State interference. The PRL programme also argued that only a 'Europe of the regions' could solve existing unevenness of industrial development in member states, but besides Regional Fund aid it only proposed the regions' representation in the EP. Some PSC candidates more furtively pronounced themselves in favour of a direct link between the regions and Commission for matters within their competence. The three traditional Flemish parties made no such demands. The SP merely stated that the development of national and regional politics had to be put in a European perspective.

The Transnational Dimension

Whereas in 1979 transnational party federations were a novelty arousing some curiosity and interest among militants and electors, by 1984 they had proved to have little impact on political life. They were hardly mentioned though some cross-national links existed. Chancellor Kohl and Dutch Prime Minister Lubbers attended the CVP 'rainbow festival' to launch the CVP campaign in Antwerp. On a smaller scale, the PSC held a 'meeting des trois frontières' in the Luxembourg province attended by French CDS and Luxemburger PCS speakers. The official opening of the Liberals' campaign coincided with the launch of the ELD campaign in Brussels. While several Liberal leaders from other member states were present, the ELD conference was a non-event as far as public attendance and national press coverage were concerned. The same cannot be said of the PRL or the PVV mass rallies whose respective leaders exchanged visits. The Flemish rally in Leuven was also attended by Dutch VVD leader Nijpels. The great event at the PRL rally was Veil's presence. On 1 June 1984 the leaders of the Socialist parties of the member states, Spain and Portugal met in Brussels and issued a common declaration. This had no more national impact than the ELD conference.

The campaign was very much a matter of national actors playing a part with their eyes fixed on the domestic consequences of the EP election. The rules of the game encouraged speculation in terms of the national and regional balance of forces. Most press comment combined such speculation with regrets over the absence of 'Europe' in the campaign. The construction of Europe was and is not a controversial issue. During the campaign all parties, including the Communists, supported the European Union (EUT) project whenever it was raised. Some uttered reservations against a two-tier EC, and others called for more federalism. All MEPs, except Beyer (PRL, and a supporter of a Europe of States), had voted in favour of EUT. Gol was reported by Beyer to have said that the Spinelli project was 'no credo' for the Liberals[7] but no controversy ensued.

Three new factors meant that the 1984 campaign had a more European flavour: first, a growing sense that whatever the policies, the current crisis could not be solved at national level; second, an increased left–right polarisation and correspondence between the national coalition in office and the centre-right majority in the EP; third, referral by outgoing MEPs to their party groups and their own record in the EP. The parties also tried to capitalise on the performances of other EC politicians. France was much referred to both by the Socialists (who praised both Mitterrand's success during the six months of France's Council presidency and his Strasbourg speech) and by the Liberals. They argued that Prime Minister Mauroy had finally understood that the only way out of the crisis was Liberal rigour (the French Ambassador protested against the PRL advertisement 'Why has Mauroy gone over to Gol?'). They also said that socialism had to be stopped before it ruined Europe as it had ruined France. The PSC used France to point up the threat to private schools. The Veil list was favoured by the PRL which in February 1984 held a conference, with top RPR personalities, where PRL leader Michel stated that 'all the forces which oppose marxism and all its collectivist by-products must meet and perhaps some day join forces'.

The European trade unions took some part in the campaign: Debunne, former secretary-general of the Fédération générale du travail de Belgique and now ETUC chairman, lent several PS and SP electoral meetings his support. He recalled that the ETUC's 'Strasbourg programme' had been accepted also by Christian trade unions. This was an argument in favour of the Socialists' efforts to attract Catholic workers' votes. Meanwhile, the European Union of Christian Democratic Workers, linked with the EPP, rejected the appeal of a Christian employees union not to vote for either the PSC or the PRL.

THE RESULTS

The steady erosion of public interest clear at the last few elections, notwithstanding obligatory voting, peaked in 1979. In 1981 a reverse trend was probably due to the bi-polarisation of the electoral campaign and may be also due to the strengthening of alternatives for the young (Ecologists) or the discontented (UDRT). 1984 turnout did not reach the 1981 level was up on 1979 (see Table 2.3). This confirmed a revival of interest in public affairs notwithstanding instructions to abstain by some parties who then lost votes to other parties.

As in 1979, Belgium had the highest turnout (92.2%) in the EC. It was up by 2.3% in the Francophone college and down by 0.3% in the Flemish college. This sheds light on the mobilising effect of some 'symbol candidates': Happart, resistance against the Flemish majority; Nols, a certain kind of xenophobia. In some parts of the country the rate of blank and invalid votes was unusually high: for example, in Comines, a territory transferred from Flanders to Wallonia in 1963 (21.4%, that is 10.4% above the national average); and even more in the Fourons (57%). In both cases many electors refused to vote for lists from the other community (incidentally, Happart was the only candidate who was not in a position to vote for himself). In the German-speaking territory (linked to Wallonia for administrative purposes), the Partei der Deutschsprächigen Belgiën runs for all national polls but recommended abstention in 1984.

TABLE 2.3   *Participation in national and European elections*

	National elections			European elections	
	1977	*1978*	*1981*	*1979*	*1984*
Turnout (% of registered electors)	95.1	94.9	94.6	91.3	92.2
Blank and invalid votes (% of voters)	7.2	8.4	7.4	12.3	11

In the Flemish community, the Christian Democrats lost heavily, the Socialists made appreciable gains and the Ecologists and the VU smaller gains. In the Francophone community, the Socialists, Liberals and Ecologists gained at the expense of the Regionalists who lost their seats (see Table 2.1). Some fluctuations correspond to national trends, notably those of the 1981 elections. Both the Francophone and the

Flemish Christian Democrats could only at the EP elections make up for heavy 1981 losses and thus end their decline. The Christian European tradition (the great ancestors, Tindemans, the EPP) probably still acts as a pole of attraction. For the Liberals and the VU the EC arena is more tricky than the national one, particularly in Flanders where both EP results were disappointing. The Francophone regionalists' division in 1981 and in 1984 prevented them from harvesting votes won in 1979 by appealing to one electoral college with joint Walloon and Brussels forces. Flemish Socialists do well in EP elections possibly because of van Miert's increasing popularity (he has only stood on two occasions). Unlike in 1979, Francophone Socialists had a flag candidate. The distinction between European and domestic spheres of functions seems to have made some headway in the PS. Lastly, the Ecologists continued to make gains at every election, whereas the Communists declined.

Preference Votes

The overall trend towards more preferential voting should normally be accentuated by large constituencies where national flag candidates can be nominated and be more conspicuous for EP elections. However, the reverse occurred because of both the ban on dual mandates and political leaders' lesser interest that deterred many leading personalities from standing in safe places. Preferential voting fell from 58.5% in 1979 to 50.4% in 1984. In Flanders, the fall from 65.1% to 47% was due to Tindemans' refusal to stand on the CVP list as effective candidate. Votes for Happart undoubtedly account for an important part of the rise from 48.1% to 58.4% in the Francophone college. A paradox was created by the combination of the Happart and of the van Miert 'effects': the two Socialist parties, which traditionally encourage list voting, secured more preference votes than the 'bourgeois' parties (see Table 2.4).

On the whole, there were more good individual results in 1984 than in 1979, but fewer exceptional performances. In 1979 three Francophone candidates – Spaak (FDF-RW), Nothomb (PSC) and Beyer (PRL) – and three Flemish candidates – Tindemans (CVP), van Miert (SP) and de Clercq (PVV) – each collected more than 100 000 votes. Tindemans held the record with nearly one million votes. In 1984, as first substitute, he still gained 338 907 votes, while CVP number one Croux got 101 384 votes, still a success for a man deemed a 'document

TABLE 2.4 *Preferential voting (per cent of votes obtained by the list)*

	National parliamentary elections		European elections	
	1978	1981	1979	1984
CVP	61	59	74	44
SP	46	47	55	60
PVV	55	50	67	42
VU	57	46	57	55
AGALEV	26	22	22	23
PSC	62	63	58	60
PS	43	44	34	60
PRL	56	48	67	59
FDF	42	39	55	56
RW				51
ECOLO	27	23	24	29
PC–KP	27	29	26	30
Extr. left	35	37	44	38

specialist'. Van Miert won 496 063 votes and Happart gained 234 996 votes.[8]

Whatever their *a priori* position on the national or strictly European significance of the election, commentators speculated on the domestic consequences of the results. Thus comparisons were made with 1981 rather than with 1979: had, or had not, the electorate sanctioned government policies and, more particularly, specific positions held by one or other political party? Flemish and Francophone electors reacted differently. The former appeared more critical and the latter more satisfied with the Martens government's centre-right policies. The image of a collectivist Wallonia opposed to neo-liberal Flanders faded as the PS vote disclosed a federalist rather than a progressist concern. It seemed to confirm Happart's attraction for a part of the regionalist parties' votes. Yet in Flanders all the opposition parties gained an extra EP seat. The end of CVP dominance is possible in the foreseeable future.

All agreed that while the government was not reinforced by the EP poll, the result did not warrant a change of coalition or policies. A severe warning had been given only to the PVV and to its uncompromising neo-liberal tendencies. However, comments pointed to certain changes in political balance both at the national and regional or community levels. Socialists, with 30.4% of the vote, became the leading political family in the country for the first time since 1936. Their leadership was confirmed in Wallonia and in the French-speaking community. They threatened the CVP in the Flemish community (see Table 2.2). Extrapolating EP results in terms of seats in the Belgian Chamber of Deputies, the government parties now with 113 seats would have won 105 seats, two less than the necessary majority unless they got external support (for example UDRT-RAD). Yet, national coalition parties held their ground in Wallonia and in the French-speaking community, where they were the minority before the event. In the Assembly of the Flemish community the CVP–PVV kept their majority. Lastly, a more even balance between communities at national level came out of the poll, since the electoral weight of the Flemish coalition parties fell relative to their Francophone allies.

Several explanations for the results were given: the message from the SP and van Miert met aspirations of Flemish youth (pacifism, dynamism and community self-assertion). A similar self-assertion allowed the PS to make up for votes lost to the ecologist 'new left'. The PVV slump was seen as the outcome of a gap between the party and its heavyweights: the latter, in government, were said to have neglected party activity. Comparisons were made with the efficient support given to the PRL by its ministers and more particularly Gol: the PRL result being shown in terms of a 'Gol effect' rather than a 'Nols effect'. From 1981 the CVP shared the PVV's concern to end what they saw as a rampant 'particratie' (government by the parties). Consequently, a similar loss of contact arose between CVP ministers and the party. The CVP's inability to make up losses since the 1970s was seen as a verdict on its leaders' lack of commitment in the campaign and loss of contact with the electors. This is an example of the 'perverse effect' of secondary elections where office holders may be compelled to turn their attention from government in order not to be sanctioned prematurely. Lastly, the Ecologists' slow and steady advance was more than a simple temporary outburst from disillusioned voters.

Several other observations were made of domestic and European import. Christian Democrats were pleased with having stopped (if temporarily) the trend towards bi-polarisation which in the long-run would threaten their existence. French-speakers pointed to Flemish parties' losses in Brussels and to Francophone parties' gains in its periphery. This risks reactivating the controversy between the two communities. Community dissent also flared up over Happart's admittance by the EP Socialist Group as an allied member. The disunity of

Belgian Socialists on that issue tarnished their electoral success and deprived Glinne (PS) of any chance of remaining in office as group leader. Meanwhile the CVP's downfall will lessen Belgian Christian Democrats' impact in the EPP.

Two more general comments will close this chapter. One was made by Perin (PRL, and a political scientist) who said these 'untimely elections' should be abolished, as they served only for national wrangling and were disastrous for the European ideal. Perin's first argument may be seen as an extreme inference from the stress on coalition governments referred to earlier. Moreover, columnists stressed the ambiguity of Socialist success won by adopting a firm and coherent 'regional' line that was only possible because both parties were in opposition. The incompatibility of a firm 'regional' stand and the need for compromise at national level makes it increasingly irrelevant to govern with coalitions supported only by regional parties. Some argue that the only solution would be to create national parties of a new kind. This would only be congruent with a party system found in federal states.

NOTES AND REFERENCES

1. For a description of the process leading to regionalisation and of the institutional reforms, see J. Brassinne, *Les institutions de la Flandre, de la Communauté française, de la Région wallonne* (Bruxelles: CRISP, 1981); P.-H. Claeys and N. Loeb-Mayer, 'Le para-fédéralisme belge: une tentative de conciliation par le cloisonnement', *International Political Science Review – Revue Internationale de Science Politique*, 4(1984). A complete constitutional analysis can be found in R. Senelle, *La réforme de l'Etat belge*, T. I, II et III (Bruxelles: Ministère des affaires étrangères, du commerce extérieur et de la coopération au développement, Coll. 'Idées et études' n°315/1978, n°319/1979 et n°326/1980).

   For a description of the party system, more specially about the emergence of regionalist parties and the splitting of the three traditional parties into separate Flemish and French parties, see P.-H. Claeys, 'Political Pluralism and Linguistic Cleavage', in St Ehrlich and G. Wootton (eds), *Three Faces of Pluralism – Political, Ethnic and Religious* (Farnborough: Gower, 1980), pp. 169–89; L. Rowies, *Les partis politiques en Belgique* (Bruxelles: CRISP, 1979); X. Mabille, *Le système de la décision politique en Belgique* (Bruxelles: CRISP, 1983).

   On the 1979 European Election in Belgium, see P.-H. Claeys, E. De Graeve-Lismont and N. Loeb-Mayer, *European or National? The 1979 Election in Belgium* (Bruxelles, Editions de l'ULB, 1980); G. van den Berghe, 'Belgium', in Hand, Sasse and Georgel (eds), *European Electoral Systems Handbook* (London: Butterworth, 1979) pp. 1–28.

2. All through this chapter, EC refers to the European Community. The single word 'community' refers to the ethno-linguistic entities (the Dutch-speaking or Flemish-speaking, the French-speaking, and the German-speaking) set up by the constitutional reforms of 1971 and 1980.
3. The last of the traditional parties to have maintained its unitary structure was the small Communist Party. In December 1982, it adapted to the new State structures by creating two regional parties – PCB and KPB – federated under one national committee.
4. Their places were the first, third, fourth and fifth for the CVP (the second was allotted to a woman); the first, second and third for the SP; the first for the PVV and for the VU; the first, second and third for the PS; the second for the PSC (where the first was allotted to the party leader); the second for the PRL; and the first for the FDF and for the PWE.
5. All survey results concerning public opinion on European matters are quoted from the *Euro-baromètres* issued by the EC Commission. Information was given to the authors respectively by the Bureau de presse et d'information pour la Belgique des Communautés européennes and by the Service d'information du Parlement européen à Bruxelles.
6. The Free European Alliance adopted a political programme in July 1981, which was ratified by nine regionalist–nationalist–autonomist parties. Contacts are now regular between eighteen parties from seven countries. The Free European Alliance will hold a statutory congress in October 1984 when decisions on membership will be taken.
7. Luc Beyer interviewed by *La Libre Belgique*, 12 June 1984.
8. Three other candidates got nearly 100 000 votes: number one PVV, de Gucht (94 496 votes), number one PSC, Deprez (90 096 votes) and number 11 PRL, Nols (92 969 votes). Several got between 40 000–80 000 votes.

3 Denmark

NEIL ELDER

BACKGROUND

The second election to the EP was held in Denmark on 14 June 1984. As in 1979, fifteen MEPs were returned from metropolitan Denmark and one from Greenland. This arrangement ceases on 1 January 1985 with Greenland's withdrawal from the EC, when the Greenland seat is incorporated in the Danish constituency.

The period between the two Euro-elections saw two general elections and a change of regime. The Social Democrats under Ankar Jörgensen left office in September 1982, to be replaced by a centre-right coalition under the Conservative premiership of Poul Schlüter. A general election on 8 December 1981 weakened the parliamentary position of the Social Democrats, who had enjoyed an uninterrupted tenure of office (singly or in coalition) since 1975. Another general election, on 10 January 1984, slightly strengthened the hold of the centre-right combination upon power and provided a convenient point of comparison with the Euro-elections six months later.[1] Domestic economic policy was a crucial factor in the change of regime and a significant influence upon the outcome of the EP elections. At least equally significant, however, was the participation in the EP elections, as in 1979, of that peculiarly Danish phenomenon, the People's Movement against the EC (Folkebevaegelsen mod EF (FB)). Inevitably this meant that the Euro-election could once again be viewed as having something of the character of a referendum upon the principle of Danish membership of the EC.[2]

73

DANISH PARTIES AND THE CLEAVAGE IN PUBLIC OPINION ABOUT THE EC

At the time of the Danish referendum on entry to the EC, on 2 October 1972, 36% of those participating voted 'No'. The turnout of 90.19% was a couple of points higher than for recent parliamentary elections. The only avowedly anti-EC party then represented in the Danish Parliament (the Folketing) was the Socialist People's Party (SF), with 9.1% of the vote in the 1971 elections. Anti-EC parties failing to clear the 2 per cent barrier to representation accounted for a further 4.7% of the vote between them. The high mobilisation of the opposition of principle owed much to the activities of the FB (the People's Movement against the EC) which had been formed with the aim of winning the support of sympathisers who normally vote for parties favourable to EC entry.

The opposition to the EC in Denmark has both familiar and distinctive features. Some four-fifths of it comes from the left,[3] where the familiar antipathy to the stereotype of a conservative, capitalist and Catholic Europe is much in evidence. Residual anti-German sentiment has played a part on both sides of the political spectrum. Fitzmaurice notes the parallel that was drawn, at the end of the embittered referendum campaign, between entry into the EC and the beginning of the wartime occupation of the country.[4] Underlying remarks of this kind can be discerned fears about a loss of national identity by a small nation with few natural resources of its own. Denmark's cultural affinities, it is felt, are with her Nordic neighbours to the north rather than continental Europe, and there has been a readiness to believe that the strengthening of Nordic ties would be a viable alternative to association with the EC. Neutralist sympathies also contribute, and not only on the left – the Social Liberals (or Radical Liberals – RV) have in particular a significant neutralist wing. The failure of the projected Scandinavian Defence Pact in 1949 was viewed with regret by those of this persuasion, involving as it did the end of the idea that Danish and Norwegian security policy would be assimilated into Swedish style neutrality.

Three of the parties with some representation in the Folketing since 1980 are overwhelmingly anti-EC. These are SF, the Left Socialists (VS) and the Justice Party (DR, often called the Single-Tax Party because of its origin as a body of adherents to the economic principles of Henry George). In the 1979 EP elections these ran their lists in alliance with that of the FB. In 1984 the Justice Party, which failed to win parliamentary representation in both the 1981 and 1984 general elections, chose not to put up a list of its own in the EP elections but to merge into the FB list. The FB only enters a list for EP elections and plays no direct part in elections to the Folketing. In EP elections, therefore, it functions as a party but otherwise as a pressure group. By adding together the votes cast in EP elections for the FB and the three (or, in 1984, two) other parties mentioned above, one can arrive at a pretty accurate estimate of the relative strength of the *committed* anti-EC vote. Very little discount requires to be made for pro-EC voters supporting any of these lists in the 1979 EP election,[5] and there is no reason to suppose that there was any significant change in 1984. Measured by this yardstick, the committed anti-EC component of the Danish electorate has remained at roughly a third of those voting in both Euro-elections. But for EP elections the turnout was only 47.1% in 1979 and 52.3% in 1984, or not much over a half of that for the original referendum on entry. So, on the evidence of the EP elections, about a sixth of the total electorate is to be reckoned as confirmedly anti-EC.

The Danish parties which are overwhelmingly pro-EC in 1979 formed the Bourgeois Electoral Alliance for the purposes of EP elections. This alliance comprises the Liberals (V), the Conservatives (KF), the Democratic Centre (CD) and the People's Christian Party (KRF). The parties mainly supportive of the EC are the maverick Progressives (FRP) and the crucial Social Democrats (S), although these last have a strong wing which is disaffected on the issue as successive EP elections have made clear. The Liberals and, less markedly, the Conservatives were indeed prepared to accept alignment with the EC in the 1960s even without Britain; for most of the others, the British application was of decisive importance. For all, economic considerations outweighed all others. The Liberals, as the main party of the agricultural interest, felt the economic costs of exclusion most keenly. The Dutch dairy industry, for example, was prospering within the EC while the Danish when outside was losing ground, and EC membership was ardently sought as a means of stabilising agricultural prices then subject to disconcerting fluctuations on the world market. Again, both Britain and the FRG were major trading partners, but for many industrialists of Conservative sympathy the FRG was becoming the more significant of the two. At the same time, Britain's accession was regarded as an indispensable condition of Danish entry by the many of Atlanticist orientation on the moderate left.

Shortly before the 1984 EP elections, on 29 May, the Social

Democrats and Radicals tabled a Folketing motion reaffirming the principles governing Danish adherence to the EC. These principles were (1) the maintenance of a right of national veto, and (2) the retention of the existing division of competence between the EP, the Council of Ministers and the Commission. By the same token the EP's draft treaty on European Union (EUT) was rejected. Earlier, at the XIII Congress of the Confederation of Socialist Parties of the EC in March, the Danish Social Democrats had joined their colleagues from the British Labour Party in withdrawing while the section of the manifesto calling for an increased role for the EP was drafted. The Folketing motion was carried by 133 votes to 30, the minority consisting of the two radical left parties (SF and VS) plus the Progressives. Since none of these supported a closer political union, the only indication of sympathy for the EUT came from the abstention of two Democratic Centre members, one of whom was Erhard Jacobsen – the party's leader and himself an MEP. This marked the first crack in the centre-right coalition government's unity on the issue.

Fears of a loss of national identity thus run right across the political spectrum in Denmark when plans for increased political integration are on the EC agenda. The salience of economic criteria for EC supporters tends to limit closer co-operation to practical sectoral business such as monetary policy. The FB maintains itself in being partly to persuade those voters who feel strongly enough about the EC issue to buck their normal allegiance in parliamentary elections to pro-EC parties when the EP elections come round. In part also it keeps a basilisk eye on the balance sheet of Danish membership, with particular vigilance for any diminutions of Danish autonomy. Thus, for example, is the Danish welfare state – a source of nationalistic pride – threatened by the harmonisation of social policies within the EC? Or is the FRG influencing the level of unemployment in Denmark, as a prominent trade union leader (Hans Rasmussen of the Metalworkers) had feared as long ago as 1961 when he was elected as a Vice-Chairman of the Social Democratic party?[6] The persistence and visibility of the opposition of principle to the EC has helped create an exceptionally stringent parliamentary control mechanism over EC business in the shape of the Folketing's Market Relations committee.[7]

DANISH ATTITUDES TOWARDS THE EC 1973–83

Within the general framework of attitudes outlined in the previous section, the evidence of public opinion surveys suggests a decline in positive support at grass-roots level for continued Danish membership of the EC since the time of entry in 1973. For example, a Danish poll of October 1977 showed 41% opposed to staying in and 44% in favour, although another in April 1978 returned figures of 39% and 47% respectively.[8] The fall in enthusiasm thus revealed as compared with the original referendum, when almost two-thirds voted in favour in a high turnout, prompted the reflection that the exceptionally acute economic difficulties experienced by Denmark since the time of entry were being unfairly blamed on the EC, not least because neither Norway nor Sweden appeared to be doing too badly outside it.[9]

Some confirmation of the same trend is provided by the series of surveys of Danish opinion cited by *Eurobarometer* as part of their general soundings of grass-roots attitudes within the EC. Here the period from late 1976 to mid-1978 shows a trough in pro-EC feeling in Denmark within a six-year span (1974–80) when fourteen polls produced an average of only 35% who considered membership a 'good thing' as against 29% who thought it a 'bad thing'.[10] Taken as a whole from 1974 to April 1983 inclusive, these surveys show supporters fluctuating fairly closely around the level of one-third of those sampled (cf. 42% in September 1973); opponents at about the 30% mark (pretty constant from September 1973 onwards, but falling to just under a quarter in the April 1983 poll); 'Don't knows' close to one in ten throughout; and the equivocal – those thinking that Danish membership was neither good nor bad – rising from 19 per cent to between 25 and 30% in the years that followed.[11] So the general picture that emerges here is one of a public opinion fairly evenly divided between supporters, opponents and the undecided. The low return of opponents from this source for April 1983 may, incidentally, be contrasted with the findings of a Danish survey taken not long before the June 1984 EP election in which no fewer than 59 per cent of the respondents said that they would vote against continued Danish membership if a referendum were to be held on the issue.[12] All in all, it is no surprise to find Denmark ranked ninth among EC members, just ahead of the UK, in respect of the degree of grass-roots commitment to the EC – nor tenth and last in respect of the measure of grass-roots support for European unification.[13]

It is, however, one thing to respond to an opinion poll and another to cast a vote in an election or a referendum. The most significant test of Danish attitudes towards the EC during the 1973–83 period was the EP election of June 1979, and in that election the proportion of opponents to supporters among those who voted was quite similar to the proportion in the 1972 referendum on entry. Thus almost exactly a third (32.6%) voted for the FB or the parliamentary parties hostile to Danish membership; rather more than a third (36.5%) voted for the non-socialist electoral alliance, overwhelmingly pro-EC; and most of the remainder voted for the Social Democrats (21.9%) or the Progress Party (5.7%) – both officially pro-EC, though the Progressives, true to their eccentric character, did allow some opponents to find a place on their list. Analysis of the results reached the conclusion that voting patterns appeared to be more akin to those of the 1972 referendum than to those of the 1977 general election, so that the electors were in effect separating the European question from 'other – and more salient – political dimensions' of Danish politics.[14]

The low level of participation in the 1979 Danish EP election has been attributed in part to electoral boredom induced by saturation coverage on the mass media during the campaign,[15] but it also accords with the longer-term poll showing an increasing number of the electorate indifferent or equivocal on the EC issue. All parties experienced declining turnout as compared with the previous general election in 1977, and the Social Democrats and Progressives were particularly hard-hit. The S share of the poll fell to a mere 21.9%, as compared with 37.1% in the 1977 election (see Table 3.1): survey data indicate that, apart from heavy abstentions, many S voters – now as in the 1972 referendum – followed the anti-EC line, with almost a quarter switching to the FB and a further 7% to the parliamentary parties hostile to membership of the EC.[16] In the following general election of October 1979, only four months after the EP election, the S vote made a full recovery and the Progressives a partial one, providing further evidence that the voters were isolating the EC issue in the June 1979 election (see Table 3.1).

The heavy losses sustained by both S and FRP in the 1979 EP election thus stemmed from internal divisions on the EC issue among both party members and supporters. Twelve out of the 65 Social Democratic members elected to the Folketing in 1977 were opponents of EC membership;[17] six joined a 'Social Democrats against the EC' group, which also had the support of the party's youth movement, in May 1979.[18] Moreover, although the Social Democrats expelled from their ranks those who stood on the FB list, and put supporters of the EC in the leading positions on their own list, they did field some opponents lower in the order. When Kjell Olesen resigned as an MEP shortly after the June election, on being appointed Foreign Minister in the Jörgensen administration, the next two in line both turned down the vacant mandate and it then went to an opponent of the EC (Ove

TABLE 3.1 *Election returns Folketing February 1977 and October 1979 EP*
June 1979

Party	Folketing 1977 % of votes	EP 1979 (June) % of votes	Seats	Folketing October 1979 % of votes
FB (Anti-EC Movement)	–	21.0	4	–
Socialist People's Party	3.9	4.7	1	6.0
Communist Party	3.7	–		–
Left Socialists	2.7	3.5		3.6
Single-Tax Party	3.3	3.4		2.6
Anti-EC Election Alliance		32.6	5	
Social Democrats	37.1	21.9	3	38.2
Social (Radical) Liberals (RV)	3.6	3.2		5.4
Conservatives	8.5	14.0	2	12.5
Liberals	12.0	14.5	3	12.5
Centre Democrats	6.4	6.2	1	3.2
Christian People's Party	3.4	1.8	–	2.6
Bourgeois Election Alliance		36.5	6	
Progress Party	14.6	5.8	1	11.0
Turnout:	88.6	47.0		85.6
Greenland				
Siumut		52.4	1	
			16	

Fich) who however accepted his party's EP election programme.[19] But
all in all the S vote in the June 1979 election can be counted as one
supportive of EC membership, with voters lukewarm on the EC issue
rallying to the party cause out of habitual loyalty because for them that
issue was of secondary importance. The practical significance of the
gap revealed by opinion polls between parliamentary/elite and grass-
roots attitudes was thus less than the survey figures might indicate, with
the net result, as mentioned earlier, that the 1979 EP election showed a
return not very dissimilar to that of the 1972 referendum, though of
course on a much reduced turnout. The case might be altered in the
event of any further referendum arising out of a revision of the terms of
the Treaty of Rome with a view to greater political unification.

A *Eurobarometer* poll of 1983 produced the result that rather more Danish respondents 'felt closer' to the FRG than to any other EC country, the UK included: 30% as against 26% for the UK, if first and second choices are aggregated.[20] It is hard to know precisely what to make of this finding, since some of those replying might well have been simply reflecting geographical fact – but certainly the anti-FRG segments of the public would never have answered thus, geographical fact notwithstanding. At all events the belief of many Danes at the time of entry into the EC that the country's natural ally within that organisation would be the UK is likely to have been weakened by the course of events. Within five years of entry, the FRG displaced the UK (and Sweden) as Denmark's chief trading partner; the Danish *krone* has shifted from the old sterling bloc to be underpinned by the Deutschmark, first within the 'snake' and latterly the EMS; Denmark has found support from the FRG against the UK in the sometimes bitter disputes over fisheries policy and the principles underlying the CAP; and she has also discovered common ground on occasion with the FRG against the UK in defence of free trading and in opposition to protectionist tendencies.[21] But these closer links with the FRG, and the economic benefits of EC membership, have not found reflection in any increase in grass-roots support for membership: it is rather as if the heart does not wish to follow the head. For one thing, quarrels over fisheries and agricultural policy have generated some adverse publicity for the EC, as for example when in December 1982 the Folketing's Market Relations Committee rejected the draft common fisheries agreement to which the Government had agreed because it proposed to keep Britain's fishing monopoly within the 12 mile limit (the Liberal chairman of the committee, Laurits Tornaes, was also the chairman of the National Fishermen's Union). For another thing, anti-FRG sentiment still draws on bitter memories that are occasionally revived, as when the Slesvig (German minority) Party candidate who was standing by agreement on the Centre Democratic list for the October 1979 parliamentary election was discovered to have been a member of the Waffen SS in his youth and forced to withdraw. It would, however, be true to say that anti-FRG sentiment has had little or nothing on which to feed as a result of the Dano-FRG relationship with the EC,[22] so that the *Eurobarometer* survey may well be significant.

Some brief reference should be made to Greenland in order to complete this section. Greenland obtained home rule from Denmark on 1 May 1979, just before the EP election. The new Landsting was dominated by the Siumut Party, a radical left party close in spirit to the

Danish Socialist People's Party and opposed to Greenland's continued membership of the EC. In the EP election Siumut won 52.4% of the Greenland poll, and so the island's seat, in opposition to the pro-EC Atassut Party. The next step for it was to arrange a referendum about whether or not to pull out of the EC. This took place on 23 February 1982. In a poll of 75%, some 52% favoured withdrawal: 12 615 votes to 11 180, with 2% blank or invalid papers. Denmark stood by the referendum result under successive governments and helped the Greenlanders in the subsequent negotiations. On 7 May 1984 the Folketing ratified the EC agreement, which contained a five-year special fisheries treaty and provision for an annual payment of 217 million krone to Greenland over the same period – together, of course, with provision for Greenland to leave the EC at the end of 1984. Fears about the loss of fishing resources were one factor weighing in the scales – as they had earlier been with the Faeroe islanders, who had got home rule from Denmark before the latter's entry into the EC and had opted out from the start. Ideological antipathy weighed more heavily than with the Faeroese. Nascent nationalism played a part in both cases – for example, Siumut had an ally in the referendum campaign in a new independence-minded party with the jaw-breaking name of Inuit Ataqatigiit.

THE 1984 EP ELECTION RESULT

The salient features of the 1984 EP election result in Denmark may be briefly summarised thus: (1) The Conservatives did better than any other party in relation to the 1979 EP election returns. (2) The Socialist People's Party also made striking gains – even more striking than the Conservatives, indeed, in relation to a much smaller original share of electoral support, but nothing like so great in terms of their share of the total number of votes cast. (3) The Social Democrats, as in 1979, lost out heavily in relation to their strength in national Folketing elections; they also did worse than in 1979 in respect of their share of the votes cast in the EP elections. (4) The Progress Party was proportionately the heaviest loser in relation to its 1979 EP returns. (5) Contrary to expectations, the anti-EC share of the vote fell slightly from the 1979 level and the committed pro-EC vote rose perceptibly. (6) Turnout rose by over 5% in relation to the 1979 EP election level, and Denmark was unique among EC member states in showing a rise. The figures underlying these points are given in Table 3.2. Each point will now be

TABLE 3.2   *Election returns Folketing December 1981 and January 1984 EP June 1984*

	Folketing 1981 % of votes	EP 1984 % of votes*	EP 1984 Seats*	Folketing 1984 % of votes
FB	–	20.8 (−0.2)	4 (4)	–
Socialist People's Party	11.3	9.2 (+4.5)	1** (1)	11.5
Left Socialists	2.7	1.3 (−2.3)	– (–)	2.7
Anti-EC†		31.3 (−1.3)	5 (5)	
Social Democrats	32.9	19.4 (−2.5)	3 (3)	31.6
Social (Radical) Liberals	5.1	3.1 (−0.1)	– (–)	5.5
Conservatives	14.5	20.8 (+6.8)	4 (2)	23.4
Liberals	11.3	12.5 (−2.0)	2 (3)	12.1
Centre Democrats	8.3	6.6 (+0.4)	1 (1)	4.6
Christian People's Party	2.3	2.7 (+0.9)	– (–)	2.7
		42.6 (+6.1)	7 (6)	
Progress Party	8.9	3.5 (−2.2)	– (1)	3.6
Turnout:	83.2	52.4 (+5.4)		88.4
Greenland				
Siumut			1 + (1)	

*Figures in brackets show comparisons with the 1979 EP elections (voting trends and aggregate seat numbers).

**Socialist People's Party will have 2 seats from 1 Jan. 1985, when it takes over the Greenland seat.

†Communist Party unrepresented in Folketing 1981 and 1984; Single-Tax (Justice) Party likewise, and neither ran a separate list in the 1984 EP elections.

considered in turn, though not always in isolation, and preliminarily it may be suggested that domestic political influences played a greater part in shaping the outcome of the 1984 EP election than had been the case in 1979.

The success of the Conservatives, who doubled their number of MEPs to four, was thus a reflection of the success that they had enjoyed on the domestic political scene in the interval between the two EP elections. By 1979 they had advanced from a nadir of 5.5% of the vote in the 1975 parliamentary elections to a position of parity with the Liberals in the Folketing and near-parity in the EP elections; by the time of the 1981 parliamentary elections they had overtaken the

Liberals to become the largest of the non-socialist parties. In September 1982 they took the premiership (in the person of Poul Schlüter) in a 'four-leaved clover' coalition with Liberals, Centre Democrats and Christian People's Party when the Social Democratic minority government suffered a parliamentary defeat over an economic policy package deal. This was the first time this century that Denmark has had a Conservative prime minister. In January 1984 the Conservatives advanced still further to poll almost a quarter of the votes cast in the Folketing elections – nearly double the Liberal share – and the government became the first ever non-socialist constellation to win an election in Denmark after displacing the Social Democrats from office. The 1984 EP election marked a slight recession for the Conservatives from this high point but still left them as the dominant grouping on the non-socialist side, with a voting share for the first time greater than that of the Social Democrats.

These Conservative successes stemmed chiefly from the leading role played by the party in combating the acute economic difficulties facing the country by the time of the regime change. At the time of the 1979 EP elections the Social Democrats were still in coalition with the Liberals, and Danish economic policy was very much the product of successive inter-party package deals undertaken on Social Democratic initiative – on occasion, with Conservative support. The 130% increase in oil prices over eighteen months contributed about one-third to a sharp increase in the inflation rate (9.5% for 1979 as a whole)[23] and helped push up the current external deficit to double the level of the previous year at over 4% of GDP. This in turn increased the level of net foreign indebtedness to 22% of GDP – double the 1973 level.[24] The projections in respect of international trade were indeed becoming so unfavourable as to raise the spectre of an intervention by the IMF in the none too distant future.[25] At the same time, the operation of automatic stabilisers during a period of low growth contributed to expansion of the public sector in excess of the rate of GDP increase, thus leading to a sharply rising budgetary deficit.

The Social Democratic government sought to contain these acute problems by tax increases and expenditure cuts and for example by introducing an early retirement scheme in 1979 which temporarily reduced the unemployment rate from 7.1% in late 1978 to 5.3% by the end of 1979. In August 1982, however, Jörgensen failed to win the backing of the Radical Liberals and the Socialist People's Party for another austerity round, and the Radicals then switched their support to a Conservative-led administration, though without entering it themselves. By this time the main economic indicators were once more showing disturbingly adverse trends: long term interest rates, for example, had reached the record high level of 21.5% and were choking off industrial investment.

The new administration set about tackling the crisis with vigour and determination, and by the time of the June 1984 EP elections could point to a large degree of success for their efforts. They managed to prevail upon most unions to accept a 4% ceiling for wage and salary increases in the collective bargaining round of March 1983: these agreements were scheduled to last for two years. At the same time they suspended the long-standing indexation of wages, salaries and social transfer payments (excepting pensions) for a similar period, subsequently extending the suspension in April 1984 until March 1987. The hope of reducing inflation, combined with the hope of tax reductions at a later date – a main Conservative election plank for many years, in Denmark as elsewhere, and an important factor in the party's electoral successes – helped to make these measures acceptable. Stringent cuts were embarked upon in public expenditure programmes, including the block grants to local government authorities and social transfer payments, and the country's exchange rate was kept stable within the EMS. Business confidence revived as these measures took effect. In the course of 1983 the current external deficit was halved to 2% of GDP; long-term interest rates fell to 13.5% by the spring; total wage costs increased by 8%, compared with 10.5% the previous year; consumer prices went up by 6.7% (10.4% in 1982), and industrial production improved by 5.5% in the last quarter of the year upon the corresponding period in 1982.[26] Simultaneously the growth in the public sector deficit was contained and the GDP continued to grow, after a decline in the second half of the year, and net foreign indebtedness rose to no less than 36% of GDP (10.5% a decade earlier,[27] but Denmark had not had a surplus on the balance of trade since 1963).

The Schlüter government had some help during this period from better external conditions for the Danish economy. The success of its economic strategy, moreover, was also a success for Henning Christophersen and Anders Andersen, respectively Finance Minister and Minister for the Economy, and both Liberals – the former, indeed, the party leader. But the role of supporting party is usually a politically unrewarding one in Danish politics. The Conservatives were also aided by the workings of the d'Hondt system of PR in the EP elections, with its tendency to favour the larger groupings at the expense of the smaller.[28]

Another factor helping the Conservatives in the EP election of 1984 was the disarray in the ranks of the Progress Party (FRP). The latter put its leader, Mogens Glistrup, at the head of its party list despite the fact that he had, in June 1983, been sentenced to three years' jail in the High Court for serious tax-evasion and excluded thereafter by parliamentary vote from continuing to sit in the Folketing. The FRP's national executive committee split evenly over the Glistrup candidature, and the party Chairman (Major Jakobsen) subsequently succeeded to form a Free Democratic Party together with one of the few remaining FRP parliamentarians: the new group is quite unrelated to the FRG's FDP. But the FRP's poor showing in the EP elections largely mirrored its performance in the January 1984 Folketing election. That election had come about as a result of the defeat of the government's budget – a budget which the FRP had had a hand in shaping, but which the party opposed when it came to a vote. Glistrup himself had been allowed out of Horserod prison for the campaign and succeeded in getting elected to the Folketing; his party, however, suffered a severe defeat and he was once more committed to jail after a 139–18 parliamentary exclusion vote. Against this background of splits and divisions – three FRP parliamentarians had earlier left the party when the High Court gave the final decision on the Glistrup case, and another had done so even before that judgment – it is not surprising that Glistrup failed to win election as an MEP even at the head of the party list. The party put out a lengthy and detailed manifesto for the 1984 EP election[29] in which it claimed, with some exaggeration, to be the only critical supporter of the EC: the Liberals and Centre Democrats were depicted as uncritical supporters, the Conservatives as too loyal to Mrs Thatcher, and the Radicals, Social Democrats and Christian People's Party as being too divided on the EC issue – a case of the pot calling the kettle black. In the event the FRP percentage of the vote fell fractionally even from its low level in the Folketing elections six months earlier, again chiefly to the benefit of the Conservatives.

The advance made by the Socialist People's Party in the 1984 EP elections is reflected in the fact that it is the grouping which will take over the Greenland seat in accordance with the PR rules when Greenland leaves the EC at the end of 1984. The total of Danish anti-EC MEPs, will thus remain unchanged at six, the same as in 1979, but the SF representation doubles to two. As with the Conservatives, domestic political circumstances go far towards explaining the SF's success. In this case the Folketing election of 1981 resulted in an upsurge in the party's vote: the rising level of unemployment, combined with a sharp fall in disposable real incomes during the previous two years of Social Democratic rule, help to account for the fact that the SF's net gains, as a percentage of the total votes cast, exactly balanced the Social Democrats' net losses (5.4%). The 1981 election, moreover, came about as a result of the defeat of a Social Democratic government proposal to channel resources from insurance companies and pension funds into investment funds for construction and agricultural use. Frustrations within the labour movement at Social Democratic inability to deliver the goods tend to be reflected in some switching of votes towards the radical left.

Mention should be made at this point of the way in which Danish foreign and defence policies have evolved since the Schlüter government took office in September 1982. In these spheres the Social Democrats, in opposition, have moved some way towards the radical left by seeking to make Denmark a lower commitment member of NATO. They have been joined in these endeavours by the Radical Liberals, whose long-standing current of international quietism has resurfaced with renewed force as East–West tensions have intensified. Consequently a whole series of measures have been passed in the Folketing on questions of foreign and defence policy which run counter to the preferences of the four-party non-socialist government. None of them have, however, been treated as issues of confidence. Sometimes the government parties have abstained in the divisions and treated the parliamentary votes as guidelines to be respected so long as the basic principle of adherence to the alliance is not put at risk. The government's main objective has been to keep its ability to manage the economic crisis, and here it has been able to survive with the help of the Radical Liberals, the Progress Party (on occasion, under threat of a parliamentary dissolution) and three out of the four North Atlantic MFs – two Faroese and one of the two Greenland members. On foreign and defence policy it has certainly suffered repeated embarrassments.

Thus in December 1982 the Social Democrats put through a motion which froze Denmark's contribution towards the installation costs of Pershing II and Cruise missiles unless agreement was reached at the Geneva disarmament talks by the deadline of December 1983. Since the Jörgensen administration had supported the original NATO double resolution on missile deployment in 1979, this marked a clear shift in the party's policy. In the Spring of 1983 the Folketing rejected the non-socialist government's call to accede to the EC proposal to extend sanctions in connection with the Polish question until the end of the year. In mid-1983 another parliamentary motion was passed which requested the government to press NATO to seek an extension of the December deadline for the Geneva negotiations and also to strive to secure the inclusion of the British and French independent nuclear armaments in the overall NATO defence calculations for the purposes of the Geneva talks. In November 1983 the government was instructed to ask for an emergency session of NATO to reconsider arms control policy before the imminent arrival of the first US missiles in the FRG. Shortly afterwards came a request for the government to work actively for the creation of a Nordic nuclear-free zone. In May 1984 – a month before the EP election – this request was repeated, but in the form of seeking a nuclear-free zone which would be recognised both by the USA and the USSR. At the same time the government was asked to press for a resumption of the Geneva talks, and the freeze on the Danish contribution towards missile installation costs was continued.

So, by the time of the 1984 EP elections, the Social Democrats had sharpened their profile on the broader foreign policy and defence front, but in respect of the EC their position was much as it had been in 1979. The aggregate number of votes cast for the party was marginally up on the 1979 level (approximately 5000 up to 387 000) but the voting share dropped by 2.5% because of the higher turnout. Social Democratic opposition to the EUT was shared by other political groupings in Denmark and thus no vote-winner. The party continued to nominate some who were cool about the EC provided they accepted the party's line. For the rest, the Social Democrats – now, unlike in 1979, in opposition – supported the cross-national Social Democratic EC programme of combating unemployment and industrial pollution and striving for an increased measure of industrial democracy. On the first of these points in particular they were able to attack the government's record in economic management. Even so, they were no more able than in 1979 to mobilise their supporters in the EP election.

The explanation for the increased turnout in 1984 as compared with 1979 is to be found in the higher mobilisation rate achieved by the pro-EC parties represented in the governing coalition – by all, that is, except the Liberals, who lost ground to the Conservatives as mentioned earlier. The considerable net increase in support for this group of parties may be interpreted in part as a counter-demonstration to the radicalising of Danish foreign and security policy through the series of parliamentary votes from late 1982 onwards: more latent party supporters were thus activated to cast a ballot than had been the case five years earlier. The only party significantly to increase its share of the votes cast in comparison with the January parliamentary election was the Centre Democratic Party, probably the most pro-EC of any of the political groupings. Another factor working to the same end was approval of the general direction of the government's economic policy. Some corroboration of this interpretation is provided by the survey data on respondents' expectations about 1984 as collated in October 1983.[30] Here Denmark features as one of the three most optimistic countries in the EC, along with the FRG and Greece, and also as a country of 'decreasing pessimism' over the 1980–83 period as a whole.

The 1984 EP election in Denmark was held under rules substantially unchanged from 1979, except for the provisions noted earlier in this chapter necessitated by Greenland's withdrawal from the EC. The Anti-EC Movement (FB) was now, however, treated on a par with parties having representation in the Folketing and, as an EP party, exempted from the requirement that validation of its list should be conditional upon the support of at least two per cent of the voters in the previous Danish general election. This was scarcely a contentious change. Once again the election was held on a Thursday, Sunday not being a permissible day under Danish electoral law.

It is hardly surprising that the turnout in Greenland was as low as 35.6% in view of the fact that the successful left-wing Siumut candidate (Finn Lynge) could only serve in the EP for the rest of the year.[31] The fact that the Greenland mandate then passes to SF under the electoral rules reflects the gain of one seat by the anti-EC forces in metropolitan Denmark but leaves the net strength of those forces in the EP unaltered. The prediction of an AIM poll commissioned by the FB shortly before the election was thus fulfilled, but not on the basis of an increased share of the poll as compared with 1979 for the combined opponents of the EC. Greenland, it may be added, will have the status of an Overseas Territory as from 1 January 1985: this concession was won by the Siumut party as part of the final package deal because Greenland is non-European, at an early stage of development, and still linked politically to the mother country. As from this date, then, the EC loses 0.02% of its population and rather more than half its land mass.

Ten sitting MEPs sought re-election (eleven, if Greenland is included), and all were successful. Three represented FB, including Jens-Peter Bonde, a leading member of the Danish Communist Party; the Social Democrats and Liberals had two apiece; the Conservatives, SF and CD one apiece. All of these except the Conservative had an increased number of personal votes cast for them as compared with 1979. Over the whole field, however, the percentage of personal votes cast fell from 69.9 to 61.4% in terms of the total vote. It was highest in the case of the CD and Progress parties (90% and 88.7% respectively), reflecting the popular salience of Erhard Jacobsen and Mogens Glistrup respectively as both party founders and party leaders. It was lowest for SF (37.1%), this being one of the minority of parties to rank-order the candidates on its list – the majority allow the personal votes to determine the order of their candidates.

Turnout, predicted at 55%,[32] was somewhat below forecast at 52.4%, but not so markedly as in 1979. Among the successful new MEPs perhaps special mention should be made of Ib Christensen, the leader of the Single-Tax (Justice) party: he was returned on the FB list. The number of successful women rose by one, to five – two Conservatives, a Liberal, a Social Democrat and one from FB. The last-named, Else Hammerich, polled more personal votes than anybody else: she had been the fourth most popular candidate in 1979. Only the CD leader, Erhard Jacobsen holds a dual mandate.

A Euro-poll of October 1983 showed that Danes were much less in favour of an increase in EP powers than anyone else within the EC: 19% of respondents, the Irish coming next at 46% and the British at 48%.[33] The CD and the Liberals probably contain a higher proportion of supporters of such an increase than other Danish political groupings. The Liberal EP election programme, for example, favours this within the framework of existing treaty arrangements:[34] it also wishes to see a less frequent use of the veto in the Council of Ministers and a greater use of the power to initiate measures on the part of the Commission.[35] Similarly, the only Danish MEP to support the EUT draft in the EP debate of February 1984 was the retiring Liberal representative, Niels Haagerup. 'Just call us the People's Movement *for* the EC', as a party sticker issued for the June election put it.

Since the EP elections, the government has been reshuffled as a result of the resignation in July of the Liberal Finance Minister and party leader (Henning Christophersen) prior to his becoming the new Danish Commissioner in Brussels. The forecast for the balance of trade deficit has increased to double the original estimate for the year, with a consequent further increase in foreign indebtedness. Unemployment, moreover, has remained high (10.5%), so that measures to combat it are scheduled to be an exception to the general freeze on welfare spending. The government's stated aim remains to bring both the domestic and foreign deficits into balance by the end of the decade, but the short-term pressures on it are now increasing rather than weakening. They are likely to be reinforced by the call from the Social Democratic party Congress in September to have the question of a nuclear-free Denmark raised in NATO. Finally, an EC Committee is to be appointed by the Social Democratic national executive to report by 1986 on, amongst other matters, the question of an increased role for the EC in both economic and political matters with increased independence of the great Powers.

NOTES AND REFERENCES

1. See Tables 3.1 and 3.2.
2. As in 1979. O. Borre, J. Elklit and O. Tonsgaard, 'The Danish Election to the European Parliament in June 1979: a New Referendum?', *Scandinavian Political Studies*, vol. 2 (New series) no. 3 (1979) 299–310.
3. J. Fitzmaurice, *Politics in Denmark* (London: C. Hurst, 1981) p. 121.
4. Ibid., p. 152.
5. O. Borre *et al.*, op. cit., p. 307.
6. T. Miljan, *The Reluctant Europeans: the Attitudes of the Nordic Countries towards European Integration* (London: C. Hurst, 1977) p. 168.
7. J. Fitzmaurice, *Politics in Denmark*, op. cit., pp. 137–44.
8. E. Bjøl, Le Danemark et la Communauté européenne, *Journal of European Integration*, 2.1 (1978) 25.
9. Ibid., pp. 25–6.
10. *Eurobarometer*, EC Commission, 19 (1983) table 31, 92 and graph 9, 95.
11. Ibid., pp. 92–3.
12. *The Economist,* June 2, 1984.
13. *Eurobarometer,* ibid., p. 94.
14. O. Borre, *et al.*, ibid., p. 303.
15. K. Menke and I. Gordon, 'Differential Mobilisation for Europe: a Comparative Note on Some Aspects of the Campaign', *European Journal of Political Research*, 8 (1980) 63–89.
16. O. Borre, *et al.*, op. cit., p. 308.
17. E. Bjøl, op. cit., p. 30.
18. K. Menke and I. Gordon, op. cit., p. 75.
19. *Nordisk Kontakt,* Nordiska radet, 14 (1979) 926–7.
20. *Eurobarometer,* ibid., pp. 107–8 and table 34, p. 109.
21. R. B. Christensen, 'Denmark: Consequences of EC Membership', *Scandinavian Political Studies* 3 (new series), 1 (1980) 79–94.
22. Ibid., p. 92.
23. OECD Economic Surveys: Denmark, July 1980, p. 10.
24. Ibid., p. 16.
25. See, for example, 'Times' supplement, The Nordic Economies, 21 May 1980.
26. OECD Economic Surveys: Denmark, July 1984, pp. 16–21.
27. Ibid., p. 28.
28. The same system was used in the 1979 EP elections, when the Liberals had benefited. In national elections the St Laguë system is used.
29. RG med Z, Fremskridtspartiet, Copenhagen, Oct. 1983.

30. *Eurobarometer,* no. 20, Dec. 1983, pp. 1–5.
31. Siumut got 7364 votes, Atassut (pro-EC) 4241 votes out of 12 532 votes cast in all.
32. *Eurobarometer,* no. 21, May 1984, p. 20.
33. *Eurobarometer,* no. 20, Dec. 1983, table 25, p. 70.
34. Et frit Europa, EF-Program for Venstre, p. 8.
35. Ibid., p. 2.

4 France

ANNE STEVENS

BACKGROUND

The first Euro-elections took place over a year after the 1978 general election, and two years before the 1981 presidential elections. The nature of the Euro-electoral system made the Euro-elections seem a nation-wide test of the standing of the main political groupings. The results were scanned for clues as to the outcome of the 1981 election, and the European dimension of the election was largely hidden. By French standards, the 60.7% turnout was low (almost 20% down on the 1978 election) and on a par with the 60.4% turnout for President Pompidou's 1973 referendum endorsing the EC's first enlargement. Neither the referendum, nor the 1979 EP election offered that fundamental *choix de société* in terms of which the outcome of general or presidential elections is often seen. In 1979 of the eleven lists of candidates those supported by the four main political groupings surmounted the 5% electoral threshold to win EP seats: the Gaullists backed a list headed by the leader of the Rassemblement pour la République (RPR), Jacques Chirac, the Liste pour la Défense des Intérêts de la France en Europe (DIFE). The Giscardian grouping, the Union pour la Démocratie Française (UDF) supported the list headed by the Minister of Health, Mme Simone Veil, the Liste de l'Union pour la France en Europe (UFE). The Parti Socialiste (PS) list was headed by the party leader, François Mitterrand and the Communist Party (PCF) list by their leader, Georges Marchais.

Perhaps the most interesting feature of the 1979 result was the gap between the two parties of the governing alliance of the time: at the first ballot of the 1978 general election the UDF won 22% of the votes and the RPR 23%. In 1979 they won 27 and 16% respectively. The clear

92

lead of the Giscardian grouping reflected the relatively high standing of President Giscard d'Estaing, a preference for an image and policies stressing a positive role for France within the EC,[1] and the great popularity of Simone Veil, representing as she did the human and humane face of a competent and modernising liberalism.

Of the two main parties of the then opposition, who in 1984 formed the governing majority, the PS achieved an important objective in holding its lead over the PCF. The PS won 24% of the votes, and the PCF 21%. The PCF campaign against the EC and especially against its enlargement had brought it, overall, no clear advantage.

The result of the 1979 election provoked controversy when officially promulgated a week after the election: votes initially classed invalid were allowed. The number of UDF votes involved was sufficient to give an extra seat to Mme Veil's list, at the expense of the PS. M. Mitterrand denounced these proceedings as 'dishonest', challenged them before the courts and resigned his seat to allow Mme Yvette Fuillet, the lowest in numerical order on his list to be initially declared elected, to continue as an MEP. The court judgment, delivered in October, reversed the previous decision and returned the seat to the PS.[2] From October 1979 the DIFE had 15 seats, the PCF 19 seats, the PS and left-wing radicals (MRG) 22 seats, and the UFE 25 seats. PCF members joined the Italian Communist members to form the bulk of the EP group of Communists and their allies, and the PS and left-wing radicals joined the Socialist group. The Gaullists linked with the sole Scottish National Party MEP, one Danish MEP and Fianna Fail MEPs to form the European Progressive Democrats (EPD). The UDF, a coalition of diverse groupings formed initially before the 1978 general election to support Giscard d'Estaing and reject any leftward move of the centre into agreements with the then opposition. Its main components were Giscard d'Estaing's own party, the Parti Républicain (PR) which, though partly his personal power base, looked back to an independent, and conservatively Liberal tradition, the Christian Democratic group, the Centre des Démocrates Sociaux (CDS), and the Radical Party. The PR and the Parti Radical Socialiste (PRS) found their clearest affinities with the European Liberal and Democratic Group (ELD) and the CDS with the Christian Democratic European People's Party (EPP). Thus nine UDF members joined the EPP and 15 the ELD.

The 1979 election did not determine French membership of the EP for the full five year term. The PS victory in 1981 meant the resignations of Jacques Delors, Edith Cresson and Yvette Roudy, for example: their appointments as ministers in the new government being incompatible with the role of MEP. Controversy followed the resignation of some Gaullist MEPs in application of the *tourniquet* (turnstile) system. Before the 1979 election DIFE candidates had pledged themselves to remove inequalities between candidates owing to their position on an 81-strong list. The *tourniquet* aimed also to prevent MEPs becoming too enmeshed in EC institutions. So, save the head of the list, Christian de la Malène, all Gaullist MEPs were to resign after a year to make way for the next batch on the list. This ought, in theory, to have allowed almost all 81 candidates to serve for a year apiece.

The *tourniquet* was challenged by other MEPs who questioned whether resignations apparently tendered under pressure by means of identically worded letters possibly signed well in advance ought to be accepted, but were not rather a breach of the EP's Rules of Procedure which require MEPs not to be bound by external instructions or mandates. From the procedural point of view the system was not formally condemned, but the Gaullist MEPs did not prove eager to operate it. Of the fourteen (other than the group chairman) initially elected, four resigned within the first year, six eventually complied while four refused. Of the ten who replaced them, four refused to operate the system.[3] However, altogether, by 1984 43 members of the DIFE list had spent some time as MEPs. Before the 1984 election the *tourniquet*'s retention, whether or not as part of a unified opposition list, was not an issue. However the Ecologists, Les Verts, anxious to avoid suggestions of hierarchy or preference among at least those members at the top of their list announced that should they, as they hoped, break the 5% barrier and gain five or so seats, batches of their members would succeed each other at twenty-month intervals, to allow 15–20 of their candidates to serve.[4]

THE NATIONAL POLITICAL CONTEXT

The 1984 Euro-elections fell after the midway point of the French parliamentary term (1981–6) but half a year before the middle of President Mitterrand's term of office. The spring 1983 municipal elections were the last major political contest, the next will be the 1986 general election. As in 1979 the elections seemed a mid-term judgment on governmental performance. Only the Socialists insisted during the campaign that the results would not affect their determination to pursue what they saw as the best course for France.[5] PCF leader,

Marchais, said that if the issues were European, the effects would be national, and the major opposition parties made it clear that a substantial lead by the opposition over those lists that could be seen as pro-government would be seen as casting some doubt on the legitimacy of the government, and might oblige it to trim its sails to the democratic wind.[6] Within domestic politics, which impinged sharply upon the European campaign, the major issues during the electoral period were the relationship between the parties of the governing coalition, the future of industrial development and employment, and the relationship between the state and public and private education.

The PCF and PS did not join forces in the 1981 presidential election until after the first ballot, when the PCF advised its voters to vote for Mitterrand. In the ensuing general election the PCF again supported the best placed candidates of the Left at the second ballot. PCF ministers were appointed by Prime Minister Mauroy after the general election. Although by June 1984, some had lost cabinet rank, four PCF ministers remained. As the government's economic policies and priorities changed, the PCF at times criticised it vociferously. Indeed by the end of March continued PCF presence in the government was questioned. It appeared as if Marchais, in criticising the errors of the government's policy and inviting Mitterrand to admit that he had been mistaken, was attempting to dissociate his party from too close an identification with the government's choices. However by the time of the elections, some of the tension had lessened. Marchais chose, for example, in a televised debate with Bernard Pons (RPR, second on Veil's list) on 24 May, to staunchly defend the government's record. It was perhaps no coincidence that this coincided with two PCF successes in what had been a disastrous run of municipal by-elections. In both Thionville and Houilles PCF mayors were returned on the basis of unity with the PS.

Future industrial and unemployment policy was a second important political issue. On 29 March the government decided to restructure the steel industry, involving closure of plants and loss of jobs. The result was demonstrations by steel workers, three resignations from the Socialist group in the National Assembly, and criticism from within the left-wing Socialist group CERES as well as from the PCF. The government and Mitterrand stressed their commitment to developing a competitive productive, dynamic and mixed economy. The discourse of the early period of the Mitterrand presidency, with its emphasis on preventing unemployment, and on the need both to export and reconquer the internal market, had been subsumed in a more general stress upon modernisation, development and competitivity, shorn, for the time being, of any overtones of protectionism.

The third issue, most likely to mobilise voters, was that of 'liberties' – a theme taking in, for example, the opposition's objections to the proposed law on press ownership and control but most strongly emphasised in the debate about the relationship between public and private education. The latter was on the table following the PS' victory in 1981 but only in mid-1983 did the government make its intentions clear. It put a bill before the National Assembly in spring 1984. The issue, presented as one of freedom and choice in education, proved an immediate rallying point. The opposition parties quickly associated themselves with the proponents of measures sought by private (that is largely church) schools. The importance this issue was expected to assume in the Euro-campaign was reflected by Mme Nicole Fontaine's inclusion for the CDS on the opposition list. She then resigned as delegate to the general secretariat for Catholic education, and was elected at nineteenth place.[7] In May the Mauroy government amended the bill to accommodate the reservations, pledged its responsibility under Article 49 of the Constitution, so that only a motion of censure (that in the event failed) could cause the bill to fall.

The leaders of the movement in defence of private schools[8] led a campaign which began on 23 May with demonstrations – ranging from an attempt by Breton demonstrators to erect and operate a school outside Montparnasse Station in Paris to traffic blockages (in Marseille) and attempts to jam the switchboard of the local educational administrations. This was linked explicitly to the Euro-elections by at least one parents' association leader who called for a major demonstration on the eve of the elections that eventually took place on 24 June. The issue mobilised people outside the normal field of party action and education featured prominently in some opposition leaders' speeches. Mme Veil referred to her 'message to young people' calling for a genuine European education. The RPR ran meetings on Europe and education. However, mobilising the Right risked a counter attack by the Left – witness the government concessions on the bill.[9] The Left-wing tradition of defence of a lay, secular and republican public education system runs very deep, and the issue was clearly two-edged.

ELECTORAL PROCEDURE

The law of 7 July 1977 regulating the first EP elections stayed in force in

1984. The prospect of a uniform electoral procedure for the Ten caused comment in early 1982, when François Goguel, a former member of the Constitutional Council, in an article in *Le Monde* argued that a uniform procedure would be unconstitutional, firstly, by enfranchising non-nationals who were nationals of other EC member states, and secondly – if multi-member regional constituencies were adopted – by impairing the indivisibility of the Republic.[10] The issue faded with the disappearance of any hope of a common electoral procedure for 1984.

The EP's provisions for party campaign finance were contested also. Parties already in the EP were entitled to funds for information purposes. Retrospective payments to those winning EP seats were also to be made. The arrangements were denounced by the Front Nationale (FN) and legally contested by the ecologists, in cases which, however, did not come before the EC Court before the elections.[11]

Retention of the 1977 law means that its provisions designed to forestall any increase in the EP's field of action remain unchanged: this did not deter President Mitterrand, in his speech to the EP in Strasbourg on 24 May, from supporting the EP's proposals for a new Treaty of European Union. The only change in the procedure governing the elections arose from the establishment, in 1982, of a new body controlling broadcasting, the *Haute Autorité de la Communication Audiovisuelle* to replace an *ad hoc* Committee that remained responsible as in 1979 for voting arrangements.[12]

THE CONSTITUTION OF THE ELECTORAL LISTS

The nature, number and organisation of lists of candidates aroused much interest. The number of lists rose from 11 in 1979 to 14 in 1984. Others had been announced in the preceding months but did not finally officially register their candidacies by 1 June as required, usually for financial reasons. A deposit of 100 000 francs was required from each list, which also had to finance official election addresses and voting slips. Only groups winning 5% of the vote and thus EP seats were entitled to the reimbursement of deposits and official expenses. One list, put up by the Rassemblement des Usagers et Contribuables, registered its candidacy, failed to pay the deposit and was disqualified by the *Conseil d'Etat*, and another, the Parti Ouvrier Européen (POE), said it would provide voting slips only in certain areas.[13] The Verts' financial problems were eventually eased by their German and Belgian partners, who underwrote bank loans.[14]

The fourteen lists – consisting of 1,134 candidates – were: Liste

Socialiste pour l'Europe, led by Lionel Jospin (PS); Liste presentée par
le Parti Communiste, led by Georges Marchais (PCF); Liste Union de
l'opposition pour l'Europe et la défense des libertés, led by Mme
Simone Veil (UDF-RPR); Liste ERE européenne – Entente radicale
écologiste pour les Etats-Unis de l'Europe, led by Olivier Stirn,
François Doubin and Brice Lalonde (ERE); Liste Front d'opposition
nationale pour l'Europe des patries, led by Jean-Marie Le Pen (FN);
Liste pour un parti des travailleurs – Liste ouvrière et paysanne d'unité
soutenue par le Parti Communiste Indépendant et des Militants du
mouvement ouvrier de toutes tendances politiques et syndicales, led by
Marc Gauquelin (PCI);[15] Liste Différents de Gauche en France – la
troisième liste de Gauche (PSU-CDU)[16] – with the Parti Socialiste
Unifié (PSU) led by Henri Fiszbin and the Communistes démocrates
Unitaires (CDU) led by Serge Depaquit; Liste Au nom des travailleurs
qui en ont assez d'être trahis par la gauche ou opprimés par la droite,
led by Arlette Laguiller (Lutte ouvrière (LO));[17] Liste Les Verts –
Europe écologie, led by Didier Anger (Verts); Liste Initiative 84, liste
des jeunes entrepreneurs, l'Europe pour entreprendre, led by Gérard
Touati;[18] Liste Réussir l'Europe, led by Francine Gomez (Réussir);
Liste Parti ouvrier européen, led by Jacques Cheminade (POE); Liste
UTILE – Union des travailleurs indépendants pour la liberté d'entreprendre, led by Gérard Nicoud; Liste pour les Etats-Unis d'Europe, led
by Henri Cartan.

THE LISTS OF THE GOVERNING COALITION

In the face of mounting unpopularity evident from polls, and from the
results of the municipal by-elections in late 1983, the PS had some
difficulty determining its strategy and personalities for the Euro-
elections. In December, the PS executive committee postponed the
party's national meeting that was due to confirm the choice of
candidates from 21 January to 24–25 March. There was some delay in
deciding who should head the list. It seemed possible that Mitterrand
would try to capitalise on the popularity and reputation for moderation, competence and realism of Finance Minister Delors who let it
be known that he had not ruled out heading the list. However, the
choice of Delors would have brought the government's economic
record into prominence and provided a focus for attack both from the
right and possibly from the PCF. So it fell to PS Secretary General
Jospin to head the list and front the campaign.

The list's exact composition was fixed in March, along lines familiar in a party that is effectively a coalition of *courants* (tendencies). The amount of support each of the main groupings at the Party Congress at Bourg-en-Bresse got the previous autumn was reflected in the number of candidates each had on the final list; each group had one among the top six on the list. The PS held to its policy of ensuring an adequate quota of women candidates; 30% of the list were women, with at the number two spot on the list Nicole Pery, an MEP since 1981 and a fisheries policy specialist. Jospin influenced the place of a few candidates on the list. Twelve of the top twenty were sitting MEPs: four appeared low down the list with little chance of re-election.[19] The press ascribed the initial relegation of the industrious and respected Jacques Moreau, who had succeeded Delors in 1981 as chairman of the EP's economic and monetary committee, to thirty-fifth place (he was subsequently restored to twenty-fourth place), partly to the fact that the group supporting Minister of Agriculture, Michel Rocard, was entitled to but two secure places, one of which had gone to Jean-Pierre Cot, who had resigned as Minister for Overseas Cooperation in December 1982. The absence from the list of the PS expert on international relations, Jacques Huntzinger, was ascribed in part to a tactless speech made in Beirut in February.[20] The list, the product of a careful balancing act between *courants*, gender, regional affiliation, and interests, proved uncontroversial and unexciting. Of 19 sitting MEPs, only three did not stand and the lowest was placed twenty-seventh. A number of leading Communists, such as the party spokesman Juquin and PCF leader in the National Assembly Lajoinie were too low on the list to be elected.

A UNIFIED LIST FOR THE OPPOSITION

The decision of the two major political groupings of the opposition to form a joint list was important and surprising. It had considerable repercussions on the nature of the electoral competition, on the themes and style of the campaign, and on the results. It marked a great change to 1979, when the election had served, *inter alia*, to allow the two parties of what was then the governing coalition to press their own identities. In 1979, the Gaullist RPR attacked President Giscard's European approach and stressed their opposition to enlarging the EC or enhancing its scope and capabilities. Given the extent of Giscardian identification with the EC's goals and some of its achievements (the

European Monetary System (EMS), for example) the formation in 1984 of a joint opposition list represented the dominance of internal political considerations and tactics over more long-term considerations, and a *volte-face* in party orientations.[21]

The suggestion that the opposition should demonstrate its united resistance to all aspects of Socialist policy by the constitution of a unified list came initially from the Gaullists, in the aftermath of the spring municipal elections when some united lists of opposition candidates won. In June 1983 the possibility of such a united list arose when the RPR central committee met and discussed European issues. Two new emphases appeared. Firstly, the Gaullists recognised that de Gaulle had taken France into the EC, and that the EC's early successes came during his period of office and could be claimed as products of Gaullist government. Secondly, the EC's current difficulties, which can partly be laid, according to the RPR, at the Mitterrand government's door, make the possibility of the EC's breakdown a more present anxiety than the fear of any supranational evolution. The EC's collapse would deprive France of an important field of activity, within which her action is already being enfeebled by the present government's activities. These two emphases enabled the RPR to lay claim to a distinctively Gaullist heritage, and to attack the government. They also made an accommodation and potentially a joint list with the Giscardians at least envisageable.

The UDF was not eager to respond to the RPR's advances. Throughout summer 1983 leading UDF figures differed slightly, but a steady intention to maintain a separate list persisted. Mme Veil, the most probable leader of a list, whether separate or united, was most favourable to a joint list. Most other UDF leaders, including UDF President Lecanuet, CDS leader Méhaignerie, and PR general secretary Léotard, argued with greater or lesser degrees of conviction for a separate UDF list. The UDF political bureau resorted to a rather unusual ploy in December 1983 by saying that it wished to consult public opinion on the matter; would therefore organise a public opinion poll; and would publish the results. SOFRES polled 1200 people between 2 and 6 January 1984.[22] This showed that two separate lists led by Veil and RPR leader Chirac would win together 52.5% of the vote, two lists headed by Veil and the RPR general secretary Pons would win 51.5% of the vote, and a common list would win 48% of the vote. Only two separate lists were thus likely to bring the combined score of the major parliamentary opposition parties to over 50%.

A number of UDF leaders made it clear even at this stage that they would prefer two separate lists to strengthen the opposition parties' overall position, without disguising their differences. However, it was decided otherwise. The decision was a personal one by Mme Veil, who had earlier made her preferences for a single list apparent. So essential was she deemed for electoral success that the price of a united list must have seemed to the UDF worth paying. Mme Veil's position seemed a strong one. The success of the Giscardian list in 1979 was largely attributed to her personal appeal. She was the first elected EP's President, acquiring high status in the EC and internationally, and would contest the presidency of the newly elected EP. From her own point of view the leadership of a broadly-based list that arrived unequivocally at the top of the poll would boost her career and, especially if it did particularly well, possibly point to the 1988 presidential elections, where a proven ability to rally support and voters across party boundaries would be a major asset in any potential candidate.[23] Veil argued that the importance of the European message and the need to avoid quarrels over European ideals outweighed any electoral considerations.

The UDF's decision to support a united list was not accepted as final, particularly by Léotard who, in January, resigned from the UDF vice-presidency. Not until mid-April did he announce publicly with PR central committee support that he would definitely not present a separate list for the PR. Once a single list had been accepted, nominating candidates proved delicate: the result was ironic and contradictory. Each party was given forty places. Mme Veil, though list leader, did not have much influence on the constitution of the list but she insisted on including President Giscard's former junior minister for women's affairs, Christine Scrivener, in the UDF contingent (at twenty-ninth place). She was keen to retain the experience and expertise of a number of sitting MEPs and to secure adequate representation of women. In the event there were only thirteen women on the list (including Veil), eight in the top half of the list; 15 sitting MEPs and five who had, under the *tourniquet*, been MEPs for a period.

The RPR eventually decided to offer five places outside its own ranks: two went to the Centre National des Independants et Paysans, the right-wing party led by Philippe Malaud, who had, in 1979, headed his own list which won 1.4% of the vote. According to *Le Figaro*, for the 33 places remaining after the selection of Bernard Pons to lead the RPR campaign as number two on the list, and EPD leader Christian de la Malène in fourth place, there were some three thousand aspirants.[24] A selection committee cut this, and an extraordinary congress confirmed the candidates on 9 March: the party machinery, in effect Chirac himself, oversaw the eventual order in which they appeared on the list, and so determined their chances of election. The list was politically far more homogeneous than had been that of 1979, profoundly renewed, and 'totalement "chiraquien"'.[25] It was notable not only for the very small number of previous members reselected, only seven of the 43 sometime Gaullist MEPs, but also for the place found for the leaders of the RPR's new wave of success in and after the 1983 municipal elections. There were no fewer than nine young mayors, typified perhaps by Alain Carignon (34) who beat the veteran Socialist Hubert Dubedout in Grenoble.

Filling the UDF places on the joint list was harder and more controversial given the need to find a just division between the various groupings that make up this federal organisation. Amongst the top twenty candidates were three sitting Radical party (PRS) MEPs, one representative each of two small groupings affiliated to the UDF, the Mouvement Social-démocrate (also a sitting MEP) and the political clubs 'Perspectives et réalités', and PR and CDS members. The CDS choice of Nicole Fontaine reflected the CDS' traditional attachment to the values of Catholic education. The choice of newspaper proprietor Robert Hersant for the twenty-third place may, as some argued, have been a symbolic rejection of the government's hotly contested bill on the freedom of the press. *Le Canard Enchainé* was more forthright; why not simply say that the largest press proprietor who supports the opposition would benefit from parliamentary immunity (against possible prosecution for offences under the existing press laws) and the opposition needs his papers?[26] Certainly the Veil list's opponents designated it the 'liste Veil ⌐ Hersant' and noted the irony of a list headed by a survivor of the concentration camps which included someone whose wartime record was less than impeccable.

THE 'LITTLE LISTS'

The remaining eleven lists were frequently called 'little lists' implying either that they were unlikely to do as well as the major parties' lists and surmount the 5% barrier, or that they did not fulfil the necessary conditions to qualify for a degree of pre-electoral television time that the major contenders would enjoy. On both counts the definition proved misleading: one of the little lists (the FN) eventually scored very nearly as much as one of the major lists (the PCF), and another of the little lists (the ERE) qualified for full access to television time.

The formation of a united opposition list produced two types of little list. One response was a centrist reaction seen first in the efforts of two sitting MEPs, *les deux Faure*, Edgar Faure (PRS) and Maurice Faure (MRG), to bring together a centre that at other elections had been divided by strategic choices of electoral alliances in a two-ballot first-past-the-post system. A decidedly pro-European theme, elaborated at a colloquium in Paris in February, along with the rejection of the idea of 'France divided in two' did not suffice to produce a list in the absence of a notable leader (who eluded them)[27] to head it. The two Faure's having given up, a centrist list did appear then (ERE – Entente Radicale Ecologiste) headed by a triumvirate of MRG treasurer Doubin, Olivier Stirn, a member of the National Assembly who promptly resigned from the UDF to form his own centrist grouping, the Union Centriste et Radicale (UCR), and veteran ecology campaigner and former presidential candidate Brice Lalonde.[28] This list was supported by MRG senators (members of the upper house of the legislature) who moved away – on a strictly temporary basis, they said – from the PS parliamentary group. The constitution of a separate group of fifteen parliamentarians to sponsor the ERE list entitled it to the same share of television time as the major lists.

Another centrist reaction flared briefly and disappeared. Philippe Guilhaume, a businessman and secretary of the national centre of young managers (the Centre de jeunes dirigeants d'entreprise) announced the formation of a new party – the Nouveaux Démocrates – and the constitution of a list, 'the third list', reflecting, he said, a middle way between government and opposition, social democratic in outlook, and close to the 1970s vision of a *nouvelle société*. Financial and organisational problems forced him and the left-wing Gaullist movement to withdraw though not before he had voiced criticisms shared elsewhere. The united opposition list was, he said, 'a retirement home for *apparatchiks* in need of an occupation'.[29] The absence from the UDF-RPR joint list of certain socio-economic milieux (that might have been expected to sympathise with the UDF-RPR list) encouraged the emergence of separate lists to include such people, the so-called *socio-professionels*. Léotard's reluctant acceptance of the impossibility of a separate PR list also encouraged independent initiatives. The *socio-professionels* eventually found places on two lists: one headed by Francine Gomez, managing director of the Waterman company, and

Gérard Touati, whose list was described as a list of young entrepreneurs. A rather different fraction of the middle class was represented in the list led by the leader of a movement of small businesses and the self-employed, Gérard Nicoud, with a political name from the past, Pierre Poujade, in eighty-first place.

The more conventionally political little lists included those of two Trotskyite parties, and of the Parti Socialiste Unifié (PSU) which made common cause with dissident Communists under Henri Fiszbin. This list also included some radical feminists. The Parti Ouvrier Européen (POE), a tiny group which appeared in the municipal by-election in Thionville in May 1984 denying that it was an extreme right organisation, campaigned on defence and moral and intellectual revival. The Ecologist vote was in some danger of being split, given Lalonde's association with a list clearly linked to the political centre. A separate list, that of Les Verts – the Greens – was linked to the transnational ecology party grouping. It included the 1979 ecologist list leader Solange Fernex but was headed by Didier Anger, who had campaigned against nuclear installations in Normandy. The extreme right vote was not split, for the parti des Forces Nouvelles which had announced a *Eurodroite* list did not reach the stage of registering its candidacy, and left the FN list led by Jean Marie Le Pen unchallenged. His list included sitting MEP, Olivier d'Ormesson, elected in 1979 on Mme Veil's list.

CAMPAIGN THEMES

The campaign officially began on 1 June. It was confused, lacklustre and dominated by other issues, notably the reform of the education system. The campaign was marked by a number of features: the degree of divergence within the opposition; a concentration on internal rather than European themes; the failure of the little lists (with the exception of the FN) to make an impact, and the steady and marked rise of the FN.

The UDF-RPR list, while made possible by some movement on European issues by the RPR, did not imply pre-existing agreement on a political or electoral programme. The list was based on a brief common declaration, that stressed the domestic theme of resistance to socialism and defence of liberties, and dealt circumspectly with EC issues like the use of the veto and enlargement. Each party then issued its own pre-election briefing or manifesto. Circumspection in the common declaration on European issues was wise: Mme Veil had voted in the EP for the

EUT and found herself hence in accord with President Mitterrand, despite the fact that the French Socialists had abstained in the initial EP vote. The RPR opposed European Union, and Chirac favoured maintaining the Luxembourg accords and the current use of the veto in the EC Council of Ministers. Similar divergencies appeared over Britain's role in the EC: Veil spoke of the need for Britain to observe the rules of the game, while RPR members were readier to envisage excluding Britain or adopting a two-speed Europe. On EC enlargement, similarly, the RPR was more cautious, speaking of the difficulty of absorbing Spain within existing structures and procedures. The PS seized on these contradictions and tried to depict the opposition campaign as confused and vague,[30] but its own campaign failed to have clear impact either, seeming both lacklustre and defensive.

This defensiveness may have been due to the extent to which the essential campaign themes derived from domestic controversy, not European issues. The government's record was one of the major issues, though the PS tried to insist on the European nature of the election, and to stress the need for the EC's development and for concerted action in some of the areas in which the government was already trying to advance, such as cutting the working week, tackling unemployment and developing high technology. The government's record also featured in the PCF's campaign that insisted that a vote for the PCF would be a sign to the government that all was not well, although when confronted directly with an attack on the government record Marchais responded, in his televised confrontation with Pons, by a determined general defence of governmental achievements since 1981. For the opposition, internal themes dominated the campaign. Freedom, compromised, according to them, under socialism, provided a steady focus, and the issue of education the opportunity to mobilise around it. A vote for the opposition could be presented not only as a protest vote, but as specific support for a policy of preserving freedom of choice, within education or elsewhere. Their campaign slogan – Pour l'Europe des libertés – evoked this.

A racist, anti-immigrant theme had appeared in, and indeed before, the 1983 municipal elections. In the Euro-election campaign it was also clear. The UDF-RPR approach was circumspect, though before the RPR special congress in February Charles Pasqua, RPR Senate leader, spoke on the immigrant problem, calling for firmer action on clandestine immigration and aid for repatriating those who were unemployed or wished to return to their countries of origin.[31] Francine Gomez (Réussir) pointed out the 'economic rationality' of repatriating immigrants whom 'many French people basically reject'.[32] A closely linked theme was that of law and order and the fear of crime – *insecurité*. Although present in the campaigning of other political groupings, they were prominent in the FN campaign which centred on the themes suggested by the title of Le Pen's book which appeared in May, *Les Français d'Abord* – the French first. He argued for law and order, for protecting citizens against terrorism and crime. Speaking in Marseille he spoke of that city, with its high concentration of immigrants, as a warning to the rest of France, an open sore. It made him think, he said, of Beirut . . . . He too used the mobilising power of the education issue, denouncing the public education system as the vehicle for ideological systems and commending the values upheld in the private education sector. In general he affirmed traditional values, especially condemning homosexuality. The growing importance of his campaign was an important feature of the pre-election period.

Until 1983 the FN's record had been one of minimal presence. In the 1979 Euro-election deft manoeuvring by another right-wing party – the Parti des Forces Nouvelles (PFN) – resulted in the failure of proposals for a joint list, and eventual presentation of a PFN list headed by veteran right-wing campaigner Jean-Louis Tixier Vignancour. This *Eurodroite* list gained 1.3% of the votes. In the 1981 presidential election neither Tixier Vignancour, nor FN leader Le Pen were able to collect the necessary number of signatures to register a candidacy. In the first ballot of the general election a month later the FN won 0.18% of the vote. In the municipal elections, largely in towns of more than 30 000 inhabitants, the FN won 0.3% of the first ballot vote. Le Pen scored a personal success, winning 11.3% of the vote in the twentieth *arrondissement* of Paris. The first sign of spectacular advance came in municipal by-elections in September and November 1983 and a parliamentary by-election, in which Le Pen stood in the Morbihan where he was born.[33] As the Euro-campaign advanced, Le Pen became a focus of media attention; the violence which his meetings attracted was widely reported. There was a bomb explosion before a meeting, and in the demonstrations at Toulouse there were forty injured, and in Marseille television pictures showed an audience (largely middle class and elderly) advancing to a meeting through the ranks of tough-looking FN 'guardians of order'.

Apart from the FN, the other little lists had little impact. This was particularly noticeable in the case of the ecologists. Linked, despite divergencies in the international field, to the European ecology movement, they had hoped to benefit from the same popular support as the

German Greens. However, their campaign won little attention, and their meetings little enthusiasm. The meeting that was supposed to be the climax of their campaign attracted only a couple of hundred supporters.

THE EUROPEAN DIMENSION

The importance of the elections in terms of domestic political balance obscured their specifically European orientations, and transnational approaches were conspicuously absent. Legislation forbids the active participation of foreigners in national election campaigns, so apart from Neil Kinnock's visit to a meeting of socialist leaders, political leaders from other countries were not seen alongside the French during the campaign. The PS adopted the CSP manifesto but stressed instead its own manifesto, emphasising the preservation of the CAP's achievements, European-wide improvement of living and working conditions, the goal of a 35 hour week, a European industrial policy and the promotion of European culture. The question of EC enlargement produced some problems for the French, well aware of doubts in some of their electorally important areas in the south and west, and manifestos omitted reference to the date of enlargement and emphasised that it would take place gradually and with guarantees.

The national characteristics of the election were reinforced, and despite a small television advertising campaign, the EC's attempts to awaken a European consciousness found little echo. This may help to explain the relative lack of impact of President Mitterrand's 24 May speech. The president and most of the government ministers had little part in the campaign, making it clear that the election was a matter for the party and (in the French tradition of trying to preserve a distinction between government and party) not the government. Mitterrand thus spoke to the EP in his capacity as president-in-office of the European Council. His speech, that stressed caution over enlargement, social policy and technological cooperation, reflected PS campaign themes but was notable for his support of a stricter definition and restriction of the veto, of the need to restore its 'authority' to the Commission, to set up a 'permanent secretariat for the political cooperation' of the Council of Ministers, and to recognise that a Europe of 'variable geometry' might 'reflect a reality'. Finally he supported the EUT initiative and suggested a conference of countries interested in it. But these themes found little echo at home. The European dimension was absent from almost all aspects of the election campaign and had a minimal effect upon the results.

RESULTS: SEATS AND MEMBERS

'Le Choc' said the *Liberation* headline on the morning after the declaration of the results: first, support for the PCF had almost halved since the 1979 EP elections and had fallen to just over 11%. Second, the FN won over two million votes (some 50 000 votes less than the PCF) and 10.95% of the votes cast, so gaining like the PCF ten EP seats.

Turnout was 56.7%, 3% lower than in 1979. The other key features of these results were firstly the united opposition list had achieved a slightly lower percentage than the combined score of both the lists in 1979; secondly, the PS list had lost ground compared to the 1981 general election, rather less relative to the first ballot of the presidential election, and even less compared to the 1979 Euro-election; thirdly, of the little lists only the FN broke the 5% barrier.

The UDF-RPR list gained 41 seats: 21 went to the UDF, 20 to the RPR. Among UDF members were twelve former MEPs, four women, and four members under forty. The RPR members included only two who had been MEPs immediately before the election, four who had been members for part of the 1979–84 session, four women and three under the age of forty. The PS's twenty new MEPs included twelve

TABLE 4.1   *Results of the 1984 Euro-elections in votes cast and percentages*

List	Votes cast	%
PCF	2 261 312	11.20
PS	4 188 875	20.75
UDF–RPR	8 683 596	43.02
PCI	182 320	0.90
LO	417 702	2.06
PSU–CDU	146 238	0.72
ERE	670 474	3.32
VERTS	680 080	3.36
EUE	78 234	0.38
REUSSIR	382 404	1.89
UTILE	138 220	0.68
I 84	123 642	0.61
FN	2 210 334	10.95
POE	17 503	0.08

TABLE 4.2   *Number of seats won by the political parties in Euro-elections*

	1984	1979
Union de l'opposition (United Opposition)	41	–
1979: UFE (Mrs Veil)	–	25
DIFE (Mr Chirac)	–	15
PS (Socialists)	20	22
PCF (Communists)	10	19
Front d'opposition nationale (National Front)	10	–

SOURCE   *Bull. EC*, 6-1984.

sitting MEPs, six women and only two members under forty. All ten re-elected PCF members were sitting MEPs, two of them were women and only one was under forty. The oldest French MEP was Mme Jacqueline Thome-Patenôtre (77) – on the RPR list.

1979 saw the election to the EP of two major party leaders whose role in the EP was marginal to their domestic political activity, Marchais and Chirac.[34] It remains to be seen whether FN leader Le Pen and Jospin, PS first secretary, will make the EP a major arena for their political activities. All the other successful candidates, including the only government minister to be elected, Max Gallo, are likely to be fairly committed to the EP's work. Gallo, on election, promptly resigned as government spokesman, and was replaced by Roland Dumas, who before and after the reshuffle in mid-July 1984, combined it with his previous role as Minister for European Affairs.

It was expected that a National Assembly by-election would result, for the MP for Puy-de-Dôme, Claude Wolff (UDF), was likely to resign his national seat to enable former President Giscard d'Estaing to stand in his home constituency. A question also arose over the eligibility of Gaston Flosse, vice-president of the governing council of French Polynesia, to retain his newly won seat on the UDF-RPR list.[35] The overall effect of the election will be further fragmentation of French representation in the EP. The PCF members will join the Communist group and the PS members the Socialists. There are no MRG members in the new EP. The UDF-RPR list will divide, twenty members going to join the newly formed European Democratic Alliance (EDA), twelve to the Liberal Group and nine to the EPP. The ten FN members, reviled in the EP, formed a new group with five Italian Social Movement MEPs and the Greek EPEN member.

REASONS AND REACTIONS

The low turnout reflected a popular perception of the Euro-elections' relative importance. Despite politicians stressing, in Simone Veil's words, that in Europe as in France the voter faced the same choice of society,[36] and encouraging the expression of opinion through the vote, it was plain that major political changes after the elections could not be expected in Europe or in France. *Paris Match* published a survey of non-voters which showed that 50% accepted as applying to them the view that the elections were of no interest.[37]

Two motives might have mobilised the electorate:[38] the desire to further the EC's development or the desire to criticise the government. Neither were likely to weigh heavily with potential PCF voters. Did the low turnout affect the PCF particularly badly? Its decline was not entirely due to transfers of votes to other lists – SOFRES showed that 88% of those who voted PCF had voted for Marchais in the 1981 presidential elections.[39] Moreover, in areas where turnout was markedly down, the PCF fared particularly badly. Nevertheless the view that the PCF would have done better on a higher turnout has to be qualified by two further observations: some of those areas where both turnout and the PCF vote fell sharply were in the East (the Haut-Rhin and the Bas-Rhin) and the West (the Manche and the Mayenne) where the communist vote has historically been low. Secondly, the *Paris Match* survey showed that only 10% of non-voters would have voted PCF. The PCF vote has to be seen against a long-term decline in its electoral support.[40] The reasons for this are complex and multiple, but clearly Euro-electoral performance cannot adequately be explained by references to factors specific to the nature of either the elections or the campaign.

Even more startling was the FN's success. Five factors help to explain it: they are the nature of the electoral system; the nature of the electoral competition; Le Pen's own image; the mobilisation to the FN's benefit of some parts of the traditional Right; and the salience of certain issues.

Certainly a proportional representation system based on a single national list helped the FN. The FN list gained over 10% of the votes in only 44 out of the 95 départements. It did particularly well in the South gaining, for example, over 20% in the Alpes Maritimes and the Var, and also in towns of over 100 000 inhabitants, where it averaged 14%. In five of the 36 towns of over 100 000 inhabitants, all in the South, it won over 20%. In some rural départements, especially those of the centre such as Corrèze, Cantal, and the Vendée, the FN won but around 3%. Furthermore, the Euro-elections provide an opportunity for registering a vote which is essentially an expression of feeling. There is no clear reason to suppose the parliamentary or presidential elections would have the same results.

Indeed, a presidential election with a rather different array of candidates might well produce very different results. The nature of the Euro-election competition influenced the FN vote. The absence of a separate RPR list and of a strong RPR leader appears to have caused a number of voters to opt for the FN. The SOFRES post-electoral survey showed that 11% of those who regarded themselves as Chirac supporters had voted FN.[41] This alone is insufficient to explain the success of Le Pen's list, for even without those RPR and UDF supporters who voted for him this time, the FN would still retain 7% of votes,[42] but it goes some way to explaining its amplitude. Personal opposition to Mme Veil because of her association with the legislation of abortion, resulting in demonstrations at her election meetings, was a feature of the campaign.

If Mme Veil was a leader with whom certain sections of the Right could not identify, Jean-Marie Le Pen proved to be an attractive figure. A smiling, white-haired avuncular figure, he was able to refer both to his experiences as a member of parliament (he was elected as a member of Pierre Poujade's Union de défense des commercants et artisans (UDCA) in 1956) and as a paratrooper who served in Indo-China and Algiers. With deceptively simple slogans – 'My ideas – the same as yours' and 'The French first' – and the Gaullist echo in his call for a Europe of the Fatherlands, he was able, without disavowing the more extreme statements of some of his associates, to convey a non-extremist image. Hostile treatment by journalists who questioned him on the television programme *L'Heure de Verité* in February provoked sharp reactions from Le Pen, who lost his temper over accusations that he had been responsible personally for torture in the Algerian war, and called for a minute's silence in memory of the victims of the Gulag, but also provoked enquiries and requests for membership at FN offices.

Surveys of the FN electorate showed that as the campaign advanced Le Pen's support was less and less confined to those mainly younger, male, working class electors typical of voters of the extreme right. As the election drew closer older electors from managerial and professional groups, though still disproportionately more men, were attracted.[43] The absence of other strong figures from the Right in the campaign and the acceptable image that Le Pen was able to convey probably helped to account for this, as did his ability to bring together a number of traditional Right-wing elements. It was not that he did particularly well in historically moderate and conservative areas, such as the Vendée or Mayenne. However, he did win over 10% in many of the départements of the South and South East where the Poujadists scored over 12% in 1956, when they gained 11.5% of the total vote. However both Pierre Poujade then, and the last extreme Right leader to attract over 5% of the national vote, Tixier Vignancour in the presidential election of 1965, also did well in areas of the West and South West where Le Pen scored below his national average.[44]

His high score in parts of the South and South East seems also to represent success in attracting the votes of a good number of those resettled from Algeria after Algerian independence twenty years ago (the so-called *pieds-noirs*). Mitterrand's gesture, in September 1982, in pushing through a law giving amnesty to the surviving leaders of the Algiers putsch in 1961 seems to have had little effect on those disillusioned about the willingness of successive governments to meet their claims, and to whom Le Pen's military record and steady support, when an MP in the early 1960s, for *Algérie Française* were attractive. Possibly a million voters can be described as *pieds-noirs*, and an analysis of the results in areas where they are particularly numerous suggests that many of them either abstained or voted for Le Pen.[45]

Le Pen did well in both communities where *pieds-noirs* were numerous and where there are a high number of immigrants. His latent racist themes surfaced clearly here. The SOFRES survey showed a clear and striking difference between Le Pen's voters and others. Asked to name the two most important issues in the election 26% of Le Pen's voters mentioned immigrants. For no other list did the percentage citing this issue exceed 3%.[46] A similar difference appeared over *insecurité*. Of Le Pen's voters 30% thought it one of the two most important election issues, compared with 17% of the UDF-RPR electorate and smaller percentages of other lists' voters. Clearly Le Pen had touched upon themes with a particular salience for certain sections of the electorate. Only with hindsight will it be possible to judge whether these issues would assume equal importance in elections of a different kind.

CRISIS OF LEGITIMACY?

From early on the opposition made it clear that it would regard a Euro-election result which put the opposition clearly ahead of the government as a substantial blow to the latter's legitimacy and credibility. The PS stressed that the government would not be swayed by a vote in an election where its future was not at stake. The opposition nevertheless quickly claimed that the plurality of votes cast for the UDF-RPR list, which, when the FN votes were added became an outright majority, called the government seriously into question.

This reaction coincided with the demonstration organised by opponents of the government's education bill for 24 June. This demonstration brought an estimated one to one and a half million people on to the streets of Paris, and was widely hailed as a further expression of discontent with the government. The Senate had before it the education bill. Always a focus for a certain resistance to the PS government, it called on a government that no longer enjoyed the confidence of a majority of electors to submit controversial measures to the democratic test of a referendum. The government's response was twofold. Firstly, President Mitterrand announced the withdrawal of the education bill and the holding of a referendum, but not upon the educational issue as such, rather upon a constitutional amendment which would enable the holding of future referendums on matters involving public liberties. Secondly, the Mauroy government resigned, Laurent Fabius was appointed Prime Minister, and the PCF announced that while continuing to support the government in the legislature it would not be taking part in the cabinet.

CONCLUSION

France's place in Europe was not an issue in this campaign, and even the nature of that Europe was little disputed; the notion of Europe was used, if at all, as a peg upon which to hang national issues, for example the rejection of socialism in Europe as in France. The election emphasised starkly the PCF's problems and dilemmas, and allowed the FN to benefit spectacularly from what was essentially a protest vote against both the Left and the moderates. The performance of the united opposition list was sufficiently strong, especially if added to that of the FN, to question the legitimacy of the government. This was partly due to the fortuitous coincidence of the election with the crisis surrounding the education bill. However, the opposition's performance was not good enough to make Simone Veil a clear front-runner for the 1988 presidential election. Jacques Chirac, himself largely absent from the campaign, may be amongst the beneficiaries of both these features. The

Euro-elections have taken their place as part of the expected sequence of political events. Their significance will be measured not in terms of their impact upon the construction of Europe, about which there is a wide consensus, but as in 1979, in terms of their impact upon the domestic political scene.

NOTES AND REFERENCES

1. V. Wright (ed.), *Continuity and Change in France* (London: Allen & Unwin, 1984) pp. 37–8.
2. The French method of casting a vote requires the candidate to place in an envelope a slip bearing the name of the candidate (or the list of candidates). Blank or non-official slips in the envelopes are counted as abstentions or spoilt papers. On 13 June 1979 over a million votes were recorded as abstentions, but on 20 June the *Commission nationale de recensement des votes*, the national returning committee, ruled that in 108 309 cases the use of an electoral address which showed both the name of the list and the names of all that list's candidates should be counted as a valid vote. This gave additional votes to five of the lists, but four of these still fell below the 5% limit. 78 958 votes were, however, added to Mme Veil's list, which caused her list to be awarded an extra seat at the expense of one previously attributed to the Socialist Party. The legal case was heard by the *Conseil d'Etat*, which adjudicates, in European as in local elections, on the conduct and validity of the elections, and which gave its decision on 21 October. It followed the views of its *Commissaire du Gouvernement* who told the Court that in his view the *Commission nationale du recensement des votes* had acted inconsistently. They had neither followed entirely the principle of respecting the choice of the electors, which would have validated all election addresses used instead of voting slips which clearly indicated a specific list, whether or not they included all the candidates' names, nor had they excluded all such addresses as invalid votes. He preferred the latter solution as being closer to the provisions of the electoral law. See *Le Monde* 22 October 1979.
3. EP Doc 1–398/82, p. 9.
4. *Le Monde,* 27 Mar. 1984.
5. *Le Monde,* 27 Mar. 1984.
6. *Le Monde,* 9 May 1984.
7. In 1979 Mme Fontaine was on Mme Veil's list, so that 'freedom of education' might be represented there, but she was placed only in the thirty-first position, and not elected. *Le Monde,* 21 March 1984.
8. Canon Paul Guilberteau, secretary-general of Catholic education, and M. Paul Daniel, president of the Union National des Association de Parents d'élèves de l'enseignement libre (UNAPEL). See *Le Monde* 25 May 1984.
9. J-M. Colombiani in *Le Monde* 29 May 1984.
10. *Le Monde,* 15–16 Apr. 1984.
11. Cases 294–296/83 Parti écologiste 'les Verts' v. European Parliament and

Case 297/83 Parti écologiste 'les Verts' v. European Council of Ministers.

12. In 1984 the ad hoc committee, the *Commission national du recensement des votes*, which supervised the vote count was presided over by a *Conseiller d'Etat*, M. Paul Rivière.

13. On the financing of campaigns see *Le Figaro*, 14 Mar. 1984 where the total outlay for a full campaign was estimated at 35 million French Francs.

14. *Le Monde,* 17 May 1984. The German ecologists guaranteed loans of 1.5 million French Francs and the Belgians loans of 0.5 million French Francs. The eventual success of some ecologist candidates, not necessarily from France, would result in EP subventions from which the loans could be repaid.

15. The list for a workers' party – a united workers and peasants list supported by the Independent Communist Party and by activists of the labour movement from all sections of the political and trades union forces.

16. The list of the different left in France, in Europe – the third list of the left of Henri Fiszbin and Serge Depaquet presented by the Parti Socialist Unifié and the united democratic communists.

17. The list in the name of the workers who are fed up with being betrayed by the left or oppressed by the right.

18. Initiative 84, the list of young European entrepreneurs: Europe for enterprise.

19. Gérard Fuchs, a prominent sitting PS MEP who found himself eventually at 35th place said to *La Croix*, 24 Mar. 1984, that to be turned out by the democratic process or one's enemies was part of political life. It was harder to accept being turned out by one's friends.

20. *L'Express,* 23 Mar. 1984.

21. Patrick Manigand and Françoise de la Serre, *Les Forces politiques et l'élection Européenne de 17 juin 1984* unpublished paper for the European Consortium for Political Research, Salzburg, Apr. 1984.

22. The results were published in *Le Quotidien de Paris*, 13 Jan. 1984.

23. *L'Express*, 6 Jan. 1984.

24. *Le Figaro*, 3 Feb. 1984.

25. See André Passeron in *Le Monde*, 6 Mar. 1984.

26. *Le Canard Enchainé*, 28 Mar. 1984.

27. *Le Point*, 25 Feb. 1984.

28. Lalonde split from 'Les Verts' over his views that ecological issues should form part of the mainstream of political life and ecologists should not hesitate to make electoral alliances where appropriate.

29. *Le Monde*, 27 Mar. 1984.

30. See Lionel Jospin's press conference of 12 June 1984.

31. *Le Monde*, 6 Mar. 1984.

32. *Le Monde*, 10–11 June 1984.

33. The FN scored 17.7% at Dreux in September, and entered into an agreement with the local RPR which resulted in the second ballot defeat of the PS mayor and the presence of FN members on the local council. At Aulnay sous Bois in November they scored 9.37%, and Le Pen took 12.02% of the vote in the Morbihan.

34. Under the *tourniquet* system Chirac remained an MEP for only one year.

35. A bill regulating the governmental structure of French Polynesia, before

the Senate at the time of the election, made his office incompatible with membership of the EP. See *Le Monde*, 29 June 1984.

36. In *Le Figaro Magazine*, 6 June 1984.
37. *Paris Match* 6 July 1984.
38. See Jaffré 'Retour aux élections européennes' *Le Monde*, 30 June 1984.
39. Ibid.
40. On the period to 1981 see V. Wright 'The French Communists under the Fifth Republic' in H. Machin (ed.), *National Communism in Western Europe* (London: Methuen, 1983) pp. 90–123. On the post-1981 period see Jaffré in *Le Monde*, 3 Apr. 1984.
41. *Nouvel Observateur*, 22 June 1984.
42. Jaffré's calculation. *Le Monde*, 1 July 1984.
43. Jaffré, 'Les fantassins de l'extreme droite' in *Le Monde*, 14 Feb. 1984 and 'Qui sont les électeurs des petites listes' in *Le Monde*, 6 June 1984.
44. The comparison between maps showing the performance of Poujade and Tixier Vignancour, such as that on p. 297 of P. M. Williams, *French Politicians and Elections 1951–1969* (Cambridge University Press, 1970) and of Le Pen (see *Le Monde*, 21 June 1984) is instructive.
45. *Le Monde*, 8–9 July 1984.
46. *Nouvel Observateur*, 22 June 1984.

5 Greece

KEVIN FEATHERSTONE*

The 1984 Euro-elections in Greece provoked a fierce campaign fought very much on domestic issues and were seen as a major test of the Socialist Government's popularity, and as an opportunity for the main opposition party, the centre-right New Democracy (ND) party, to show that it had recovered from its defeat in the 1981 national elections. In the event, the Socialists (PASOK, the Panhellenic Socialist Movement) remained the largest single party, though ND did narrow the gap. Earlier opposition suggestions, that a major swing from PASOK to ND might prompt President Karamanlis to call fresh national elections, therefore evaporated when the results were declared, and the Papandreou Government looks set to run its normal course until October 1985. One direct consequence of the election results was that Averof resigned as ND leader, less than three months after the party's electoral disappointment.

The vitality of the campaign owed more to domestic considerations than to interest in the EP, but the manner of the debate that did take place on the EC reflected the nature of Greece's recent membership of the EC. In assessing the implications of the EP elections, it is therefore important to relate the discussion to that experience.

INTRODUCTION: GREECE AND THE EUROPEAN COMMUNITY

Greece became the EC's first associate member in 1962, and the terms of its agreement with the EC included a provision which remains unique: namely, the envisaged accession of Greece to full EC membership. The terms of the Association Agreement had the character of a

117

pre-accession accord pending full membership. Signed on 6 July 1961, the Agreement had been negotiated for almost two years. It explicitly provided for the integration of large and important sectors of the Greek economy, particularly agriculture, into that of the EC.[1] The Agreement established a customs union between Greece and the EC, and sought to make resources available to the Greek economy so that it might develop at a faster rate and thereby permit accession to full membership 'at a later date'. Moreover, Article 35 had as its aim 'to ensure equality of treatment between [agricultural] products of member states and like products of Greece on the markets of the contracting parties'.[2] Other provisions of the Agreement concerned the free movement of persons and services, rules of competition, and the co-ordination of trade policies. Unlike the three new member states of 1972, therefore, Greece has a much longer experience of involvement with the EC, and its representatives had attended meetings of the Council of Association until days before the April 1967 military coup in Athens.

With the establishment of the Colonels' regime in Greece, the Six decided not to dismantle the Association Agreement, but to 'freeze' it. The 1962 Agreement's provisions were never realised, but both sides continued to follow the timetable for the elimination of tariffs. Thus, 'Greek industrial exports have enjoyed free access since 1968, earlier than originally envisaged, while by 1974 two-thirds of EC exports entered Greece duty-free.'[3] After the restoration of democracy in 1974, Karamanlis as head of the ND Government applied for full EC membership on 12 June 1975. With the successful completion of the negotiations – Greece was deliberately given preference over Spain and Portugal – Greece's Treaty of Accession was signed in May 1979 and later ratified by all ten national parliaments. Consequently, Greece became a full EC member in January 1981.

GREECE AND THE EUROPEAN PARLIAMENT

In January 1981 Greece sent its first representatives to the EP: its 24 MEPs being nominated by the national parliament on a proportional basis, pending the holding of Euro-elections at the time of the next domestic poll. ND had 14 nominated MEPs, and they sat independent of any party group in the EP; PASOK had seven MEPs in the Socialist Group; the Union of the Democratic Centre (EDIK) had one MEP sitting independently; the Social Democrats (KODISO) also had one

MEP sitting independently; and the Communists (KKE) had one MEP in the Communist Group.

The first Euro-elections were held in Greece on 18 October 1981, on the same day as those for the national parliament. The results of both the national and the Euro-elections are given in Table 5.1. PASOK gained three seats, ND lost six seats, KKE ('pro-Moscow') gained two seats, KODISO retained one seat, and the Progressive Party (KP) (extreme right-wing) and KKE-es (Euro-Communists – see below) were represented for the first time.[4]

Some intriguing contrasts were highlighted between the results of the national and the European elections. In comparison with the national elections, PASOK's vote was nearly 8% lower, whilst the ND vote was also lower (by almost 4%). By contrast, the vote for the pro-EC Euro-Communists was up by 3%.[5] In addition to the greater dispersal of popular support in the Euro-elections, domestic comment highlighted voters' hesitation in endorsing PASOK's EC policies, and some suggested that the implications of this lower vote were not been lost on the Papandreou Government.

After some initial delay, the Greek parties represented in the EP began to be assimilated into the EP's institutional structures. ND MEPs sit in the EPP Group, after having considered joining the Liberal Group instead. They are also full members of the European Democratic Union (EDU), which includes United Kingdom Conservatives. The MEPs from both Greek Communist parties sit together in the Communist Group. PASOK is a member of the EP Socialist Group, but it is not affiliated to either the Socialist International, which it regards as too moderate, or to the CSP, which is tied to the International. Recent signs are that PASOK might reconsider its attitude towards the International, but it could not be formally admitted as a member until the next Socialist International Congress in 1986.

The 1981 Euro-elections in Greece were held on the basis of a party list system in a single national constituency, which is different from the normal 'reinforced proportional representation' system used in national parliamentary elections with 56 local electoral districts. However, as with national elections, voting in the Euro-elections was compulsory. Foreign EC nationals living in Greece were not allowed to participate in the domestic Euro-elections. The 1981 Greek law on the Euro-elections also disallowed any successful candidate holding a dual-mandate between the EP and either the unicameral national legislature, or a post as a professor in higher education. The order in which candidates appear on a party's list is determined by the party itself, and any party must forfeit a deposit of Dr150 000 if it fails to obtain 3% of the national vote or, alternatively, to win at least one seat. The 1981 law did not contain any references of the French variety seeking to protect the national parliament from an increase in the EP's powers.[6]

Several Greek MEPs resigned between October 1981 and June 1984. The original KP MEP died, a PASOK MEP became Ambassador to Sweden, and another PASOK MEP became a government minister. Under the 1981 electoral law, a retiring MEP is replaced by 'substitutes from the same list in the order in which they were declared' (Article 7(4)). The political careers of the Greek MEPs in the pre-June 1984 EP reflected the experience of their respective parties.[7] Amongst the ten PASOK MEPs, four were former members of the national parliament (though only one had been a deputy before 1967, and that was for the Centre Union in 1963 and 1964), and two were members of the party's national executive committee. By contrast, ND's eight MEPs had the advantage of longer right-wing rule at home. Four of the eight were ex-ministers, seven ex-MPs, one a member of the party's national executive committee, and one was an ex-member of the EC's Economic and Social Committee (ESC). Of the other MEPs, one of the three KKE MEPs was a former national deputy from 1951, for the United Democratic Left (UDL), the one Euro-Communist-KKE-es MEP was a UDL deputy from 1961 and a member of the party's Executive Bureau, and the one KODISO MEP was an ex-MP for the Centre Union from 1974 and a former cabinet minister. Only two Greek MEPs were women, both for PASOK.

In the 1981 Euro-elections, the EC office in Athens adopted a low-key role, concerned with public information. However, the scope and finance of its endeavours were in no way comparable to the type of campaign undertaken in 1979 in the other EC member states. Given the circumstances of its accession, only from 1984 onwards would Greece be exposed to a cross-national EC election campaign.

PASOK's sweeping victory in 1981 altered the balance of the Greek party system. The new government appeared to enjoy a long honeymoon with the voters, though by the municipal elections of October 1982 there were warning signals from the electorate.[8] PASOK again won a clear victory over the two rounds of the elections, with Socialist mayors victorious in 89 of the 136 towns and cities. However, this success was only made possible by the tacit alliance apparently made between PASOK and the Communists, which neutralised the effects of a substantial switch of left-wing votes from PASOK to the Communists (KKE). In the 89 towns won by PASOK, only 20 of them were gained without Communist help. Interestingly, in the 37 towns where PASOK was left to fight the Communists on the second round of voting, PASOK lost in 23, seemingly reflecting anti-government sentiment. One consequence of the elections was to make the Papandreou Government aware of the importance of winning back its disenchanted voters, and it has made a number of symbolic radical gestures. Whilst the Communists at the start of 1984 maintained a strong left-wing challenge to the Government, ND appeared still not to have recovered from the trauma of losing power in 1981. ND's appeal lacked coherence and direction, and it appeared uncertain as to its future policy initiatives, despite public criticism of the Papandreou Government.

PASOK

From the party's formative years onwards, PASOK's policy towards EC membership had strong undercurrents of both populism and nationalism, captured in the party's early slogan of 'Greece for the Greeks'.[9] At the time of Karamanlis' negotiations for accession to the EC, PASOK opposed membership. The party's anti-EC appeal was part of a more general campaign aimed at a disparate electorate which, when faced with membership, was worried as to the impact it might have on Greece's increasingly fragile economic growth. PASOK warned of the dangers to rural communities from what it saw as the inadequate protection of the CAP, which paralleled the problems of the urban economies facing tougher competition from European multinationals. All sectors of the Greek nation would be exposed to the ruinous exploitation of monopoly capitalism. Instead, PASOK argued that, 'Greece must seek ... to create a non-capitalist Mediterranean Community which will constitute a sufficiently powerful entity to resist the pressures of the superpowers, and meet its basic needs by itself'. However, although the Mediterranean dimension was attractive to many party supporters, the party dropped this notion as it was becoming increasingly apparent that it had little support abroad, let alone domestically, in the countries that mattered most.

By 1977, PASOK's policy had become one of putting Greek membership to a referendum and of favouring a special relationship with the EC similar to that of Norway. However, the parallel with Norway seemed limited given the alarm PASOK had voiced over the impact of tariff reductions on the Greek economy, and the limited influence in EC decision-making. The further example of Yugoslavia's 'special agreement' was also raised, and dropped, after the 1981 elections. Moreover, the referendum policy also faced difficulties: only the Greek President, Karamanlis, can call a national referendum, and he is strongly committed to continued EC membership. At the 1981 elections, Papandreou stated that he expected Karamanlis to bow to the 'will of the people' and authorise a referendum, but others were sceptical as to whether he really believed this to be a realistic prospect.

Such a legacy has meant that since coming to power, PASOK has been critical of the conditions of Greek membership whilst it has also seemingly accepted its continued participation in the EC. Before its election in 1981, PASOK declared that EC membership involves an unacceptable 'transfer of national sovereignty concerning crucial economic matters to foreign decision-making centres'. In March 1982 the Papandreou Government submitted a memorandum to the Council of Ministers asking for a modification of the terms of entry and for 'special arrangements' to meet Greece's need for economic development. It sought increased agricultural and regional aid, and to establish the possibility that individual member states could, temporarily, derogate themselves from particular EC regulations. Such 'special arrangements', the Government said, would 'constitute the minimum possible' basis on which membership would not be 'in conflict with basic Greek national interests'. In February 1983, the EC Commission allowed Greece a special derogation which authorises it to block imports of eight groups of products from other member states. These special measures were taken after the devaluation of the drachma, but they were allowed for under the Treaty of Rome. At a more comprehensive level, the EC Commission in March 1983 published its reply to the Papandreou Government's 1982 memorandum and the reply received a favourable response from Athens (though minor differences remained). The Government indicated its intention of staying in the EC. In its reply, the Commission accepted PASOK's five-year economic plan which included a number of protection clauses to help small businesses that run counter to EC rules on competition policy. The Commission also proposed establishing a number of special projects to give specific economic aid to Greece. More generally, the Commission saw most problems being reconciled within the context of a developing EC Mediterranean policy.

In less than two years, then, PASOK's EC policy developed from one which foresaw Greek withdrawal to one which still appears content with something less than a renegotiation of membership terms. This development reflects a wider change in attitudes towards Western

Europe, whilst it also responds to domestic opinion which seems unprepared for the upheavals of leaving the EC. Asked as to the apparent inconsistency of its EC policy, the party emphasises that it has never favoured immediate withdrawal, rather that since Greece became a member it has sought a special agreement. The 1961 Association Agreement would have required renewal by 1984, in any event, so PASOK has endeavoured to achieve the same aims as it had set itself before EC membership became a reality.[10]

Not surprisingly, parties both to the left and right of PASOK have not accepted this defence. However, the current effect of the Government's policy is to place PASOK in the electorally advantageous position of being able to accept strong criticism of the EC (so long as it does not seek immediate withdrawal) and at the same time to portray itself as playing a positive role within EC institutions, alongside other socialists, defending Greek interests.

In line with its wider foreign policy aims, the Papandreou Government has sought to establish its political independence from both the USA and the USSR, and to pursue its own approach. Within the EC this made attempts at political co-operation difficult at times. The Papandreou Government has been relatively muted in its criticisms of events in Poland. At the Stuttgart summit in June 1983 Greece, which had previously opposed 'unblocking' a very small EC loan to Israel (over Lebanon) abstained, so it went through. On 12 September 1983, however, at the Foreign Ministers' meeting on the downed Korean airliner, Greece refused a tough anti-Soviet motion, and other EC governments came away frustrated with the more carefully worded motion that had eventually been approved. Domestically, though, PASOK presents incidents such as these as evidence of a more assertive independent Greek foreign policy, and one which breaks away from past disappointments at the hands of Washington.

Papandreou had been criticised for his handling of the December 1983 EC Summit in Athens, which ended without agreement on the EC's pressing problems. He had, though, attempted to put together a compromise, the effects of which would have included exempting Ireland, Italy and Greece from cutbacks in milk production, and to have provided 'medium-term' alleviations of the British and West German budget contributions until 1989. Given the particular Greek interests he wanted to protect, however, the role of intermediary was a difficult one to adopt and the Summit's failure appeared to confirm some of Papandreou's own criticisms of EC membership. Certainly his Government's EC policies have kept the main opposition party, ND, on the defensive and made it difficult for it to present a coherent alternative.

NEW DEMOCRACY

Following his return to Greece in 1974, and the restoration of democracy, Constantine Karamanlis founded a new party, ND, to facilitate his exercise of power. This was the second party he had formed, and many of its adherents had been members of the old National Radical Union which Karamanlis had established whilst in government in 1955. After his return in 1974, the Karamanlis Government was quick to lodge Greece's application for full EC membership, which it saw as a means of stabilising the new regime and as a long-term strategy for modernising the economy, though it accepted that Greece had distinctive agricultural interests that needed safeguarding. Furthermore, the political link with Western Europe was useful at a time of domestic anti-USA sentiment.

With the successful completion of the EC negotiations, on which he had placed so much stress, Karamanlis resigned as Prime Minister and became President in May 1980 for a five-year term. His successor, George Rallis led New Democracy into the 1981 election campaign, amidst evidence of increasing public support for PASOK, the main opposition party. Having put accession to the EC first on its foreign policy agenda, ND defended that decision in its 1981 manifesto by maintaining that EC membership enhances rather than restricts Greece's sovereignty, by rendering the country an equal partner in a powerful community of nations.[11] At the time of accession, Premier Rallis stated that Greece would 'simply be occupying a place in Europe that has rightfully been its, by dint of both history and culture'. New Democracy scorned the idea of Greece being able to negotiate a 'special relationship' with the rest of the EC as suggested by PASOK; no such relationship could be imposed on the EC solely on Greece's terms so as to be more favourable than the existing Treaty of Accession. New Democracy also criticised what it saw as PASOK's populist appeal to anti-USA sentiment. 'Greece's place', New Democracy's 1981 manifesto declared, 'can only be in the West, with which Greece has allied itself politically and economically as well as in defence matters'.

Following its sweeping defeat in the 1981 elections, ND and its leadership had to adapt to the new experience of opposition. From 1974 onwards, and for most of the pre-1967 period, the Right has enjoyed political power. Out of government, it has found it difficult to present a coherent alternative with popular appeal. Its task was not helped by the prolonged illness of its aged new leader, Evangelos Averof in 1982, and the uncertainty over the direction in which the party wished to be led.

Forced to respond to the initiatives of the new government, New Democracy tried to criticise what it saw as the dangerous tone of PASOK EC policies, whilst at the same time claiming that its more popular measures derived from the impetus given by its own earlier administration. As one senior New Democracy MP explained, 'the EC Memorandum essentially up-dates the spirit of what we said earlier, though we disagree with the rhetoric associated with it'.[12] The fact that New Democracy has felt itself obliged to respond in such a manner is a measure of PASOK's own success in shifting the focus of domestic debate on the EC. New Democracy calls for added emphasis within the EC on regional development, a review of the impact of EC membership on Greek agriculture, and a general reorientation of EC policy towards the Mediterranean, all within the context of an expanded budget. As the party which took Greece into the EC it is portrayed as a fervent supporter of the EC ideal and responsible for Greece being given preferential treatment over Spain and Portugal. It also reminded PASOK of the hesitation shown by socialist voters in the 1981 Euro-elections and uses this as evidence of public concern over the prospect of EC withdrawal.

THE COMMUNISTS

In 1968 the Greek Communist Movement split into what has now become labelled the Communist Party of 'the exterior' (Marxist–Leninist, 'pro-Moscow', KKE) and the Communist Party of 'the interior' (Euro-Communist, KKE–es). As has been indicated already, KKE had three MEPs before June 1984, together with 13 seats in the national parliament, and KKE–es had one MEP and no national MPs. The national electoral success of KKE–ext. (as it does not accept the label 'exterior', references here are to KKE) has given it greater domestic visibility and influence, especially in the trade unions.

KKE has always opposed Greek membership of the EC, which it sees as representative of USA-dominated Western capitalism, acting against the interests of Greek workers and threatening Greek independence. It has strongly criticised what it sees as PASOK's change of policy on the

EC, and it has struck a chord as PASOK's own left-wing, which has never been sympathetic to the EC. By contrast, KKE-Interior (it labels itself 'Interior') in its 1981 election manifesto declared itself in favour of EC membership, but criticised the transitional terms of entry.[13] It did noticeably better in the 1981 Euro-elections than in the national elections, but since then it has had some difficulty in reacting to PASOK's developing EC policy in a distinctive fashion.

THE 1984 EP ELECTIONS

The EP elections of 1984 were the first to be held in Greece in synchronisation with other EC member states. As the EC's newest member, with a government that was critical of the terms of Greece's existing membership, and at a time of crisis over the EC's future, it was perhaps inevitable that the campaign should focus on domestic considerations. The 1981 electoral procedure was used for the 1984 elections. Foreign EC nationals in Greece were not able to vote for Greek MEPs, though Greek nationals abroad could vote for Greek candidates. As is traditional in Greek law, the polling stations were open to coincide with the period between 'sunrise and sunset'. One change allowed a maximum of two national MPs to appear on any one party list; this facilitated the candidature of George Mavros and others (see below). The election campaign was one of the most impassioned for years, concentrating as it did on the performance of the PASOK government. Party activists stuck campaign posters up seemingly everywhere, and in the competition between the parties incidents of violence were reported on a number of occasions.[14] In some cases, poster gangs were shot at with hunting guns and an explosive device was hurled at ND headquarters in Kastoria. ND accused the police of bias and unnecessary brutality and asked the Prime Minister to replace the Athens police chief. Papandreou accused ND of cooperating with undemocratic right-wing elements to subvert law and order, and he rejected an ND offer to set up a joint committee to monitor incidents and attacks.

Both PASOK and ND selected senior figures to head their respective party lists, and their stature was a sign of the importance attached to the domestic contest. George Mavros, the former leader of the Union of the Democratic Centre and a well-known member of the old Centre Union party, headed the PASOK list, a choice designed to maintain PASOK's appeal to centrist voters. Of PASOK's 24 candidates, only five were sitting-MEPs, three of which were re-elected. The party's selection procedure for candidates emphasised control from the centre, with decisions being taken by the Central Committee, and particularly Papandreou as leader, after representations from various party organs. For its part, ND chose its leader Evangelos Averof to head the party list. Some observers suggested that former Premier Rallis might head the list to signify a reconciliation between his own moderate supporters and those of the more right-wing Averof, but Rallis apparently refused. Second in the list was Ioannis Boutos, another leading moderate. ND's selection of candidates followed at least as hierarchical a process as that of PASOK, with the leadership determining the rankings after receiving representations. At an election rally in Thessaloniki, Averof publicly announced that, 'I drew up a fully reformed, more broadly representative and carefully selected list of candidates.'[15] Indeed, of ND's 24 candidates, not one was a sitting-MEP.

Among the minority parties, the biggest change was that a new party, the National Political Union (EPEN), was formed in January 1984 by the ex-dictator, and still imprisoned, George Papadopoulos.[16] His extreme right-wing party list was headed by Chrysanthos Dimitriadis, and it competed with that of the older Progressive Party (KP). EPEN's main objective appears to be Papadopoulos' release.

No major foreign speaker came to Greece to support any of the parties in the Euro-elections. New Democracy endorsed the EPP's common manifesto, though PASOK did not formally endorse the common socialist manifesto, and very little reference was made to it in the campaign. Before the campaign got underway, ND sought advice on its tactics from both the British Conservative Party and the advertising agency, Saatchi & Saatchi. ND was advised to improve the co-ordination of its organisation and to stress the quality of its collective leadership, but in the event much media attention focussed on Averof as party leader, as would normally have been the case.

The EC office in Athens conducted a non-partisan information campaign on the elections until mid-April. Press and television advertising was used to herald the elections, and the party campaigns followed on. The Government refused to allow the European Parliament's own 8-minute video film to be shown on television, so it was only used in cinemas. Media coverage of the elections was probably higher, in quantitative terms, than in many other EC countries. The national television organisation, ERT, claimed that it gave a more generous allocation of broadcasting time to the parties than most other EC systems. Both PASOK and New Democracy held three public rallies which were covered 'live' by ERT, and for the month before June 17 television time was allocated proportionately between the parties. As more than a dozen parties were contesting the elections, the generosity of television time may have been of some help to the minority parties, though some, such as KKE–es, were still critical. Certainly television news coverage outside of election time has been criticised for its pro-Government bias and for its superficial account of opposing views.[17] Press coverage was also more extensive than in many other EC states, and the range of partisan commitment of the Greek press in recent years has helped to reflect the breadth of public opinion.

At the start of the campaign, public opinion still seemed sceptical about EC membership. In a *Eurodim* Poll in Greater Athens in April 1984, only 30% of those interviewed said they would now vote 'Yes' if a referendum were held on continued Greek membership of the EC.[18] However, a *Eurobarometer* survey at the same time found that 41% of Greek voters supported the idea of 'European Union', a higher percentage than in Denmark, France, Ireland, or the United Kingdom.[19] The same survey showed a decline, though, in the number of Greek voters believing that EC membership had been 'a good choice': down from 47% in October 1983 to 38% in March–April 1984. The poll also suggested that Greek voters would be particularly concerned with national issues: only Denmark registered a lower proportion saying that they would vote on European, as opposed to national, matters, though this was still more than half those interviewed; and, 69% of Greeks said that their MEPs should put national interests first, and European considerations second. Overall, public opinion was still cautious about the EC and the party campaigns were conducted against this background.

THE CAMPAIGN: A CHALLENGE TO THE PAPANDREOU GOVERNMENT

The campaign was a fierce contest over the Papandreou Government's two-and-a-half years of office, with each of the main parties seeking public endorsement of their own domestic strategy. It centred on the Government's record, and distinctly 'European' issues were clearly of secondary concern.

As with their opponents, PASOK campaigned on a broadly based theme that covered foreign and domestic policies, and emphasised key elements of the party's philosophy. Papandreou invited the voters 'to gather round the popular, patriotic Movement for National Independence, Popular Sovereignty, Democracy and Socialism'.[20] He said that PASOK supporters were 'First Greeks and then Europeans', and indeed the party's campaign slogan was 'Greece First'.[21] 'A strong PASOK in the European Parliament', said the party, 'means another strong front for defending our national interests. It also means popular support in the continuous and crucial battle being waged by the Government of Change in Brussels. A victory [would] definitely support the Change in Greece and decisively support the struggle for a change in our relations with the EEC.'[22] PASOK thus stressed its role as a defender of Greek interests and the toughness of its approach towards 'the EEC', to which it ascribed a distant, competitive image.

At a large rally in Thessaloniki, Papandreou declared his government to be 'unyielding' on three key policies. These were: 'the complete adoption of the Greek Memorandum, which changes the terms of accession'; 'the promotion of the integrated Mediterranean programmes, to narrow the gap between North and South'; and 'the implementation – through EEC financing – of the Five-Year Development programme, which PASOK considers a foundation for Greece's self-sufficient economic development'. At a rally in Patras, Papandreou took pride in the fact that PASOK had received more money from the EC than had New Democracy, and he concluded that his government's approach was more effective in safeguarding Greek interests.[23]

Moreover, PASOK remained committed to a change in Greece's relations with the EC. Papandreou declared in Thessaloniki that Greece's position was 'for an autonomous Europe between the two superpowers', and the way forward for the EC was for a 'new Messina' to be held to discuss the future. PASOK would keep Greece's EC role constantly under review, however. Theodore Pangalos, Foreign Under-Secretary for EC Affairs, explained in a press interview that he hoped Greece's relations with the EC would develop smoothly. 'If, however, we face insurmountable problems', he went on, 'we will adjust our relations in such a way as to protect the interests of our economy and those of the Greek people. Naturally we will inform the people in time and ask their approval of any significant change.'[24] There thus remains a conditional and ambiguous element in PASOK's attitude towards future relations with the EC.

During the campaign PASOK bitterly attacked the Right (New Democracy), though it paid far less attention to its differences with KKE. 'The people do not forget what the right-wing means', declared Papandreou, accusing ND of right-wing extremism, fanaticism, and of seeking to polarise and divide Greece.[25] He accused Averof of 'lying' about PASOK's EC achievements, and of being 'a shadow from the past'.[26] ND was too Atlanticist, too subservient to foreign interests, and its pro-Europeanism was damaging to Greece. The virulence of Papandreou's attacks were matched by those of Averof, and each were broadcast in full on national television. New Democracy presented itself as the only genuine pro-European party; it saw EC membership as the 'only solution' for Greece in the future:

> The people correctly see that the forthcoming elections are not a simple process of choosing the Greek representatives to the European Parliament. They are an opportunity for all citizens to warn, punish and condemn the Third World inconsistencies, the incompetency and inadequacy, intolerance and the fanaticism of the apprentice magicians with their grandiose promises, those who are destroying the Greek economy and compromising the nation.[27]

Averof, at a rally in Thessaloniki, criticised the 'hazy Social-Marxist experiments' of PASOK, and attacked its lack of a clear EC policy which contrasted with ND's 'unwavering commitment'.[28]

ND claimed that Greece's accession to the EC had been on more favourable terms than those negotiated for the three new EC members in 1973 or was likely for either Spain or Portugal. Moreover, a 'special relationship' with the EC was not possible under the Treaty of Rome, and PASOK's anti-EC attitude was damaging to Greek interests. In many respects, ND's campaign was a reaction to PASOK initiatives. It was thus partially shaped and fought on a terrain of the Government's rather than ND's own choosing.

KKE's election slogan was 'No to the European Community, Yes to Change', and its campaign offered little that was new. 'Our party', it declared, was 'against Greece's accession to the EEC, and today [it] stands for disengagement as the only solution for the country's prosperity and for change'.[29] KKE had emphasised the grave economic consequences that membership would bring, and had been proved right. Moreover, PASOK by itself had failed to bring about real change, and therefore needed a strong KKE alongside it to ensure that progressive policies would be pursued. KKE's attacks on PASOK were a little muted, returning the favour which PASOK had shown to them. KKE severely condemned the legacy of the Right.

The various minority parties on the whole supported Greece's participation in the EC. The policy of KKE–es had much in common

with the substance of what PASOK had pursued itself, but differed in
style and rhetoric. It said, 'Yes to Change, with a new momentum. As
far as ignoring the European dimension of the election goes, it declares:
Together with the workers of the EC for a Europe of peace and labour,
and against the Euro-right, missiles and unemployment'.[30] The party's
campaign slogan was 'Yes to a Workers' Europe'. KODISO called for
a more positive approach within the EC to overcome the current crisis,
and it set out a number of 'sweeping reforms' for the EC, some of which
were specifically tailored to Greece's own economic situation. The
Union of the Democratic Centre (EDIK) was even more ambitious,
and it declared 'if Western Europe does not become a federation, then
in a few years it will turn into a province either of the USA or of the
USSR'.[31] It was unequivocally in favour of a 'United States of Europe'.

THE RESULTS: THE CHALLENGE THAT FAILED

Overall, the results of the 1984 EP elections suggested little dramatic
change with no party having performed spectacularly well or badly (see
Table 5.1). PASOK increased its share of the vote on the 1981 Euro-
elections (+1.4%), but it had lost support in comparison to its higher
vote in the 1981 national elections (−6.5%).[32] The Papandreou
Government stressed that it was satisfied with the outcome, and it was

TABLE 5.1   *The 1981 and 1984 election results in Greece*

	1981 national election %	1981 European election %	1984 European election %	1984 Seats (1981 in brackets)
PASOK	48.1	40.2	41.6	10 (10)
New Democracy	35.9	31.4	38.1	9 (8)
KKE	10.9	12.8	11.6	3 (3)
KKE–es	1.4	5.3	3.4	1 (1)
Progressives	1.7	2.0	0.2	0 (1)
KODISO	0.7	4.2	0.8	0 (1)
EDIK	0.4	N.A.	0.3	0 (0)
EPEN	–	–	2.3	1 (0)
Turnout*		81.5	77.1	–

*Voting compulsory by law.
SOURCES   Greek Press & Information Office, London; Athens News Agency.

undoubtedly heartened by the fact that ND had failed to make much of an advance upon its 1981 performance. ND's vote increased, as compared to the national elections of 1981 by only 2.2%, though its vote was up 6.7% on the previous Euro-elections. ND was the only party to increase its representation at Strasbourg. However, its aim had been to regain electoral superiority over PASOK and its failure to do so, despite the tribulations of the Papandreou Government over the previous three years, provoked considerable debate within the party. Indeed, by September 1984 Averof had resigned as ND leader and was replaced by Constantine Mitsotakis, as the party sought a fresh image for the forthcoming national elections.

The elections also produced mixed fortunes for the other parties. Both communist parties did better than in the national elections of 1981, but worse than in the 1981 Euro-elections. The total vote for the Extreme Right remained stable, but was transferred from the Progressive Party (KP) to EPEN, with the effect that Georgios Alexiadis' seat went to Chrysanthos Dimitriadis. The elections were an unqualified failure, however, for the Centre in Greek politics: KODISO's vote fell to 0.8% and it lost its seat in Strasbourg.

Now there are five rather than six Greek parties in the EP, two of which are not currently represented in the national parliament (KKE-es and EPEN). Indeed, the Greek assembly has deputies from only the three largest parties. With the substantial turnover of candidates on the various party lists, the 1984 elections resulted in seven (of the ten) elected PASOK MEPs being new to the EP; each of the nine ND MEPs are new; one of three KKE MEPs is new; and the EPEN MEP is also new. With the exception of Leonidas Kyrkos of KKE-es, each of the parties will have fresh personnel in the EP. Only PASOK's Spyros Plaskovitis has served in the EP continuously since Greek entry in January 1981. This rapid turnover of personnel means a relatively large number of party members have experience and knowledge of how the EC works, but it suggests also that the major parties do not value length of service at Strasbourg very highly. The inclusion of Averof at the head of the New Democracy party list and of Mavros at the head of PASOK's list now means that they can bring considerable political experience to the EP, but their participation in their respective party campaigns undoubtedly owed much more to domestic considerations, for and against the Papandreou Government, than to the prestige of a European political career. Similar considerations also undoubtedly explain the inclusion of Leonidas Kyrkos, a long-serving KKE-es deputy at the head of the KKE-es list.

The domestic party struggle clearly revolved around the popularity of the Government, and PASOK's loss of support since the 1981 national elections seemed to flow in various directions. Whilst PASOK's aggregate vote was down 6.5%, New Democracy was up 2.2%, and the combined Extreme Right up 0.8%; on the Left, KKE–es was up 2.0%, KKE up 0.7%. The primary source of satisfaction in the 1984 results for PASOK must be that their limited net loss of support appears to have transferred to four different parties; that is, they face a diverse and mutually competitive opposition, both to its Left and to its Right. Of more specific concern to PASOK will be the location of its lost support. The electoral support for both PASOK and New Democracy across the country varied more in 1984 than in the 1981 national elections. The regional variation in each party's vote is shown in Table 5.2. PASOK in 1981 managed to increase its vote in areas of traditional Right-wing support, such as Peloponnesos and Thrace, and this was a major element of its sweeping success.[33] In 1984, PASOK lost support in an area associated with the Left (Greater Athens), but did relatively better in rural districts, suggesting some interesting change in the

TABLE 5.2   *The 1981 national election results and the 1984 European election results in Greece, by region*

		1981				1984			
		ND	PASOK	KKE	EPEN	ND	PASOK	KKE–es	KKE
1	Greater Athens	30.3	48.8	16.5	1.8	36.1	39.7	6.4	16.1
2	Rest of Central Greece, Euboea	37.7	51.2	8.7	2.6	41.0	44.0	2.5	10.0
3	Peloponnesos	41.6	48.4	7.0	3.9	41.9	43.6	2.5	8.3
4	Ionian Is.	35.7	47.3	14.9	1.5	34.8	44.0	3.5	16.2
5	Epirus	41.3	46.5	10.4	2.2	40.5	40.9	2.8	13.6
6	Thessaly	37.1	46.2	14.2	3.5	36.4	41.7	2.7	15.7
7	Macedonia	40.6	47.4	9.1	2.2	43.0	42.3	2.7	9.9
8	Thrace	41.9	47.2	4.6	4.8	50.3	37.3	2.0	5.6
9	Aegean Is.	37.7	47.8	12.7	0.9	36.8	45.9	2.9	13.5
10	Crete	24.8	65.1	9.1	0.4	26.8	60.2	2.4	10.2
	National	35.9	48.1	10.9	2.3	38.1	41.6	3.4	11.6

NOTE   Percentages are based on the votes for the three largest parties in 1981 and the five largest parties in 1984. Figures given are row percentages calculated on the basis of the average vote for each party in each region. The figures may not total 100 due to rounding-up.
SOURCES   Greek Press & Information Office, London; *ΕΛΕΥΘΕΡΟΤΥΠΙΑ*.

composition of its electorate. PASOK's largest losses were in Thrace (−9.9%), where it had done particularly well in 1981, and in Greater Athens (−9.1%) and Rest of Central Greece & Euboea (−7.2%), with more urban electorates. Greater Athens, which has the largest electorate of any of the regions, has traditionally favoured the far Left to a disproportionate extent (United Democratic Left in 1963 and 1964, United Left in 1974, and the Communists thereafter), but not the Centre-Left, for example the Centre Union in 1963 and 1964. PASOK itself has never performed disproportionately well there, though the size of the region's electorate makes it important to any victory.

In 1984, ND increased its vote relative to the 1981 national elections in every region, though in half of them its vote rose by less than 1.0%. ND beat PASOK into first place in its two highest regions, Macedonia and Thrace, both areas of traditional Right-wing support. The largest increases in ND's support came in those regions where PASOK suffered its most significant losses: Thrace (ND up 8.4%), Greater Athens (+5.8%), and Rest of Central Greece & Euboea (+3.3%). ND's net increase in these regions did not match PASOK's net loss, and to some extent the far Left appears to have benefitted: in Thrace, the KKE vote was up 1.0%; in Greater Athens, KKE–es received its highest vote; and in Central Greece KKE's vote increased by 2.1%. Again, PASOK's losses appear to have gone in opposite directions, though mainly to the Right.

KKE had been expected by some observers to significantly increase its vote, but in the event it proved relatively stable. Its two highest votes were in Greater Athens and the Ionian Islands, as in 1981, though only in the former did its vote fall (0.4%). Across the country, its vote fluctuated less than it had in 1981, though it will be frustrated at not having been able to pick up more PASOK votes and at the continued existence of its sister communist party, KKE–es, which did well in urban areas.

The Greek party system remained relatively unchanged after the 1984 Euro-elections, and this will reassure the Papandreou Government, though it will worry ND as they both face the national elections due before October 1985. PASOK claimed that had the 1984 elections been for the Greek Parliament, it would have been returned with a small overall majority, though others disputed this.[34] The challenge to the Papandreou Government in June 1984 failed, and afterwards it looked to be in a more secure position than most of its EC counterparts.

THE AFTERMATH

The Euro-elections had a number of short- and long-term consequences. After the elections, the PASOK Government could declare that it was 'fully satisfied' with the results and that it would continue to implement its 1981 programme.[35] However, Papandreou did announce that he would establish a mini-cabinet to make his government run more effectively and to improve its coordination. The Government also indicated that it plans to hold national elections in October 1985, at the end of its four-year term, and it must be facing those with confidence. It reiterated its pledge to introduce a 'simple proportional representation' system for the 1985 elections. If implemented, PASOK would no doubt see itself as being the largest single party after the elections and one which would be critical to any government. A PR system might also give PASOK the opportunity to seek allies both to its left and to the centre, or possibly both, whilst New Democracy might well be unable to establish any workable coalition.

ND's challenge to the Papandreou Government failed, in that PASOK was still the largest party, though ND had managed to increase its own vote. The failure of ND's challenge led directly to Averof's resignation as party leader, and his successor, Mitsotakis, a man of liberal origins, seems keen to make a fresh start.

Another leader in trouble, KODISO's Pesmazoglou, announced his resignation and his temporary withdrawal from active politics almost immediately the results were known. The 1984 elections were also disappointing for the Centre in Greek politics: they confirmed its decline since 1974 and gave little sign that its situation could be ameliorated in the near future. One possible consequence of the 1984 elections for the remainder of the present decade is that the Greek party system will continue to be stronger on the Left than on the Right, and very weak in the Centre.

Although the Extreme Right in Greece retained its one MEP (transferred to EPEN), its vote remained stable and low. With the success of the Extreme Right in France, the EP will see a new political group formed around these new MEPs, but the prospects for close collaboration may not be very strong, given differences in their domestic appeal. Neither racism nor immigration are as strong issues in Greece as they currently appear to be in France, and EPEN is not fascist.

With respect to the EC, a further consequence of the 1984 elections may also be that Greece's relations with the rest of the Ten will remain conditional, in that a PASOK Government will be anxious to secure a 'good deal' for Greece from the EC budget and may keep under review Greece's role in the EC. However, the EC's difficulties in 1984 suggested that other member governments may follow a similar strategy and so PASOK may be following a wider trend. In terms of the EP though, the 1984 elections in Greece provided the opportunity for a lively and fiercely conducted campaign on essentially national concerns, and in particular the popularity of the Government, rather than an outlet for a more substantive debate on the future of the EC. Given the opportunity to talk of Europe, the Greek parties opted, like others, for a domestic tug-of-war.

NOTES AND REFERENCES

* Research for this paper was carried out in Athens with the help of a grant from the Carnegie Trust, for which the author would like to record his gratitude. The author would also like to thank D. K. Katsoudas and Vassilis Kapetanyannis for their help in preparing this research. Any errors are the author's sole responsibility.

1. See S. Stathatos, 'From Association to Full Membership', in L. Tsoukalis (ed.), *Greece and the European Community*, (Farnborough: Saxon House, 1979).
2. Quoted in S. Stathatos, ibid.
3. L. Tsoukalis, *The European Community and Its Mediterranean Enlargement*, (London: Allen & Unwin 1981) p. 31.
4. As explained later in the text, there are two communist parties in Greece. In this discussion, 'KKE' will be used to refer to the larger, more orthodox communist party, and 'KKE-es' will refer to the (Euro-communist) Communist Party of the Interior.
5. See K. Featherstone, 'Elections and Parties in Greece', *Government & Opposition*, 17, 2, Spring 1982.
6. See 'The Law on the Direct Election of Greek Representatives to the European Parliament', in the Report of Parliament's 163rd proceedings of 2 July 1981, Athens.
7. Information taken from the list of members published by the EC Office, Athens.
8. See K. Featherstone, 'The Greek Socialists in Power', *West European Politics*, 6, 3, July 1983.
9. See K. Featherstone, (1983), ibid. Discussion here relies, in part, on that article.
10. Obtained from personal interview with a party MEP in February 1984. This interpretation may be a little idiosyncratic.
11. See K. Featherstone (1982) ibid. Discussion here relies, in part, on that article.

12. Transcribed from a personal interview in February 1984.
13. Information taken from publications of Greek Embassy, London.
14. See *The Times* 4 June 1984, 16 June 1984; *Le Monde* 19 June 1984.
15. Taken from text of speech given on 2 June 1984 distributed by Athens News Agency (No. 164).
16. See *The Guardian*, 31 Jan. 1984.
17. For a discussion of the Greek media, see article by D. K. Katsoudas in the forthcoming special issue of *West European Politics* on the media in Europe.
18. A national KPEE poll showed 47.5% supporting EC membership, however, with only 29.1% against.
19. *Eurobarometer*, no. 21, (EC Commission: Brussels, 1984).
20. Speech given on 5 May 1984 in Thessaloniki; text distributed by Athens News Agency (no. 157). Later references to Thessaloniki speech are taken from this text.
21. Thessaloniki speech, 5 May 1984.
22. Statements from each of the parties on EC policies, Athens News Agency (no. 165), 8 June 1984.
23. Speech given on 26 May 1984, text distributed by Athens News Agency.
24. Athens News Agency, 15 June 1984.
25. Thessaloniki, 5 May 1984.
26. Patras, 26 May 1984.
27. Athens News Agency, 8 June 1984.
28. Speech on 2 June 1984, text distributed by Athens News Agency.
29. Athens News Agency, 8 June 1984.
30. Athens News Agency, 8 June 1984.
31. Athens News Agency, 8 June 1984.
32. See K. Featherstone (1982), ibid.
33. See K. Featherstone and D. K. Katsoudas, 'Change and Continuity in Greek Voting Behaviour', *European Journal of Political Research*, forthcoming.
34. Statement to Athens News Agency, 20 June 1984, by Government spokesman Dimitri Maroudas.
35. Statement by Dimitri Maroudas, ibid.

6 Ireland

NEIL COLLINS*

The two EP elections have been similar in form but different in significance for Ireland. The election of 1979 was important for the Republic of Ireland not so much for the resolution of any political debate at home, but because it marked a further assertion of national identity abroad. Ireland was taking full part in this important international event on an equal footing with the other older European nation states. The most striking points in the 1979 election results were that the two independent candidates polled 14.1% of the popular vote; the Fianna Fail party suffered a heavy setback compared with its showing in the previous general election; and, the Labour Party gained 27% of the seats with only 14.5% of the popular vote. By 1984 the Republic was far more familiar with Europe and with elections. The wrangling over finance which seems to typify the EC is a constant feature of Irish news coverage and the electorate had been to the polls for three general elections in a period of 18 months in 1981/82. In addition, there had been a very divisive constitutional referendum in 1983. Another wearily familiar Northern Ireland contest was being watched with special interest from Dublin mainly to assess the electoral strength of Sinn Fein, the Provisional IRA's stalking horse entering a European race for the first time.

In the main the Irish election to the EP was a very low-key affair. It was only to a limited extent about what the *Irish Independent*'s political commentary declared it should be about.

The European elections should be about the performance of [MEPs] during the first term of the directly elected parliament. They should be about the effectiveness of the different political groupings and their policies. They should be about future progress towards a better balance of power between national governments and the EEC, between politicians and bureaucrats, between European democracy and the curious oligarchy of Councils and Summits over which Margaret Thatcher tends to preside like the Black Queen in Snow White, we being one of the dwarfs.[1]

The outcome of the 1984 EP election was an increase in seats for the two largest parties, Fianna Fail and Fine Gael. A complete rout for the Labour Party. The current disposition of Irish members from the Republic of Ireland is eight Fianna Fail, seven Fine Gael and one independent. In Northern Ireland the balance of representation was maintained at two unionists and one nationalist.

The 1984 poll in the Republic was only 47.6%, a sign perhaps of how little public interest the election generated. In 1979 the figure was 63.6%. A referendum to change the constitution to allow legislation giving non-nationals a vote in Irish elections was held on the same day, Thursday 14 June. The need for a constitutional amendment was not challenged by any of the main parties and there was very little public debate on the issue. A by-election was also fought in Laois–Offaly, a Dail constituency in Leinster.[2] Voting was, as usual, on the single transferable vote (STV) system in multi-member constituencies. As in the 1979 EP election, there were four constituencies, returning a total of fifteen MEPs. The largest representation is five seats for Munster; Dublin returns four, and Leinster and Connacht/Ulster three each. This arrangement of seats gives an advantage to the western and more rural constituencies with 138 215 and 157 192 electors per member in Munster and Connacht–Ulster respectively, but 176 218 and 181 959 in Dublin and Leinster. The voter in the STV system may mark the ballot paper according to his order of preference between candidates, irres-pective of party. His vote can be transferred if his number one candidate is eliminated from the contest with too few first preference votes, or if he is elected with more votes than necessary. From each candidate's point of view the important considerations, therefore, are both first preference votes for himself and, failing that, transfers from other candidates.

The EP election was held at a time of rising popularity for the leader of the opposition, C. J. Haughey and his party, Fianna Fail. Opinion surveys published before the election showed a very significant increase in satisfaction with Mr Haughey's leadership during 1984. Even so the Taoiseach (Prime Minister) remained two percentage points ahead with 48% of the electorate expressing satisfaction with his performance. Dr FitzGerald's popularity was, however, not reflected in support for his party, Fine Gael, which was 11% below that for Fianna Fail at 38%.[3] The Labour Party maintained its level of support at around 8% although its leader Mr Spring was gaining popularity. On the whole, Fianna Fail entered the final weeks of the campaign in its most satisfactory position for several years.

THE CAMPAIGN

The EP election procedure was essentially the same as for all Irish contests. There was, however, one novel feature. During the life of the first EP a problem arose concerning the filling of casual vacancies. Under Irish law, vacant seats were filled on the nomination of the Dail, acting on the recommendation of the party in which the vacancy had occurred. Because of the various changes of government and other political developments during 1981 and 1982, it fell to the Labour Party to operate the system. The four seats they won in 1979 had eleven occupants. The Irish procedure was challenged in the EP. An Act was passed before the second election providing for named substitutes for each candidate. In 1984 each party published names of substitute candidates before the election. If an elected member vacates his seat, then that place is to be taken by the first substitute of the elected member's party.

The new substitute procedure added interest to the nominating conventions which each party held in March and April. The main selection problems are usually in the governing parties; a seat in the cabinet or the prospect of it, is more attractive than 'exile' in Strasbourg. Thus, in 1979, the Fianna Fail candidates were generally regarded as political light-weights. In Opposition, however, the party was able to field eight former holders of government office. Fine Gael, on the other hand, was represented by five candidates who had not held office of any kind at a national level. The Labour Party, defending its major successes of 1979 but with little real prospect outside Dublin, nominated one candidate per constituency. Each Labour candidate was well known in his or her area and included a former leader and the current chairman.

The substitute lists included the names of the nominated candidates so that a defeated party representative will take over should an elected colleague vacate a seat. The substitutes' names did not appear on the ballot paper and it is unclear whether the EP will accept the validity of the new procedure when it is first used to fill a vacancy. The minister who introduced the necessary regulations in the Dail said that the substitution system was a temporary measure and that it was possible that an entirely new system of voting would be in place by the next EP contest.

The eight Sinn Fein candidates in the Republic changed their names before their nomination. This device was resorted to because Sinn Fein is not a registered political party and would not normally be named on a ballot paper. Thus, the Dublin constituency was contested by John Sinn Fein Noonan. Name changing is not a new feature of Irish elections. As the candidacy of Sean Dublin Bay Rockall Loftus or Tony Gregory Independent at previous elections demonstrates, candidates have used this method before to get their message across. The Green Alliance is a registered party, but it is not clear that its name helped clarify the message of its one candidate. In Northern Ireland Sinn Fein did not meet any name restrictions.

The Euro-campaign was very short because public attention had been diverted in the previous months by the publication of the report of The New Ireland Forum and the visit of President Reagan. Both these events received massive media coverage and both had caused far more political controversy than had been anticipated. Fine Gael opened its campaign on 16 May and the other parties followed within days. The New Ireland Forum was an attempt by the nationalist parties on the island to draw up a blueprint for Irish unity. It included representatives of the three main parties in the Republic as well as the Social Democratic and Labour Party (SDLP) from Northern Ireland. The Forum Report itself was full of the rhetoric of unity but it provoked immediate dissension between Fianna Fail and the other parties on the significance of its various proposals. The Reagan visit generated a great deal of public protest and was particularly divisive within the Labour Party because some of its leadership were among the protestors while others were in the official government welcoming party. The protest action was led by an unusual alliance of Catholic bishops and left-wing politicians. In the main the controversy was concerned with US defence and Latin American policy. Many Irish missionaries are based in Latin America and this is the one area of American foreign policy to excite real interest in Ireland. Surprisingly, neither the Forum Report nor the Reagan visit were issues in the EP campaign. Some commentators speculated that there was an understanding between party leaders in the Republic to soft-pedal on the Report to avoid electoral difficulties for the leader of the SDLP in the North.

The major issue in the election was the Government's handling of the economy. The Fine Gael/Labour coalition[4] had been embarrassed in the Dail by serious miscalculations in the economic indicators but more pressing for the electorate were unemployment, prices and taxation. The last is a particularly important issue because of the widespread belief among urban workers that the farming community does not contribute sufficiently to the public purse. The emphasis on these issues suited Fianna Fail because on the EC front the picture was not so bleak. In particular, in April Ireland was able to secure an increase of over 4% in its allowed production of milk under EC rules in an agreement that introduced a super-levy to reduce production by up to 7% in other EC states. Ireland's relative success in the negotiations on the milk super-levy weighed in the coalition's favour. The Government made various cheering announcements about the factory openings, hospital places, state subsidies etc before the polling date with an eye to more localist issues. For example, to coincide with the by-election, as well as the Euro-election, the Labour leader Dick Spring announced the reprieve of a turf-burning power station in the Laois–Offaly constituency.

The issues that got less intense treatment but were nevertheless widely discussed were a possible military commitment to European defence, the broader issue of neutrality and the powers of the EP. Fianna Fail urged the electorate to protect Ireland's neutrality, but it was hard to see that their opponents were any less vigilant. CND, which had gained much publicity during the Reagan visit, also warned about the foreign military entanglements. A pledge to support neutrality and resist the deployment of nuclear weapons in Europe was circulated by CND and signed by all Fine Gael and Labour candidates along with three Fianna Fail hopefuls.

The drop in turnout at the 1984 EP election is in part explained by the absence of local elections which, though scheduled originally for the same day, in line with the 1979 arrangements, were postponed because a local government reform measure is expected in 1985. Critics suggested that the Government was merely trying to minimise the possible effects of its poor election prospects. Other explanations for the low poll centred on the media coverage. Television especially is an important element in Irish elections and coverage in 1984 was less than in 1979. Nevertheless, poll data shows that interest in the election was low so even the air time the election got was probably less effective. Disinterest was particularly marked among the upper middle class and larger farmers, groups usually highly participative, and in Munster where the independent T. J. Maher was defending his seat. The EP office in Dublin provides a constant stream of information and documentation to the media. The same phrases occur frequently in different papers and under different by-lines. Nevertheless, the bulk of the EP election budget was spent directly by the politicians and the EP official advertising campaign ended in April, well before the election. If poor advertising and media coverage was a feature of the 1984 contest the blame probably lies with the parties themselves. It was only in the final stages that the EP election got front page attention in the national dailies and even then the coverage was hardly sympathetic.

On the whole the EP election had little to do with the EC; rather it was a mid-term test of the Government. In this respect, the 1984 contest was like the 1979 election when many of the issues were the same. The result, therefore, says more about national politics than attitudes to EC institutions.

TABLE 6.1   *EP election results*

	1984		1979	
Political parties and groups	*% votes cast*	*Seats won*	*% votes cast*	*Seats won*
Fianna Fail	39.2	8	34.7	5
Fine Gael	32.2	6	33.1	4
Labour	8.4	–	14.5	4
Independents	10.1	1	14.1	2

SOURCE   *Bull. EC*, 6-1984.

RESULT IN NATIONAL TERMS

The long-term significance of the election in terms of national politics is likely to revolve around the reaction of the Labour Party to its defeat. The party had made disproportionate gains in 1979, winning 27% of the seats with only 14.5% of the popular vote. The loss of all its seats may strengthen the hand of those within the party who reject the coalition with Fine Gael on the basis that it is electorally ill-judged and ideologically unsound. According to the anti-coalition faction, Fine Gael will squeeze Labour out of all its Dail seats in the same way that it gained at the party's expense in elections to the EP. The party's image as a separate force is diminishing and, say the critics of coalition,

Labour will lose out to more radical parties on the left, especially in urban working-class areas. The Labour Party's chairman and candidate in Connacht/Ulster, Michael D. Higgins, is the best-known anti-coalitionist. His reaction to defeat was to call on the party to oppose the growth of 'the enormous conservative force that is Fine Gael' as much as it has been opposing Fianna Fail. To those, a majority in the parliamentary party, at least, who favour the coalition arrangement, the EP election defeats will show that while the party could not afford to precipitate an election now, it must be seen to win more concessions from its partner before the next general election.

Despite losing all four of its seats, Labour's popular vote fell by only 1.0% compared with the November 1982 General Election which brought it to government. Compared to the 1979 EP result Labour's vote dropped from 14.5% of all first preference votes to 8.4%. This pattern of falling support may not be as alarming for Labour's parliamentary numbers as it seems. The Labour vote varies very widely between constituencies partly because most of its TDs[5] can secure large personal first preference totals. Thus, for example, though their candidate, Eileen Desmond, failed to halt a decline of almost 4% in the party's overall vote compared to the 1982 general election, most of the seven sitting Labour TDs in the Munster constituency are probably secure. What the Labour politicians in national elections have to rely on is sufficient transfers from other elected or eliminated candidates. The party will probably remain within the coalition and hope for an electoral up-turn. Labour has never brought down a government despite its constant soul-searching. In 1979 the leader of the governing party which performed badly resigned shortly after the EP election; no such dramatic events occurred in 1984. An interesting corollary to the Labour dilemma is the question of Fine Gael's attitude to Labour. Some Fine Gael TDs argue association with Labour is holding the party back in its struggle to overtake Fianna Fail. On the evidence of the EP election, however, it is difficult to see Fine Gael forming a single majority party government for some years yet.

Although both Fianna Fail and Fine Gael improved their number of seats at Strasbourg they each suffered a significant decline, 6% and 7% respectively, in their vote compared with the 1982 Irish general election. Fianna Fail's votes improved relative to 1979 by 4.5% while Fine Gael fell by 0.9%. For a governing party in recessionary times, the Fine Gael performance is possibly less worrying. At a general election, still some time away and with a higher turnout, they may well do much better. For Fianna Fail, however, their inability to profit from the Government's unpopularity is a cause for concern. In the key battleground of Dublin, where one third of the electorate live, their vote continues a steady decline. Where Fianna Fail's vote looks strongest in Connacht-Ulster the room for improvement in Dail seats is small. The party leadership made the most of their top of the poll placing and Labour's discomfort but they realised clearly that the coalition is going to battle-on for some years yet.

The minor parties all increased their proportion of the vote but neither the Workers' Party nor Sinn Fein made a significant break-through. All eight Sinn Fein candidates in the Republic lost their deposits. Independents (Maher and Blaney) sustained a 4% drop in support in national terms though their 10.1% was gained in only two constituencies. Blaney lost his seat in Connacht-Ulster, but Maher held on in Munster.

The demise of Neil Blaney is an interesting illustration of how hard it is for politicians to survive outside the main parties. Blaney was first elected to the Dail in 1948 at a by-election caused by the death of his father. He has been returned as a TD ever since. Until 1970 he was a leading member of Fianna Fail and often served in the cabinet. He left the party after a controversial trial involving the importation of arms for use in Northern Ireland. He is a master of brokerage politics and when he left Fianna Fail his personal machine remained intact and formidable. In 1979, he ran as Independent Fianna Fail and was returned as MEP for Connacht-Ulster at the head of the poll. He has not been able to follow up that success by establishing a firm base of support outside his native Donegal where he is supported by a team of four county councillors. As an independent MEP, Blaney was an almost constant attender but he rarely voted. Between December 1982 and April 1984, for example, he attended on 81 days of a possible 93 but voted only 15 times. The equivalent figures for T. J. Maher were 83 and 53. Maher, as a member of the Liberal EP group, was clearly under more pressure to vote than Blaney, who was attached to the TCG. Blaney's contributions to debates were limited to the topics of agricul-ture and Northern Ireland. As in the Dail, Blaney was an isolated figure in the EP. Faced with an almost certain decline in his vote in view of his outstanding success in 1979 and Fianna Fail's subsequent revival, Blaney in 1984 was going to need transfers from major party candi-dates. To stop the leakage of its vote, Fianna Fail nominated a former minister of agriculture with a public image for being even tougher than Blaney on Northern Ireland. Blaney's vote on the first count was substantially down on 1979, but he could still have secured election with good transfers. In the event, he got votes from the Sinn Fein and left-wing Labour candidates and from Joey Murrin, Fine Gael's Donegal-based candidate. Fianna Fail's vote, however, stayed in the fold with the 1979 dissidents returning. The power of partisanship and the decay of the localist effect in large European constituencies was too telling for a hard-working but isolating candidate. Even so he might have survived in 1984 had he been in a five-seat constituency like fellow independent T. J. Maher. Blaney's fate demonstrates again the irony of proportional representation and the inability of minor parties to break up Ireland's two (and a half) party system.

As in all Irish elections, projections for the future depend greatly on estimates of how votes will transfer between parties. The Labour Party has to look carefully at the pattern of transfers both between the coalition partners and from other left-wing parties to themselves. It was the relatively low transfer of votes from the Workers' Party to Labour that ultimately cost Labour a seat in Dublin. A third of Sinn Fein voters who did not express non-Sinn Fein preference votes in its key constituencies, makes Labour even more dependent on Fine Gael, if the EP election is a guide. The transfers from Fine Gael to Labour, however, were significantly down in the only case where a higher figure might have saved a Labour seat.

EUROPEAN LEVEL

During the election campaign Fine Gael attempted to make capital out of its participation in the EPP. In their final pre-election broadcast on Irish television the Fine Gael leader emphasised that as part of the largest non-socialist group Fine Gael has an influence in the EC denied to Fianna Fail. Their opponents were marginalised by their link to the French Gaullists in the EPD. The Fine Gael broadcast also stressed the importance of their parliamentary group in placing Irish members on key committees. The milk super-levy success was attributed in part to EPP influence. With Fine Gael in the EPP, Ireland could, their slogan declared, 'keep winning in Europe'. Fianna Fail's campaign was geared to the government's domestic performance, but its counter-attack on the European front centred on the Christian Democrat's defence policies. Fine Gael, through its reliance on the EPP, would ultimately be forced to compromise Ireland's neutrality. Further it was claimed, since Fianna Fail comprised a larger proportion of the EPD than Fine

Gael of the EPP, its influence on its EP group policy was proportionately greater.

The impact of Irish MEPs is bound to be limited because eighteen (including the Northern Irish) in a membership of 434 is relatively insignificant. Fine Gael probably made the best use they could, therefore, of what success they had had. There was little 'European' impact even in 1979 despite an extensive publicity campaign by the EP and the Commission. In 1984 EC issues were even more tangential. Few non-Irish MEPs other than Haagerup, author of the EP's report on Northern Ireland, made any impact on Ireland. A major problem facing Irish members was convincing the electorate that the EP was worth voting for and that membership was not, as numerous press reports suggested, simply a 'gravy-train'. In the general view, Irish candidates should be chosen for their ability as ambassadors for Ireland in Europe. A good MEP was one who could bring back increased benefits to Ireland, improve on an already good deal while thwarting unpalatable EC legislation. Irish candidates put little stress on the EC's future, or its relevance to the European-wide issues of unemployment, inflation, currency stability, defence, East–West relations or the environment. Rather, the Irish MEPs presented themselves as being able to pursue issues of local and regional importance through parliamentary questions and by joining other Irish interests in pleading for the recognition of Ireland's special problems. The Irish political parties both in 1979 and 1984 stressed the benefits of the CAP and Regional and Social Funds. There was no mention of any need to make sacrifices for a European cause as may be the case in, for example, Germany. Some sitting MEPs showed an awareness of the European dimension of the election, of the need for monetary union and reform of EC institutions. This did not, however, seriously challenge the dominant ambassadorial outlook. Even in the Labour Party, though its international links through the Socialist International predate the EP groups, electioneering was essentially localist.

The Irish parties were not particularly fortunate in the EP groups they joined and this may have contributed to the lack of emphasis on Europe. Fine Gael found themselves as the only English-speaking MEPs in a fairly cohesive and large German and Italian bloc with strong Christian and individualistic ideals unfamiliar in Irish political debate. The Gaullist domination of the EPD was similarly difficult for Fianna Fail though they did share a common tradition of nationalism and pragmatism. After the election Fianna Fail fairly openly looked for other partners in the EP, they were even reported as considering a link with the Socialists. Labour was affected by numerical weakness accentuated by a high turnover in its EP membership. Nevertheless, the Irish gained from the notion among party managers that a national balance in spokesmanships, rapporteurships, committee memberships and speaking time should be maintained. National 'opting-out' of group decisions is also generally accepted.

EP groups to which Irish members belonged between 1979–84 were generally united in defence of the CAP and a wish to allocate more resources to the Social and Regional Fund. Where this was not the case, as with the Socialist criticisms of CAP, Irish members made their own dissenting opinions clear. On the Spinelli proposals, only Fianna Fail voiced opposition but this issue was never more than a footnote to the election campaign.

The Irish MEPs may be playing a long-term educative role for the Irish electorate but its effect is far from obvious to date. While a member state is ensured prominence in the powerful Council of Ministers, the Irish public is likely to see this body as far more relevant than the EP in which its representation is so small. The only issue on which the EP consistently engenders interest in Ireland is national sovereignty and on this all Irish parties are united. Fears for Irish neutrality, a feature even of the referendum campaign before EC entry in 1972, remaiñs a constant theme in Irish politicians' pronouncements on Europe but it was insufficiently incisive to impact significantly upon the EP election.

STRASBOURG VERSUS DUBLIN

> The Strasbourg Parliament is a weak enough instrument. It should grow in strength. We like to hug an heroic and romantic concept of ourselves as the one time saviours of the soul of Christendom. . . . The monks who sailed from these shores for Europe in dark days have indeed left a mark on European civilisation and thus the world. . . . Today there is as much need, in a secular way, to reaffirm our faith in Europe. Everywhere in this Republic there is groaning and moaning about our economic plight. Here today is a chance to do at least a little something to shift the scales towards sanity and balance in our part of the world.[6]

Irish MEPs are quite active in that they are generally good attenders.

Clinton (Fine Gael) and Maher (Independent) in particular, spoke regularly in debates on a wide range of issues. An active EP presence does not appear, however, to impress voters at home. Indeed, of the four worst attenders who ran again in 1984, Ryan (Fine Gael), Flanagan (Fianna Fail), McCartin (Fine Gael) and O'Donnell (Fine Gael) all were re-elected, despite the publication of their attendance records in the national papers.[7]

Irish election campaigns have to be understood at two levels of competition between the parties. Nationally the parties compete for attention with promises, predictions and favourable interpretations of their current and previous performances in government. In the constituencies, the parties attempt to organise the vote which is 'due' to them into the most effective pattern with respect to the transferred surpluses or the vote of eliminated candidates during the count. In Munster, for example, Fine Gael called in its publicity for its supporters to 'balance the vote'. In Cork and Waterford, where one of their candidates had a local base, he was to be given the first preference vote. Deputy O'Donnell, a better-known party standard-bearer from Limerick, was 'Number One' elsewhere. As far as possible the major parties try to ensure that their candidates are from various parts of the constituencies so as to maximise the benefits of localist loyalties and minimise intra-party rivalry. They also attempt to divide their first preference votes evenly between their candidates so that none are eliminated too early to benefit from the transferred surplus votes of elected colleagues. Smaller parties put up fewer candidates so that their partisan vote is not divided between candidates in such a way that they are eliminated before any possible benefit from transfers. Thus, for example, in 1984 Fianna Fail put up three candidates in Dublin, all existing members from the Dail, from the south, west and north of the constituency; each of whom received almost the same number of first preference votes, 11% of the total.

At the level of candidates the competition is mainly between members of the same party. The party may be in favour of a well-disciplined vote so that its votes are used more effectively, but no candidate wishes to be the harvester of votes which will ultimately only help his running-mates. Thus, every candidate will try to maximise his own first preference vote, within the confines of party discipline and public unity. To compete with colleagues while appearing to care only for the party's overall performance, it is necessary for the candidates to garner votes across party lines from among the opposition's supporters. This personal campaigning is usually done by appealing to localist, clientelist, and charismatic relations. All these factors were evident in this election as they are indeed between elections when a candidate can assiduously build up his personal following.

The above observations are widely accepted conventional wisdoms of Irish politics, but they are most clearly challenged in EP elections by the enormous constituencies, and, for the incumbent MEP, the lack of clientelist or localist benefits from the distant EP. The successful incumbent must make unusually broad, personal appeals possibly being associated in some way with major projects featuring EC funds or the protection of current benefits. The one successful independent, T. J. Maher, effectively did both, but his percentage poll was down on 1979. Sean Flanagan, who retained his seat for Fianna Fail, announced a proposed £500 million development programme for his constituency just before the election, although the source of the money was rather unclear. Richie Ryan (Fine Gael), attacked in the press for very extensive foreign travel and very little contribution to debates, claimed in his election literature some of the kudos for Dublin's success in receiving a third of Ireland's share of EC regional and social funds. He never spoke on urban matters in a parliamentary session.

The Irish public's perception of politicians as a whole is uncomplimentary, but their loyalty to individual politicians can often be high, based as it is on family loyalties, personal contact and particular favours. Irish political parties do not divide on class, religious or ethnic lines, except in Northern Ireland. In the Republic, the partisan division reflects indirectly attitudes to the constitutional settlement of 1922 rather than socio-economic cleavages. The existing party division is a product of the enduring partisanship of the Irish electorate. The elites of the parties differ little in their attitudes to many major political issues. The electorate also see the parties as essentially similar, though the Labour Party is recognised as relatively left wing. Partisan identification, as reflected in regular and consistent party voting is well developed. The great majority of Irish voters are lifetime partisans. Irish politicians are also intensely loyal to their party label. Candidates for election, therefore, compete for their support via personal political machines with an emphasis on regional availability and brokerage ability. Politicians must create social or ideological barriers between themselves and the electorate. In this respect, incumbent MEPs were at a double disadvantage at this election. The public image of the MEPs is of 'men on the make' with high salaries, foreign trips and substantial perks; their personal profiles are, however, low because the electorate is too large for any personal network to be as significant as it may be in domestic elections. Among those to suffer from these disadvantages was sitting MEP Noel Davern (Fianna Fail).

He is a classic Irish politician who inherited a Dail seat from his brother which had previously been held by his father. He was then elected an MEP in 1979 with 37 647 first preference votes. In 1984 his vote increased by over 5 000 but his seat went to a party colleague Gene Fitzgerald who was a current member of the Dail for Cork and who gained transfers disproportionately from other candidates in his part of Munster. The first Fianna Fail surplus went to Fitzgerald and Davern in the proportion of three to one as a successful Corkman helped elect another. The defeated incumbent was recognised as having worked hard in Strasbourg by his party and informed commentators, but he lost because his party colleague was better known at home and better placed to pick up transfers from other candidates.

For the individual MEPs the main lesson of the election must be the importance of maintaining a high profile at home. Until there is a change in the basis of Irish electoral competition, good EP work is unlikely to insure survival in the absence of specific benefits for a large group of personal supporters. If there is to be an agreed common electoral procedure for the next election, successful Irish MEPs will look to it for greater protection for incumbents. The two successful challengers who were not already members of the Irish or European Parliaments were both from Fine Gael. Mary Banotti is well-known on television for her advice on social welfare and is a campaigner on women's and family issues. Her colleague, Tom Raftery, a former senator and currently professor of agriculture, has also received wide publicity through his involvement in the establishment of a new national wildlife park. They both benefitted from transfers from established party figures and good organisational support, but their success also points to the benefits of wider public recognition than the EP affords.

Perhaps because of the emphasis on individual competition, and the need to reaffirm links with the voters regularly, eight of the Republic's MEPs also sit in Dail Eireann. Only two of Fianna Fail's eight MEPs are not also TDs. In all parties, the dual mandate has been under heavy criticism. Fine Gael announced its intention to end it during the campaign. Fianna Fail, while putting forward TDs as candidates, has announced that the dual mandated MEPs will have to declare (by the end of 1984) in which parliament they intend to sit. In the meantime, it is said that their party colleagues in each constituency will help to relieve them of their case load. One successful candidate promised to give half her Dail salary to employ a person to work in her Dail constituency on her behalf. Subsequently it seems a local charity may benefit. For the rest of Europe the trend is away from dual mandates. Nevertheless, in Ireland's case, the advantage of a seat in the Dail is likely to remain important for candidates to the EP.

NORTHERN IRELAND

The 1984 contest in Northern Ireland produced a very predictable result with the three sitting MEPs – the Rev. Ian Paisley, Democratic Unionist Party (DUP), John Hume, Social Democratic and Labour Party and John Taylor, Official Unionist Party (OUP) – all being returned. The most notable feature of the election was the candidacy of Danny Morrison, Sinn Fein. The Sinn Fein presence put considerable pressure on the SDLP which had established itself as the major representative of the nationalist community. Sinn Fein, after a long period of electoral abstention, returned to contest the elections with the strategy of the ballot paper in one hand and the Armalite rifle in the other.

In 1979 John Hume, SDLP leader, had won over 24% of the first preference votes. Since the last EP election, however, the SDLP's share of the poll in other contests had fallen to around 18%. Hume had personally received a boost from the outcome of the New Ireland Forum but his party organisation was widely criticised as inept. In the campaign he stressed his outstanding record as an MEP.

The Unionist politicians used the Forum Report as an opportunity to emphasise the dangers to the Union. The DUP and OUP produced their own counter proposals. The main contest among unionists, however, was for the leadership of their community between Paisley and Taylor. The campaigns of the DUP and OUP emphasised the Catholic nature of the EC, and the potential treachery of the London government. Taylor represented himself as the mature voice of unionism and castigated Paisley for 'childish pranks' and counter-productive extremism. The DUP called for a massive vote for Paisley as a warning to Sinn Fein and the British government.

There were eight candidates in Northern Ireland but the main struggle was Paisley versus Taylor and Hume versus Morrison. The poll at over 65% was higher than in 1979 (57%). The result was much the same and represented huge personal successes for Paisley and Hume, who won the battle to lead their communities. Sinn Fein, whose participation contributed to the high turnout, received over 13% of the poll about the same as in other recent elections in Northern Ireland. The remaining candidates all did badly, especially the Alliance Party whose vote collapsed.

CONCLUSIONS

The major features of the EP election were: a 16% drop in the poll; gains in seats by Fianna Fail and Fine Gael, despite vote shares; and the demise of Labour, all its seats lost and a further decline in its electoral strength. The importance of party organisation and vote management were further underlined. Both Fianna Fail and Fine Gael made good use of their established candidates and divided their voting strengths effectively. To retain their hold on the electorate all MEPs will have to keep their names before the electorate by furthering local causes even at the cost of involvement at Strasbourg. The fifteen Irish members are likely to be more TDs for the EC than MEPs.

NOTES AND REFERENCES

Fianna Fail: literally means 'soldiers of destiny', is Ireland's largest party, led from December 1979 by Charles J. Haughey.

Fine Gael: literally means 'family of the Gaels', successor to the party which accepted the Treaty with Britain in 1922 and formed the first government, led by Garret FitzGerald.

Labour: oldest but smallest of the major parties; led by Dick Spring.

Workers' Party: previously Sinn Fein the Workers' Party, renamed in 1982.

*I thank Philomena Murray of the EUI for her help with this chapter.

1. *Irish Independent*, 19 May 1984.
2. Fianna Fail won the by-election increasing their vote by 3%. The constitutional change was carried by a large majority – 3 to 1 in favour in most counties.
3. The survey quoted was conducted by Market Research Bureau of Ireland for the *Irish Times*, 21 May 1984. The sample of 1000 electors was taken on 9 and 10 May, a week after publication of the Report of the New Ireland Forum.
4. Fine Gael is the larger party in a coalition with Labour which came to office after the general election of November 1982. The two parties with 86 seats have a majority of 6 over all others in the Dail, the Irish parliament. The main opposition, Fianna Fail, which has been the biggest single party since 1932, failed to win an overall majority for the third time since June 1981. The 1982 election brought an end to 18 months of unusual political instability.

5. TD (Teachta Dala) – a deputy in the Irish parliament, literally means 'messenger to the Dail'.
6. *Irish Times*, 14 June 1984.
7. See M. Kelly, 'The 1984 European Election in the Republic of Ireland', paper presented to the *Third International Symposium on European Elections*, Mannheim, Nov. 1984 for a discussion of media coverage.

7 Italy

GEOFFREY PRIDHAM*

EUROPEAN ELECTIONS AND THE 'INTERNALISATION' OF COMMMUNITY POLICY

There is a paradox in Italy's position towards the EC. While she has long been one of the most pro-European – if not *the* most pro-European – member states, as measured by polls on attitudes to European integration and by views of political élites, the concerns behind this pro-Europeanism are at least on the part of the latter first and foremost domestic ones. Can this simply be explained by a difference between conceptual attitudes towards integration on the one level which are positive and actual political behaviour on another which may be called instrumental? This scenario was well illustrated by the 1984 EP election campaign which was highly 'internalised' in terms of the issues and the real motives of the politicians involved. But, in fact, the 'internalisation' of European policy has a long tradition in postwar Italy.

The parties have been the essential determinants of the content and dynamics of European policy. The consequent 'internalisation' has been no more evident than in the link between party approaches to integration and party strategies at home. This link may be seen as strategic in so far as this has required a re-thinking of policy goals, and the outcome has been a convergence of party approaches to EC affairs.[1] Furthermore, the paradox noted in Italy's position towards the EC and the accusation of her, 'verbal Europeanism' are misleading and naive in that they postulate a distinction between 'EC issues' and 'national issues' that is artificial, or at least has become more so, given politicisation and widening policy concerns in the EC, whereby most policies now have an EC dimension. At one end some areas – notably

155

agriculture – are recognised as essentially an EC concern, and at the other end certain areas are indisputably a national matter. Otherwise, there has been a growing overlap between European and national perspectives on individual policy matters – certainly by political leaders.

Clearly, this pattern of 'internalisation' coupled with the later politicisation of EC policy concerns was likely to be promoted or given a specific twist by the direct introduction of a popular mandate for the EP. This is not to overrate the politicising or 'Europeanising' potential of direct elections as such so much as to note that EP elections became fitted into the national political calendar and offered some opportunity to debate EC matters. Since the first EP elections they have become 'routinised' and form one stage in the series of elections that occur at local, regional and national levels. This was clear after the June 1983 general election which saw an unprecedented fall in support for the governing Christian Democratic party (DC), when politicians and journalists alike started to speculate about the outcome of the 1984 EP elections. Electoral and party competition worked for the EP elections *despite* the absence of the power factor in the EP. As one PCI leader said, it is 'stupid and mistaken to maintain that European elections are separate from the national situation'.

Yet the 1984 campaign failed to create the chance for a debate on the EC in any comprehensive or serious way. This led to criticisms of the 'trivialisation' of the EP elections, but that misses the point about the game of electoral·politics and avoids the question again about the boundaries of European policy and the problems of its projection at the national level. In fact the lack of controversy over the basics of integration, as well as the intrinisic complexity of EC policy, opened the way for national issues (assuming they can be distinguished from EC ones) to come to the forefront. If everyone agrees at both élite and popular levels about the value of the EC and the importance of its further development – as is undoubtedly the case in Italy – then the dynamics of party and electoral competition is likely to revolve around issues that *are* controversial, notably in the domestic arena. This is one clue to the paradox in Italy's position towards the EC but it needs qualification.

It is true that party-political convergence over integration has reduced the scope for difference over broad policy lines (for example, support for EC enlargement, the decision on direct elections to the EP and the question of strengthening its constitutional powers and more recently the idea of European Union). However, when one turns to specific policy proposals differences do emerge. Hence there is some scope for debate over European policy in the way parties may take up, project or exploit issues as a legitimate feature of electoral competition. A party's willingness to do so will depend much less on the abstract value of policy content than on a multiplicity of factors which may or may not apply in a particular election; for example, a party's political role such as whether or not in government and hence coalition with other parties, the particular concerns of a party's electorate, the perceived advantages of EC membership at a given time and naturally competition for attention from other political issues during the election period. Moreover, the parties will not always or automatically be in control of the agenda of debate in election campaigns, for undoubtedly the media are an important determinant of this. Finally, there is the question of effective public interest in or knowledge of European policy. A significant characteristic of Italian public attitudes towards integration is that alongside continuous and overwhelmingly positive support for integration (the conceptual level) there has been very limited knowledge of both how the EC works and its policies, as shown by opinion polls. It is easy, therefore, to conclude that party leaders and election organisers found little incentive to debate EC affairs; but the interflow or overlap between what is a 'European' or a 'national' issue is such that any pure projection of the former is not realistic or likely, especially in the heat of an election campaign.

From the foregoing, one can construct a categorisation for the 'internalisation' of European policy:

a. *Party strategy* (the most long-standing aspect of this ('internalisation'): the priority accorded integration in party strategy or, more concretely, activity in EC institutions, and as a reflection of this whether a party claims or can be said to have a European strategy as distinct from regarding European policy merely instrumental;

b. *General issue salience*: the relative weight accorded EC issues *vis-à-vis* other policy areas, both internal and external, where in the long-term widening policy concerns in the EC have strengthened the former, while in the short-term (such as the immediate context of a particular election) the balance of attention between different policy areas, including the European, evidently varies;

c. *Electoral politics and behaviour* (the most significant recent addition to this categorisation): institutionally, the introduction of EP elections at five-yearly intervals has created an oppor-

tunity for direct mobilisation over EC issues, although this
potential has not yet been utilised;

d. *Issue-specific*: as distinct from general issue salience (European
policy as a whole), certain particular issues might at given times
lend salience to the EC depending on media reaction or government involvement in a 'good news' or 'bad news' fashion (for
example, frustrations with Britain over the EC budget), or they
might underline the direct link between European policy and
domestic political considerations (for example, the question of
reforming the electoral law for Strasbourg might well be seen as
a rehearsal for the more controversial national electoral reform).

A broad distinction in the above can be made between macro- and
micro-political factors, with (a) and (b) more likely to feature among
the former and (c) and (d) among the latter: the routinisation of EP
elections against the background of politicisation in the EC in general
has done more than anything else to bring this 'internalisation' of
European policy more directly into the orbit of everyday politics.

THE NATIONAL POLITICAL CONTEXT OF THE 1984 EUROPEAN ELECTION

It should be a truism to say that the national political context or actual
time-period in which an election falls is crucial to the chemistry of the
campaign which follows, in the sense of the issue salience of the
moment, the standing, state of morale and organisational preparedness
of individual parties and generally the way 'campaign events' influence
the outcome. Growing dealignment and volatility have meant that the
scope for the impact of the immediate situation on voters' political
awareness has increased. However, despite this being a truism, recognition that it must also apply to EP elections has been slow in coming.
Supposedly this is because they are still a relatively new exercise, and it
may also continue to reflect the European idealism attached to the 1979
EP election. But it is very doubtful that the parties' line in pro-
European rhetoric now turned polemical provided a major or in any
way significant determinant of the vote in either of the two EP elections
in Italy. The particularity of the election situation – notably the absence
in 1979 of a PCI challenge, in contrast with 1984 – was crucial in
understanding voter movements in the two EP elections. This had
apparently little or nothing to do with the European policies of the

respective parties or the official European name of the election. Italian voting behaviour in general has become relatively more volatile, but not essentially because of the EP elections. Issue consciousness, in so far as it features in dealignment, has helped to loosen traditional voting patterns, and it may or may not focus on European themes in a given time-period such as an election campaign.

These general traits cast a fresh light on trends of public opinion on European integration. In view of the two major trends noted – very positive espousal of the EC, but low knowledge about its specifics – it is worth elaborating on this as it clearly is related to the possible impact of a European campaign. The two trends are not necessarily incompatible, and the opposite may obtain as some surveys have suggested that a growth in knowledge about the EC sharpens a critical awareness (a rise in issue consciousness). In recent years, and certainly since the 1979 EP election, news about the EC has inclined to be 'bad' rather than 'good'; for example, the EP has been something of a disappointment at least compared with Italian expectations of its role once directly elected, the frustrations in official circles and bad impression created publicly by the intermittent though persistent dispute over the EC budget, a quarrel with France over restrictions on wine imports, Italy's differences with EC partners over restraints on steel production during 1983 and generally the stagnation in integration in the years leading up to the 1984 election. Italian reactions to Mitterrand's Strasbourg speech in late May 1984 on moving towards a European Union were predictably very favourable, but this came probably too late to reverse some growing disillusionment with the EC in Italy up to the vote.

Looking more closely at trends in public opinion on the EC in the years between the two EP elections, various features may be highlighted. Firstly, it is worth trying to identify reasons for strong adherence to European integration in general. According to a Doxa report of 1984 summarising opinion polls on this question, the following rational and emotive factors were operative: a favourable attitude towards the idea of the free movement of labour and goods; a lack of trust in the efficiency of Italian national institutions; and the hope of drawing advantage from involvement in a larger community and from collaboration with countries which enjoy a very positive image in Italy.[2] One might also add, although *Eurobarometer* (via Doxa) has not done research on this, that a low attachment to the idea of the nation state in Italy (in contrast, say, with France) must provide a 'cultural' reason for the very positive support for integration. Possibly connected with this is low esteem for national institutions or government performance. Based on a late-1983 poll, Italy emerged as among those with the most reservations about the national parliament and compared with views on the EP was almost equally favourable – 64% thought the national parliament 'much or rather important', 59% in the case of the EP.[3] One must stress that such positive views of the EC are not based merely on some form of European idealism, but encompass a good element of national self-interest in regarding the EC, for instance, as a source of welcome funds for domestic policies, a motive that has become clearer in the past decade and more with Italy's greater economic difficulties. Yet the same Doxa report had a hidden warning in its conclusion: 'Altogether, Italian voters think that Italy presently draws more advantages than disadvantages from [EC] membership ... but ... opinion is rather widespread that the advantages gained by Italy are inferior to those gained by other countries.'[4]

Secondly, the low level of knowledge about the workings of the EC – including the activity of the EP – also sheds light on the relationship between the conceptual level (for example, stong majority support for the EP as an 'important' institution and for giving it more power) and indicators of actual political behaviour. As to the latter, there was a mixed picture with Italy having one of the highest voting intentions for EP elections among the EC member states (76% 'certain to vote' in May 1983, a year beforehand'[5] but a drop registered in those seeing this event as having important consequences for integration (50% in October 1983, compared with 63% in October 1978, the same distance from the first EP elections.[6] Also perhaps indicative are reactions to the question on having read or seen news on the EP: a decline from the high point of 77% in April 1979 shortly before the first elections (when the EP was enjoying fairly intensive coverage with the novelty of the event) to 66% in October 1979, 52% in October 1982 and 50% in April 1983.[7] Undoubtedly, inadequate media coverage of the EP and the EC in general contributed substantially to this trend. According to the director of the Doxa Institute, the EP had been 'explained very badly' by the media because it 'does not make news, and when it does this is bad news'.[8] The 'meetings of the Council of Ministers make news, not the European Parliament';[9] and 'Italians expect more from Brussels than from Strasbourg'.[10]

The problem is that the low visibility of the EC and of the EP in particular comes from the sense of distance. This is geographical, but also more significantly it is psychological and probably political – Brussels, and certainly Strasbourg, is seen as being remote from the country's immediate concerns. While support for the EC and for strengthening it is among other things stimulated by a relatively low view of national institutions, this is supposedly with an eye on the future, for meanwhile the focus of the power game continues willy-nilly to be Rome.[11] There is another aspect of Italian life that often affects political perceptions. This is the attachment to locality, which was highlighted during the 1984 EP campaign. Reports from the regions during the weeks in question emphasised the EC's distance from local problems, such as those of the port and transport system at Genoa, of agriculture in Puglia and the multiple problems which continue to hit Naples (high unemployment, housing those displaced by the earth-quake of 1980).[12] Revealingly, this sense of distance applied too in areas where EC funds had been of some assistance in dealing with some problems. In the central region of Abruzzo, the EC had provided useful funds for public works and occupational training but these had been presented as regional achievements!; while in the southern region of Calabria people were expecting the EP itself to intervene decisively in order that the EC finance the projected bridge across the Straits of Messina[13] (a case no doubt where the idea of a stronger EP had simplistically affected concrete political perceptions in a way that would be likely to rebound against the EP).

The point is that party élites and campaign organisers accepted this public mentality as a fact, adjusted their electioneering accordingly and chose not to make any real effort to 'educate' Italian voters about the EC's reality and complexity. Typical of this was the comment of Maurizio Valenzi, a top candidate for the PCI in the southern constituency who as former mayor of Naples had been active in procuring EC funds for his needy city, that the public was indifferent because 'Europe is not felt' at the grass-roots.[14] One candidate and national organiser of the Radical Party was asked whether they would be publicising the activities of their MEPs during the campaign and replied: 'The fact is that Strasbourg is not felt at the popular level' and the public would not understand this if they did.[15]

This curious mixture of the material, the provincial and an apparent European idealism did not suggest the automatic and firm support for integration assumed by many observers. When attitudes were probed beneath the surface, the EC's legitimacy was confirmed but it was linked to a strong element of national interest (instrumentalism) and a distinction was intimated between legitimacy (the conceptual level) and credibility (where practical experience could affect actual political perceptions of the EC). Public attitudes are usually complex at heart and often anything but logical, but if one were to describe this situation schematically one could say that in Italy the EC had much goodwill to draw on based on traditional or long-standing reasons but that this could be strengthened or weakened or merely confirmed by experience. One could go so far as to argue that Italy's political culture supported integration, but that political culture itself was always subject to modification in the light of political reality, usually over time. The scope for political reality affecting perceptions of the EC had risen with such developments as EP elections, as its activities had come that much nearer everyday politics. The basic problem was that, while objectively this tendency could be identified (notably by political experts in European affairs and by academics), subjectively this made little or only distorted impact on the public, not least because of the very complexity of EC business. These different factors lie behind a new trend seen in polls, showing a relative drop in support for the EC even though Italy continues to register high approval for membership in the region of 70% (the figure for April 1983, compared with 78% in April 1979).[16] Similarly, on the importance attributed to EP elections, 63% thought this was an event 'thick with consequences' in the autumn of 1978 compared with 50% exactly five years later.[17]

It follows that the potential for any direct impact of European themes on the electorate (or rather themes seen to be 'European') was limited, that the projection of EC affairs was at best likely to be partial and fragmental and that their influence on voters depended on longer-term trends and on the more immediate situation both in the EC at large and in Italy itself. Basic changes in voting behaviour, notably the growth of volatility, opened up more scope for impact by the latter, underlined the importance of the national political context, and confirmed the 'internalisation' thesis.

This being so, what therefore was the national political situation on the eve of the 1984 EP election campaign which occurred at a time of political and social strife? The historic appointment of the first Socialist prime minister in Italy. Bettino Craxi, the previous summer had been followed by speculation about the effect this could have on the balance of electoral strength between the parties. The scene was therefore set for heightened party rivalry a year before EP elections took place. Pessimists predicted shortly after the June 1983 parliamentary election, when the DC suffered an unprecedented drop in support from 38.3% to 32.9%, that the DC was now vulnerable to a further slide downwards. Certainly, the DC leadership seriously heeded such warnings and there were signs of nervousness about the forthcoming EP elections. At the DC's congress in Rome in late-February 1984, the prospect of EP elections powerfully affected the discussion about the DC's direction and fears were expressed about its support beginning to evaporate.[18] The first year of the Craxi government was also marked by intense activity on a number of policy fronts, of which the most controversial in the immediate run-up to the EP election campaign was the anti-inflation decree. This split the trade union movement and produced mass demonstrations by that section opposed to the policy, provoked hostile opposition from the PCI and led to a fierce parliamentary battle right up to the opening of the campaign, including an initial rejection of the decree following PCI obstructionism and its eventual approval after its re-presentation and a vote of confidence in the government towards the end of May.

This domestic political conflict detracted from the EP election campaign, for leading politicians were held back in Rome by the extension of the parliamentary battle before leaving to speak at rallies. However, this focus of attention was not at variance with pressing public concerns – unemployment, the cost of living, criminality and public order[19] – pinpointed by a Doxa report on opinion trends up to spring 1984. This background of policy controversy plus inflamed party rivalry created a situation at the outset of the EP election campaign ripe for bitter polemics and even a 'government crisis' (officialese terminology for the fall of a coalition government). Craxi's government was approaching the average length of Italian governments of less than a year, and already on 17 May *La Repubblica* was talking of a possible *crisi di governo* being postponed until just after the European vote. Media commentary soon adopted this as the overriding theme of the campaign, which came to be seen as an 'internal referendum' on the government, if not, in more personalised form, a referendum on Craxi as prime minister, encouraged by Craxi's own strong-arm approach and widespread talk of his style as *decisionismo* (a new word added at this time to the vocabulary of Italian politics).

Already on 9 June 1984, the British *Economist* reported that 'the European campaign in Italy is growing less European by the minute; the main issue has become not representation in Strasbourg, but leadership in Rome'. Invariably, EP campaign reports featured on the inside pages of newspapers, except when election speeches picked up related themes. The P2 scandal over the masonic lodge had by early June come to dominate the news, particularly as it now pointed directly at Pietro Longo, Budget Minister and PSDI leader, leading to calls for his resignation and bitter accusations between him and other ministers, especially Spadolini of the PRI, which was intent on exploiting the so-called 'moral question' for electoral reasons. P2 only gave way to other headline news when Berlinguer's sudden illness on 8 June 1984, three days' struggle to live and death followed by the mass turnout at his funeral on 13 June 1984 dramatically changed people's attention in the last week of the campaign. In general, one could only agree with the comment of *Corriera della Sera* at the end of the campaign that what a few months before was a vote for a 'supranational parliament' had turned into a 'dramatisation' of Italian politics, behind which was 'the chronic instability of the government majority and the incessant competition between parties which are allies in Parliament and rivals in the piazzas'. One wonders how much this 'dramatisation' was really a media event rather than the tenor of political debate determined by the parties, so it is the role of the latter to which we now turn

THE 1984 CAMPAIGN: A NATIONAL ELECTION WITH EUROPEAN COLOURS

A campaign for EP elections should perhaps ideally provide a special test of how far European policy has been brought within the orbit of everyday politics. We have seen that the timing of the 1984 campaign against the immediate domestic political background, together with the complexities and motives that lie behind positive public attitudes towards integration, already indicated that the projection of European policy on to the (albeit 'European') electoral scene was in any clear or complete form unlikely if not impossible. This confirmed the 'internalisation' thesis, for any really separate profile for European policy was not obtainable because of the close interplay between domestic and EC issues. Therefore, one cannot merely dismiss the 1984 campaign in Italy as virtually a national election and no more, despite the media attempt to portray it as such.

Since the political parties are the essential agents in the content and dynamics of European policy – as indeed of any policy area – their role in the EP election campaign must be assessed. The fact that all, from radical-Left to extreme-Right, were unreservedly pro-European in supporting integration and EP elections (this was so when direct elections were first seriously projected in the mid-1970s, and thus was no novelty in 1984) did not say very much about this problem of the 'European' character of the 1984 campaign. It was more a 'descriptive than an explanatory point, if only because the relationship between conceptual attitudes towards integration and actual political behaviour was not straightforward. The method chosen here is to take up the four-point categorisation for the 'internalisation' of European policy introduced at the end of the first section and apply it to the case of the 1984 election in Italy. The campaign will now be examined from various standpoints – organisation, party strategies, issues and the specific nature of the 'European colours' – and then conclusions will be drawn in direct answer to this categorisation.

Organisationally, party organisers began to wind up their electoral machines well before the political leaders turned their belated attention to the campaign. The exact date was set for EP elections early in 1983, but organisational preparations only commenced a year later, as required by electoral procedure. Certain arrangments were clearly the state's responsibility, such as implementing provisions for Italian voters living in other EC member states (according to one report there were as many as 940, 000 such voters), while party preparations were taken up with candidate selection. One issue that surfaced but briefly was the question of reform of the European electoral law. The law that applied in the 1979 EP elections was simple in outline: Italy was divided into five large constituencies (North-West, North-East, Centre, South and the Islands) with the 81 seats apportioned between them according to population size; candidates were presented by party lists in each constituency; and voting was by proportional representation with provision for preference votes.

Candidate selection was a fairly routine affair and deserves no more than a brief mention. Eleven parties competed and the 774 candidates were marked by the presence of many top leaders heading the lists (for example, Andreotti, de Mita and Forlani for the DC, Berlinguer, Pajetta, Natta and Spinelli for the PCI, Pannella for the Radicals and Almirante for the MSI), a fair sample of mayors from big cities such as Milan, Turin and Venice (there was no incompatibility rule preventing this), intellectual figures, notably Alberto Moravia (PCI), and some politicians who had failed in 1983 to get elected to the national parliament.

The presentation of top figures as 'flag candidates', also a feature of the 1979 EP election, clearly was with a view to electoral appeal even though they usually could not be expected to play any active part at Strasbourg, if at all. Italy retained the dual mandate only for such major figures, allowing them a flexibility and the freedom to continue their national careers (there were 13 such cases in the outgoing EP). It was predictably these famous politicians who were the most visible MEPs back home, even though their regular attendance was low (for example, Berlinguer made a few speeches in the EP, notably on Afghanistan early in 1980).

There was a handful of controversial candidacies provoking media attention, strictly for particular reasons relating to Italian politics. For instance, a priest with unorthodox views (Baget Bozzo) was placed high on one PSI list and this caused a sharp reaction from the Vatican, while the Radicals made a great play with the candidacy of Enzo Tortora, who had been imprisoned because of charges of links with the Neopolitan mafia (this was in the style of the suspected terrorist Negri, who had stood for the Radicals in the 1983 national election). Apart from these details, the only particularly new feature of the party lists was that the Republicans and Liberals combined theirs. This had a certain transnational significance in that both parties had belonged to the same EP party group and party federation, and they boasted the same firm commitment to integration and federalism. They consequently presented the same programme to the voters (the common programme of the ELD), and held common rallies with leaders of both parties.

Party strategies were more or less evident depending on the party in question. The PCI had tended to develop the most conspicuous European strategy, in recent years called the 'European Left' involving more intense contact with Socialist parties in the EC, and this was given an airing during the campaign in slogans and posters. There were various motives for this strategy adopted since the 1979 election: the general desire by the PCI to further its legitimation as a political force and overcome the danger of 'isolation' (more pronounced in domestic politics since the end of its support for the Andreotti government in 1979 and the subsequent DC-PSI axis in government); more pronounced differences with other Communist parties, especially the PCF, over European integration; the opportunity through contact with Socialist parties to try and outflank the PSI, now more aggressive towards the PCI, and maintain its position as the senior party of the Italian Left; and, finally, the greater attention to foreign policy in the EC, specifically the concern over worsening East/West relations, the PCI's more critical line towards Moscow following the imposition of martial law in Poland late in 1981 and the emergence across Europe of the peace movement which brought the PCI and many Socialist parties together. This strategic line was reflected in the PCI's slogans during the 1984 campaign: 'A vote in Italy for the Left in Europe', 'To the Left, the Future of Europe'. Electorally speaking, the maximum aim for the

PCI was both the 'overtaking' (*sorpasso*) of the DC as the largest party and a setback for the PSI.

The DC lacked any particular strategy as a party in the sense of an active role in transnational contacts or fresh thinking on European questions. Instead, the party advertised its pride in its European tradition, as expressed in the slogans 'DC, Champions of Europe' and 'We have made Europe, now we must make Europeans'. Its essential aim was unquestionably the electoral one of at least maintaining its 1983 level of support. This became only too apparent over the issue of abstention and its projected differential impact on the votes for the parties, for one early poll in the campaign indicated it would hit the DC hardest. The DC could not fully veil its nervousness, and this became even less manageable once Berlinguer's death brought forth strong emotional sympathy among the public at large and made the *sorpasso* a real possibility.

The strategies of the other parties – if that is the right word – could be described concisely. Late in 1983 for the PSI, one of the vice-secretaries, Valdo Spini, stated 'for us Italian Socialists, the elections of next year are fundamental: our objective is finally to obtain that large increase in votes that up to now has escaped us'.[20] So far as it brought transnational links into its campaign, this was to counter the PCI's pursuit of relations with Socialist parties like the SPD and PASOK. Among the small parties, perhaps the one with the most visible strategy was the PRI which, hoping to capitalise further on Spadolini's popularity as an honest politician following its success in winning floating voters in 1983, exploited the P2 scandal alongside emphasising its European credentials. In general, electoral competition aroused party leaders and organisers irrespective of the EP's institutional weakness. The campaign became increasingly bitter because it was maintained all-round that the European vote would have probable consequences for the individual party strategies whether long-term or more immediate: the parties' strategies so far as these existed became more electoralistic.

On the question of issues, the intermixture of European and national themes was illustrated by the parties' slogans: 'A Europe of peace and work for those who will be 20 years old in 2000, vote PCI', 'We will not bring to Europe the Italy of the P2' (PCI), 'A clean Italy in a clean Europe' (PRI/PLI – also a reference to P2), 'For Europe, vote Italy' (MSI), 'Do you want to run the risk of an Italy represented in Europe by the Communists?' (DC – a variation on an old electoral theme of this party) and 'No unemployed, in Europe there is one more unemployed every 15 seconds, vote PCI for work and growth'. Yet, while the media influenced the course of issue debate in the campaign, apparently forcing party leaders to respond to their demands, did the parties try to fix the issues and gear them to questions of concern to the EC?

There are various standard ways of trying to assess this. If one takes the parties' programmes, then European themes were very prominent. This was true of those using the common programmes of their respective transnational party federations – the DC with the EPP programme, the PLI/PRI with the ELD programme and the PSI and PSDI with the CSP programme. The ELD programme, for instance, gave elaborate attention to an EC role in overcoming the economic crisis and promoting economic development. The PCI was the only major party not to have a transnational programme as there was no equivalent Communist party federation, but it could hardly be faulted for failing to present its own version of European policies. It produced a 'Memorandum for the European Voter', covering such matters as the peace issue, CAP, the Third World, environmental problems and citizens' rights; as well as a small folder of one-sheet briefs covering EC concerns. The Radical Party produced a special issue of *Notizie Radicali* which emphasised 'choosing the Europe of freedom, of life, of peace, of ecology against the Europe of merchants, of cannons, of pollution, of plutonium' and gave coverage to a variety of its policy positions. Even the PSI, widely suspected of being instrumental about EP elections for boosting Craxi's power position in Rome, produced its own 'Socialist Proposals for Europe' outlining its views on 'problems of Europe' with much attention to defence issues.

But what did all this mean? One might well be as sceptical about party programmes as in national elections, if not more so, because of the lack of executive power vested in the EP. Some party programmes are more detailed than others (the ELD's more than the EPP's), and some may be seen as more commercial window-dressing than genuinely programmatic (the PCI being a case of the latter), so variation between the parties must be part of the answer to this question.

One further way of testing the parties' projection of EC issues is by looking at the content of campaign speeches. For lack of any systematic study in this respect, only various indicators are offered. In practice, the parties chose to be customarily selective in projecting certain issues – the PCI over unemployment, defence and the importance of integration as such, the Radicals with their stress on civil rights in Europe, and the PLI/PRI on European federalism, defence economic integration and a foreign policy for the EC. The parties' television appeals focussed predictably on the effect of the vote on the domestic scene, although some of their broadcasts were 'European' in style. In speeches, European themes inevitably came across more often than not in generic and abstract terms, but altogether any assessment of the content of publicity of the parties only confirms the intermixture of domestic and European themes, and hence 'internalisation'.

The laconic remark of one newspaper editorial on 20 May 1984 that the campaign was marked by 'more polemics than passion' in the sense of attachment to the issues[21] seemed to be borne out subsequently but the competitive factor was most likely to produce such an effect. The ultimate problem with the parties' attempt to project questions of concern to the EC was their dependence on the media. This was unavoidable in order to reach the mass public, as distinct from party activists or the limited numbers who attended party rallies. But a distinction should be drawn between the two forms of the media. The press showed little or no interest in EC affairs during the campaign, except for certain weeklies which featured background articles on the EP or particular common policies of the EC; rather differently, the broadcast media did give more extensive coverage to party policy positions on the EC, perhaps not really surprising because of combined party control over the public radio and television company.[22]

Finally, the 'European' nature of the campaign cannot avoid reference to transnational party links, which had taken a qualitative jump with the process towards the first EP elections. These offered the most direct 'European colours' in that they advertised the parties' own links with structures within the EC. In line with previous trends, they took a variety of forms. Apart from the common programmes as the most important contribution of the transnational party federations to the campaign, the Italian parties utilised publicity of their EP party groups detailing their parliamentary records and in some cases included short reports on the same in material for party activists. In some instances, transnational links became controversial and were sucked into polemical exchanges. The supposed statement by SPD leader, Ehmke, that the PCI was the only party of the Left that was 'really European' was proudly mentioned in PCI propaganda, but was decidedly rejected by the PSI. As in 1979, small parties emphasised their links with the major political movements in the EC clearly to overcome their minor status domestically.

Generally, transnational links were less prominent than in the 1979 campaign when several parties had amply, even enthusiastically, used them.[23] Few foreign speakers were invited by the parties to take part in the 1984 campaign. The DC booked several for the party's Festival of Friendship in Milan, an annual event brought forward from the summer to coincide with the European campaign, though this was primarily for activists. One PSI leader in the region of Lombardy was dismissive about the idea, claiming he did not know of plans for foreign speakers: 'It is not as if this thing has a great electoral importance – a meeting conducted in German, to what purpose?', he said laughing.[24] While the PCI was, according to the head of its EP election office, sending speakers to Greece (to support PASOK) and would have meetings with the PCF in France, but he commented: 'Transnationality is not guaranteed so much by the presence at rallies of deputies from other countries ... transnationality is above all, should be assured by the content of debate, by the capacity to pose European questions connected with national question – that is the real point'.[25] One particular Italian feature of transnational links should be mentioned here, namely the extension of party organisations abroad to maintain contact with emigrant workers. The PCI, the best organised case in point, held the first large-scale *Unità* Festival (an annual party event in Italy from national down to local levels) outside Italy at Brussels in May with visiting speakers from Rome. The PCI said it would attempt to elect a candidate representing emigrant Italian workers[26] (several emigrants were included on the PCI list, and one was elected – who had been living in Brussels since 1963).[27]

Such transnational 'colours' were low grade and showed no further development over the first EP elections, if anything the opposite. This corresponds to the EC information campaign which in 1984 was much less ambitious than in 1979, when the exercise was to exploit the novelty of the event. EC institution offices in Rome produced some standard booklets (for example, 'The European Parliament, Your Voice in Europe'), and according to a spokesman of the EP office there the information campaign was limited, for the decision was to leave the main part of the propaganda to the Italian parties,[28] which received some finance *via* their EP party groups but relied more on state finance. Overall, there was evidence of party variation in the use of transnational links, but these suffered from lack of popularity or exposure among the public at large. Here was a particular instance where the lack of consistent media attention in the previous five years had meant no progress since the 1979 elections.

In conclusion, in reference to the four-point categorisation for the 'internalisation' of European policy one may note the following:

a. *Party strategy*: there were no real surprises compared with 1979 as to the degree to which the various parties emphasised that they had European strategies (here the parties differed as before), while they again all chose to give some publicity to their activity in the EP; the PCI, the party as having the most pronounced European strategy, had changed the direction of this towards the 'European Left' since 1979, but this was not with any direct regard to EP elections.

b. *General issue salience*: the 1984 campaign confirmed the distinction between 'European' and 'national' issues as artificial, but so far as there could be variation in the balance of attention between more strictly EC issues and more strictly national issues then this was tilted distinctly towards the latter; however, it is worth noting some differences here between media interpretation and coverage and the efforts by the parties to project policy questions.

c. *Electoral politics and behaviour*: the routinisation of EP elections was evident in the way the parties set about organising the campaign and in the competitive element, for the parties were predictably electoralistic in all cases irrespective of their European strategies and the degree of their active commitment to the EC; but, politically, the opportunity for mobilisation over EC issues provided by EP elections showed no advance over the 1979 campaign.

d. *Issue-specific*: the obvious case of 'internalisation' was the last minute attempt to reform the European electoral law, but this was brief and aroused no extended conflict; speaking more generally, the possibility that 'campaign events' highlighting palpably EC matters did not occur (Mitterrand's speech at Strasbourg produced positive reactions from Italian political leaders, but it did nothing to alter the tenor of the campaign).

Altogether, an examination of these four categories underlines that 1984 brought no radical or significant change in the style and substance of 'internalisation' in Italian European policy, except for noting that general issue salience happened to be pitched this time towards more obviously national problems, because of the domestic situation which preceded these elections. Otherwise, the 1984 campaign confirmed previous trends. Obviously, therefore, this campaign brought European policy within the orbit of everyday politics, but one has doubts about the depth to which this happened.

THE RESULTS: MUCH ADO ABOUT NOTHING?

The automatic government crisis regarded widely as inevitable immediately after the EP elections failed to transpire, although a forthcoming demise of the Craxi government seemed odds-on, bearing in mind internal division and rivalries and growing signs of policy stagnation. But the EP vote itself did nothing to provoke such a crisis, mainly because the results did not seriously disturb the balance of strength within the government camp. Ciriaco de Mita, the DC leader, had warned early in June 1984 that a PSI advance at the cost of the DC would have a 'de-stabilising' impact on the government, and shortly before election day (and after Berlinguer's death) this became a threat of a government crisis in the event of both such a Socialist advance and an 'overtaking' (*sorpasso*) of the DC by the PCI.[29] As it turned out, only the latter occurred and then by a fraction of 0.3%. The aftermath of EP elections contrasted with the dramatisation of the campaign, especially with the outbreak of warfare inside the coalition and the emotional outburst over the PCI leader's death. In the short term, the whole event did appear to be 'much ado about nothing'.

The results did not provide any definite signals to the various parties and their strategies in a longer-term sense, although expectations had been high that they might. Most notably, this was present on the part of the PSI because of its historic acquisition of the leadership of government the previous year, obviously linked as this was to ambitions for challenging the DC's dominance. But the failure of the Socialists to advance – in fact, compared to the 1983 election they lost 0.2% – could only be interpreted as a blow to Craxi. PSI failure to come anywhere near meeting its aim was a relief to the DC, which despite predictions to the contrary maintained its percentage of 1983, and it took the sting out of the fact that for the first time in a national election the PCI 'overtook' the DC. It appeared that the sympathy vote the PCI derived from Berlinguer's death was counter-balanced by concern afterwards among Centre-right voters about a rise in Communist support. Smaller parties lost votes to the DC, the main anti-Communist bulwark, as a consequence. The same electoral syndrome had operated in the 1976 national election when the prospect of a substantial rise in the PCI vote had in the end stabilised DC support.

The most interesting detail and the most commented upon election result was the *sorpasso* of the PCI. This allowed the PCI to claim credibility for its European strategy, though leaving very much open whether its new status as first party would eventually improve its

TABLE 7.1   *EP election results*

	1984		1979	
	% votes cast	Seats won	% votes cast	Seats won
PCI (Communists)	33.3	27	29.6	24
DC (Christian Democrats)	33.0	26	36.4	29
PSI (Socialists)	11.2	9	11.0	9
PLI (Liberals	6.1	5	3.5	3
PRI (Republicans)			2.6	2
MSI–DN (Italian Social Movement – National Right)	6.5	5	5.4	4
PSDI (Social Democrats)	3.5	3	4.3	4
PR (Radicals)	3.4	3	3.7	3
DP (Proletarian Democrats)	1.4	1	0.7	1
SVP (South Tyrol People's Party)	0.6	1	0.6	1
Union Valdôtaine – Partito Sardo d'Azione (Val d'Aosta Union and Sardinian Action Party)	0.5	1	–	–
PDUP (Proletarian Unity)	–	–	1.2	1
Others	0.5	–	0.9	–

SOURCE   Adapted from *Bull. EC*, 6-1984 and *EP News*, no. 55, June 1984.

domestic role. The prestige of becoming first party certainly lifted party morale, and it could only help its full legitimation as a political force. The PCI daily newspaper, *L'Unità*, featured on its front page the next day the word 'FIRST' in red letters five inches deep, for the term *sorpasso* had long acquired a strong psychological value. The fact that the five parties in the Craxi-led coalition had together lost two million votes compared with the 1983 election was convincing backing for the PCI's frontal attacks against many of the government's policies. It certainly erased for the time being fears that the PCI had nursed since Craxi's elevation the previous summer that the PSI might start getting the political edge over itself. The PCI lost no time in trying to capitalise on its new status: its parliamentary leader, Giorgio Napolitano, demanded that one of Italy's two EC Commissioners should come from the PCI.[30] It was also noted that the PCI position in municipal government was strengthened, such as in certain cities where relations with the PSI and the smaller parties had worsened so that the latter, embittered by PCI attacks on national government policies, were looking for an opportunity to eject the PCI from local administrations.[31]

The PCI's probable benefit from the 'Berlinguer effect' suggested that its newly acquired status might be difficult to sustain. Indeed in the regional elections in Sardinia a week later the PCI lost ground, having moved ahead of the DC in the European vote there. However, seen regionally and sociologically, the PCI vote showed evidence of gains in areas worst hit by the recession and unemployment, with particularly strong rises in southern cities (up 5–6% in Naples, Bari, Palermo and Catania), while reinforcing its support in the northern conurbations.[32] Similarly, behind the consistency of the DC vote compared with 1983 lay some warning signs – while gaining slightly in northern cities and towns, it lost substantially in the South, especially in Sicily where the DC continued to drop even over 1983 (notably in the regional capital of Palermo, with −4.4%).[33] While the PCI made big gains in both advanced and backward urban areas as well as those which were not particularly urbanised, the DC declined in areas where it had traditionally been dominant through its mass clientelistic use of state power. The PCI showed that it could exploit discontent with the DC, even though it might temporarily be riding a Berlinguer sympathy vote. There was some talk after the election of a return of bipolarism, in view of the losses by third and small parties. Statistically, this involved a reverse of the growth in support for the latter during the national elections of 1979 and 1983, but any firm conclusion here cannot really be made because a crucial factor which had traditionally buttressed bipolarism (namely, the institutionalised sub-cultures of the PCI and DC) had been progressively weakening over the previous half decade or more. The result of this had been a steady growth in opinion, voters, and volatility, but evidently in the 1984 EP election strong polarisation between government and opposition on essentially domestic grounds had moved voters back to the major parties.

The EP election therefore confirmed recent trends. There is, of course, a variety of angles for judging individual elections – statistically, sociologically, psychologically and politically. The EP vote, like any national election, gave food for thought on the first three, but politically it was difficult to argue there was any impact. Even though politicians and journalists alike made comparisons with the 1983 national election rather than with the 1979 EP election, the obvious difference this time from a national election was that there followed no extended coalition government formation – as is usually the case – to keep the election's political effects alive. The parties during the campaign appeared to want to pre-determine political repercussions from the eventual result, but this did not happen in the end. A relative surprise of the result in statistical terms was the turnout – at 83.9% a small decline from 85.5% in 1979, and one of the highest in the EC (marginally behind Luxembourg and little over 8% less than Belgium) and way ahead of the other EC member states. This was contrary to expectations and predictions, for in the previous half decade abstention had appeared as an issue and grown, reaching an unprecedented level in 1983 with turnout down to 89%.

CONCLUSION

Among the reasons for expecting a lower turnout had been the technical fact that for EP elections there was only one day for voting instead of the two set aside for national elections. In fact, the 83.9% turnout was by Italian standards relatively low, although by and large the practised habit of high turnout was not seriously dented. This takes us back to our main theme of Italy's European policy, its 'internalisation' by the political parties and the less easily determinable effect of both on the Italian electorate.

A *Eurobarometer* poll published in spring 1984 showed Italy to be very evenly divided between those who considered the forthcoming EP election to be of 'EC interest' or 'national interest' (45% for the former and 44% for the latter, with 11% no comment).[34] But the intensification of national party battles in the intervening months together with basic doubts about such a distinction undercut the value of this poll. The scope for the impact of the EC and its activity and policies on the public was limited, notwithstanding Italy's general and long-standing reputation for being a very pro-European country. The latter has been seen as involving a conceptual attitude and is really a descriptive point, while the question of actual political behaviour in relation to European themes is much harder to gauge because it broaches depth and intensity.

It is of course the role of political parties and also the media as well as governments to mediate between the EC and the national publics. In Italy, the first of these did in the EP election campaign of 1984 make some effort to project EC issues, albeit rather partially and often polemically, but their impact was probably weakened by the increasing gulf between society and the parties as structures of mediation.[35] This study of the EP election suggests very strongly that it was an event very much more for the party elites than it was for the public. All this of course throws serious doubt on the extent to which the EC has acquired any form of 'grass-roots'. So far as the elites were concerned, this survey has sought to explain why the 'internalisation' of the European campaign should have been no surprise, simply because this related to a long-term pattern in postwar Italy. The various positions of the parties illustrated how European and national political considerations were closely linked. Assessed against this background, the 1984 EP elections confirmed continuities in the motivation and presentation of Italy's European policy back home. But some change was also apparent, notably in the evolution in party-political differentiation over EC affairs and its gradual replacement of the bland pro-European rhetoric that had tended to predominate in party statements in the past.

NOTES AND REFERENCES

I should like to thank Antonio Agosta of the Italian Ministry of the Interior's electoral office for his assistance with collecting material, James Walston for his kind hospitality during my stay in Rome in May 1984 and the Bristol University's academic staff travel fund for welcome funds for the trip.

1. G. Pridham, 'Italy' in C. and K. Twitchett (eds), *Building Europe: Britain's Partners in the EEC* (London: Europa, 1981) pp. 105ff.
2. Doxa Institute, *Sintesi dei risultati di alcune indagini periodiche sull'informazione e gli atteggiamenti degli Italiani nei confronti della Comunità Europea e del Parlamento Europeo*, 1984, pp. 5–6.
3. Ibid., p. 14.
4. Ibid., p. 8.
5. *Le Parlement Européen et l'Election de 1984: état de l'opinion publique européenne en avril 1983*, Faits et Opinions, Paris, 20 Aug. 1983, p. 67.
6. Euro-Barometre, Brussels, *L'Opinion Publique dans la Communauté Européenne à l'automne 1983*, no. 20, Dec. 1983, p. 75.
7. *Le Parlement Européen*, 20 Aug. 1983, p. 59.
8. Interview with Ennio Salamon, director of Doxa Institute, Milan, 18 May 1984.
9. Interview with Giancarlo Mencucci, servizio verifica programmi, RAI, Rome, 23 May 1984.
10. Interview with Ennio Salamon, op. cit.
11. For example, the report on Sicily in the European election campaign in *Corriere della Sera*, 10 June 1984, that 'as at the national level the parties here are proceeding towards the elections on Sunday looking more to Rome than to Strasbourg', and that the focus in the region was the inevitable question of control over state patronage.
12. *Corriere della Sera*, 3, 4 and 11 June 1984.

13. Ibid., 4 June 1984.
14. Ibid., 3 June 1984.
15. Interview with Micaela Buonfrate, headquarters of the Radical Party, Rome, 24 May 1984.
16. *L'Opinion Publique*, Dec. 1983, Appendix, p. 63.
17. Doxa, *Sintesi dei risultati*, appendix, table 9.
18. *Corriere della Sera*, 24 Feb. 1984.
19. Doxa, *Sintesi dei risultati*, p. 7.
20. *Panorama*, 28 Nov. 1983.
21. *Corriere della Sera*, 'L'Europa senza passione', 20 May 1984.
22. See discussion of this in G. Mazzoleni, 'The Italian European Election of 1984', *Electoral Studies*, Nov. 1984.
23. G. Pridham and P. Pridham, *Transnational Party Co-operation and European Integration: The Process Towards Direct Elections* (London: Allen & Unwin, 1981) pp. 238 and 250.
24. Interview with Walter Marossi, PSI regional vice-secretary for Lombardy, Milan, 19 May 1984.
25. Interview with Renato Sandri, head of the PCI's European Elections Office, Rome, 24 May 1984.
26. Europe Agence Internationale d'Information pour la Presse, Brussels, *European Election Special*, 17 May 1984.
27. Ibid., 30 June 1984.
28. Interview with Erberto Stolfi, European Parliament office, Rome, 22 May 1984.
29. *Corriere della Sera*, 11 and 19 June 1984.
30. *Panorama*, 2 July 1984.
31. See report in *Corriere della Sera*, 19 June 1984.
32. See table on regional breakdown of PCI support in *Panorama*, 2 July 1984, p. 38.
33. Ibid., pp. 38–9.
34. Europe Agence Internationale, op. cit., 2 June 1984.
35. On this, see L. Morlino, 'The Changing Relationship between Parties and Society in Italy', *West European Politics* 7 (1984).

8 Luxembourg

JOHN FITZMAURICE

Luxembourg is the smallest member state of the EC, with a mere 384 000 inhabitants. It is perhaps the most 'European' minded, with the least reticence about integration and supranationality and with the fewest specific national interests to defend. Yet, paradoxically, the 1979 and 1984 Euro-elections had less impact in Luxembourg than in almost any other member state.

Luxembourg's 'European Vocation' is an early one. She was a signatory of the Benelux Treaty in 1944, a founder member of the Brussels Treaty Organisation, later Western European Union, in 1948 and of NATO. She joined the Council of Europe in 1949. She entered the Schuman Plan negotiations with enthusiasm and became a founder member of the European Coal and Steel Community (ECSC) and later joined the EEC and EURATOM. Luxembourg supported all attempts at greater integration, including the ill-fated European Defence Community. She supported enlargement and European Union and her Prime Minister Pierre Werner was the author of the first plan for an Economic and Monetary Union. At a more concrete level, the EC's institutions soon had high visibility in Luxembourg City, where the ECSC High Authority was set up from 1952, with Jean Monnet as its first President. This was followed by the EP Secretariat, the Court of Justice, the European Investment Bank, the Court of Auditors and several Commission Directorates, especially those dealing with borrowing and lending operations, and the Statistical Office and Health and Safety. Currently, over 5000 EC civil servants are based in Luxembourg. Above all, on the political level, Luxembourg has a very clear sense that national sovereignty can, in the modern world, at best be a very relative term. Her history,[1] small size and economic dependence have all taught this basic lesson. The independence of Luxembourg and indeed her existence has always been precarious and dependent on others as expressed through the nineteenth century settlements reached by the great powers.

HISTORY

The 'large' Grand Duchy (the present Grand Duchy plus the present day Belgian Province of Luxembourg) was awarded to William I of the Netherlands as compensation for the loss of Nassau and at the same time was included in the German Confederation, which replaced the defunct Holy Roman Empire after 1806. From 1830–39, following the Belgian Revolution of 1830, Luxembourg was the subject of very difficult diplomatic negotiations, in which Belgium sought to obtain both parts of the Grand Duchy, if necessary by purchase. Eventually the issue was resolved in 1839 by the XXIV Articles Treaty. Walloon Luxembourg was included in Belgium, and the present area of the Grand Duchy remained in a personal union with the Dutch Crown, whilst remaining a member of the German Confederation. With the demise of the Confederation in 1866, the issue was re-opened. The Netherlands offered to sell Luxembourg to France, whereas Austria proposed that France should receive Namur, parts of Hainaut and Walloon Luxembourg and that Belgium should be compensated with Luxembourg. The Conference of London (1867) resolved the issue by leaving the Grand Duchy with the Dutch Crown, but neutralised and guaranteed by the great powers. Prussian forces were withdrawn, but she remained a member of the Zollverein. In 1890, the personal union ended and a separate Luxembourg dynasty came to the throne. Already, there are the seeds of a form of *de facto* 'Europeanisation' and in any event a form of state with less than total sovereignty.

In the first world war, Luxembourg was the first state to be invaded by the German steamroller of 1914. Her internationally guaranteed neutral status proved valueless. Following four years of German occupation, she was occupied by French troops in 1918 and became the object of dispute between France and Belgium, who both sought territorial aggrandisement. Her own wish for an economic union with France, coupled with the maintenance of the dynasty, as expressed through the referendum of 28 September 1919 was not respected, as it did not accord with the overall designs of the allied powers. Instead, in 1921, a customs union and a monetary union with Belgium was imposed, which remains in force today. Luxembourg therefore lost control over her currency and thereby over the major determinants of macroeconomic policy. Belgian failure to even consult Luxembourg over currency realignments became so flagrant at the time of the 1982 devaluation, that the denunciation of the agreement became a political issue in Luxembourg.

In 1940, Luxembourg was overrun in one day by the Nazi Wehrmacht. Her intended fate was worse than in 1914. Nazi Germany was not content with occupation, but to Germanise the Grand Duchy and incorporate it into the Reich, under the notorious Gauleiter Simon. The results of a Nazi-organised popular consultation showed an overwhelming majority against incorporation and thus were never published. As in Alsace-Lorraine, young Luxembourgers faced conscription into the Wehrmacht, whilst the legal government had fled to London to continue the war on the side of the allies. People faced very difficult personal choices, which opened up wounds, which have yet to heal.

As a barely sovereign state, with such a traumatic recent history, which had suffered so much from the excesses of nationalism, to whom neither total independence, nor annexation to one of her three immediate neighbours, represented a solution to her future, it is natural that she embraced the European idea with enthusiasm. This was reinforced by the fact that one of the first concrete manifestations of this new concept was the ECSC, which concerned an industry of major direct interest to Luxembourg, as a major steel producer and exporter.

The main economic activities of the country are steel production, agriculture and tourism. Agriculture still remains relatively important, with about 6% of the work force involved, which is close to the EC average. She produces no energy, not even coal. The Grand Duchy produces some 1.6% of the iron ore mined in the EC; 3.5% of the crude steel; 3.9% of the pig iron. This production is largely for export. These figures do not appear impressive, but should be compared with the size of the country. Her production exceeds that of Sweden, Norway, Ireland, Denmark, Greece and Austria.[2]

Thus, apart from the initial almost *pro forma* opposition of the Communists, all parties in Luxembourg were strong supporters of the Communities and further integration. Supranationalism was welcomed. As a small country, with few specific interests to defend, and a strong national consensus around the European idea, Luxembourg's role has been to act as a mediator between the conflicting interests of the larger powers, in the general interest of the EC as a whole, whilst pressing for greater integration. Her statesmen have sought to play a role in EC affairs, which her size could not justify and they have been relatively successful in that aim. To name but the most well-known, her

Foreign Minister, M. Bech, was one of the architects of the 1956 Messina Conference; Pierre Werner chaired the committee which proposed an economic and monetary union; and Gaston Thorn has played a major role in European affairs, first as Prime Minister and Foreign Minister and then as President of the Commission. The international performance of Luxembourg leaders is also often a political issue in elections.

ELECTORAL SYSTEM

The Grand Duchy is a constitutional monarchy, in which the Grand Duke is a mere figurehead.[3] Political power is exercised by a small cabinet, led by a Prime Minister and responsible to the unicameral, 59-member Chamber of Deputies, elected for a maximum of five years. Parliament usually runs its full term (1974, 1979, 1984). The electoral system is very complex.[4] The country is divided into four multi-member districts with seats allocated according to population size as follows: South (the industrial area) 24 seats; Centre (includes the capital) 20 seats; East six seats; and North nine seats.

For Euro-elections, the country is one constituency, returning six members and party lists must contain twelve names, in order to provide adequate substitutes. Voting is compulsory. Each voter has a number of votes equivalent to the number of members to be returned in the constituency – in the EP elections, six votes. Voters may accord all their votes to one list; or split them among different lists ('panachage'); or 'plump' for certain candidates, giving them two votes. The seats for each list are then distributed by the Hagenbach-Bischoff method. A quota is determined by dividing the total vote of each list by the number of seats to be filled plus one. Each party's vote is then divided by the quota and one seat allocated for each whole quota thus obtained. Remaining unallocated seats are distributed by dividing each party's vote by the number of seats that it has so far gained plus one, two and so on. Seats are allocated according to the highest remainder resulting from each of these divisions. This system is marginally less generous to small parties than the d'Hondt system used in Belgium and considerably less generous than Scandinavian systems.

Parties

The party system is in effect a three-and-a-half party system, with several smaller parties also obtaining some parliamentary seats.[5] Only three parties – the CSV (Christian Democrats), LSAP (Socialists) and the DP (Liberals) – enter into coalition formation processes. The CSV is the largest party and was established in its present form in the immediate post-1945 period of party renewal, but had existed since 1914 as the Partei der Rechten. Indeed, it had lived up to its earlier name, with repressive measures against the Communists, which were in turn rejected by a referendum in 1937. In the 1930s it flirted with corporatist ideologies. Since its reorganisation in 1944, it has been a broad based 'Volkspartei' of the centre, with a trade union wing like the CDU and other Benelux Christian democratic parties. Its key figure over the last decade has been Pierre Werner, who resigned the leadership to Finance Minister Jacques Santer at the last Congress in December 1983. It enjoys its main support in the North and East constituencies.

The Socialist Party (LSAP) has mostly been the second largest party in the country and occasionally the largest (1928, 1951 and 1964). It was initially a radical party, but faced several major handicaps in the inter-war period: its 'revolutionary' position in the general strike of 1921 (which failed); its republicanism and its unclear stand on the issue of national independence. Only since 1968 has it been able to attract a sizeable middle class electorate. It has participated in centrist coalitions with the CSV and in coalitions with the anti-clerical liberal DP. Now it has become a moderate reformist party, which nevertheless seeks important changes in society. In its last period of power from 1974–79 with the DP, it was handicapped by the lack of leadership figures and by too close identification with the trade unions. Its main support lies in the southern constituency, where it usually obtains between 35 and 40% of the vote. The Parti Démocratique (here called the DP after its Letzeburgisch name) also emerged out of the resistance. Liberalism had faced a severe crisis in the pre-war period, splitting into many factions. A modern liberal and patriotic party was formed in 1945. Its traditions are strongly anti-clerical, though this is now of less importance. Its main stronghold is in the capital and the central constituency in which it lies. Here it gains up to 35% of the vote, but the party's electorate is very volatile, depending on floating middle class voters. It is committed to the market economy, but supports the welfare state. It is a strong supporter of NATO and the EC. Its main assets have been its fluidity in policy terms and the charismatic personality of Gaston Thorn, its leader until 1981.

Some other small parties have been able to hold on to a modest level of representation in the Chamber, but have played no part in parliamentary politics. The most venerable is the PCL (Communist Party), which has long been dominated by the Urbany family. Its main support has been in the industrial south constituency, especially the area of Esch, where it still obtained 15.8% of the vote as late as 1974. In 1945, the party obtained 13.5% of the vote nationally and five seats. In the rest of the postwar period, its vote has stabilised at around 9 to 12%, but with a high of 15.5% in 1968. In 1979, its vote fell to a mere 4.9% and two seats.

The Social Democratic Party (PSD), formed in 1971 as a breakaway from the LSAP, in protest against local government alliances with the PCL and too close links with the trade unions, took several leading LSAP personalities and vote-getters such as Astrid Lulling and Henri Cravatte. It won 10.6% of the vote and five seats in 1974, but fell to two seats and 6.4% of the vote in 1979. It has now been wound up and Astrid Lulling is a candidate for the CSV in the centre constituency.

Coalition possibilities in Luxembourg are limited. The most common coalition has been the 'grand coalition' of the CSV and the LSAP, predominant in the 1950s and 1960s. There are as alternatives the centre-left anti-clerical LSAP–DP coalition in office under Gaston Thorn from 1974–79 or the present CSV–DP coalition.

EUROPEAN ISSUES 1979–84

In Luxembourg, genuine European issues are hard to discern. There is a generalised permissive consensus in favour of the EC and a degree of élite support for greater integration not found in most other member states.[6]

Outside election times, EC issues are little apparent. There is, it has been said, no 'European public opinion in Luxembourg'. There is little or no debate or divergence of view, but rather a passive consensus in favour of the EC. European activity, be it by ministers or leaders of opposition parties, is seen as a means of increasing their 'presence' or international stature as statesmen and as such figures heavily in electoral propaganda, especially in that of the government parties. Some issues have become more prominent in the last five years. First and perhaps most significant, though not as significant in the actual election campaign as could have been expected, was the situation of the steel industry. The arrangements between ARBED (Luxembourg) and the Belgian concern Cockerill-Sambre and the 410 000 tonnes capacity cuts demanded by the Commission have been a source of controversy.

The LSAP and the PCL have strongly criticised the Commission quotas under the Davignon plan, but the LSAP's credibility, at least, has been limited by the fact that re-structuring of the industry, with significant capacity cuts, began under the LSAP–DP coalition in 1974–79. The CSV is more nuanced in its attitude than the DP. Only the DP expounds radical re-structuring in response to market forces.

The second visible issue related to the EP's seat. Since 1981 no plenary sessions have been held in Luxembourg and there is no prospect of any being held there, in view of the 1982 Zagari Resolution, which even envisaged transferring some EP staff to Strasbourg and Brussels to meet sessional and committee needs. The Luxembourg government twice took the EP to Court.[7] In the first judgement honours were in a certain sense even: the EP could hold sessions in either Brussels or Strasbourg and transfer an undefined but limited part of its staff to these working places. However, the competence of the Court and the interest of Luxembourg were recognised, as was the fact that the whole EP General Secretariat had to remain in Luxembourg. Transfers had to be limited to what was necessary for meetings. All the Luxembourg parties criticise lack of effort by other parties on this issue and present themselves, whether in government or opposition, as defenders of the cause of Luxembourg on this issue, which is electorally important, at least in the centre constituency.

Enlargement, to which Luxembourg is otherwise strongly favourable, raises a problem in relation to the free movement of labour. This concerns Portugal in particular. There are over 91 000 foreigners in Luxembourg, of which 40 000 are Portuguese, representing an obvious pole of attraction for other Portuguese immigrants in the event of accession. Thus, the Luxembourg government has sought certain special provisions, by way of a longer transition period. Agriculture and in particular the impact of measures to control milk production have been issues, but debate has been limited and no clear government view has emerged. On the broader issues, such as CAP reform, the financing of the EC or the European Union Treaty, there has been almost no debate and few clear positions have emerged.

THE 1984 CAMPAIGN

As in 1979, so in 1984, the EP elections were held on the same day as the General Election. As a result there was no distinct Euro-campaign, but all the political parties weaved European elements into their campaigns. In this context it should be remembered that Luxembourg political parties have very limited resources and skeletal organisations. For example, the headquarters of the DP and the CSV are only open on a half-day basis. Furthermore, despite changes in the electoral law and stronger anti-dual mandate rules in the LSAP,[8] the European election lists were not seen as distinct entities by the parties, but as part of an overall political jigsaw puzzle or game plan, enabling the party leaders to keep their options open as to ministerial office, the national parliament or the EP, depending on the outcome of the elections and of post-election coalition bargaining. Thus in all cases, the party leaders (Jacques Santer for the CSV; Jacques Poos for the LSAP; Colette Flesch for the DP; and René Urbany for the PCL) led both the national and EP lists. All six sitting-MEPs sought re-election, but only Victor Abens (LSAP), in second place on his party's list, obtained an immediately 'electable' place. The others had much lower placings. All CSV Euro-candidates were also candidates for the Chamber of Deputies. The political leaders wanted to act as political locomotives, whilst remaining available for national office.

There was little distinct EC policy debate, although EC issues were often raised in election meetings: the EP's seat, steel and milk production quotas being the favourite topics. The parties included short 'European sections' in their national election manifestos instead of adopting specific Euro-manifestos. The DP and CSV issued the ELD and EPP manifestos and distributed them widely. Luxembourg parties which belong to a transnational party federation (CSP, ELD or EPP) are eager to identify with their respective federation and its policy positions, as these are seen to confer wider influence on the obviously very small Luxembourg parties and at the same time are evidence of their internationalist credentials and wider links. This was a major motive for the LSAP in ensuring that the CSP pre-election Congress was held in Luxembourg.

The nature of political debate in Luxembourg is paradoxical. It is a mixture of extreme parochialism and open internationalism. The European and international dimension is a ready and natural element of the political debate. The obvious interdependency is easily understood and accepted by public opinion. Debate is too much influenced by events in neighbouring France and Germany, which are often taken as either positive or negative models, according to political preference. The press and media give extensive coverage to EC events, which in any case often take place in Luxembourg, but strangely offers little by way of a specifically Luxembourg position on such events. More than in any other member state, European events and issues are part of everyday life and an integral part of the stuff of politics, but only rarely emerge in their own right as concrete issues, except perhaps the crisis of the steel industry. Even this figured less in the 1984 campaign than might have been expected, despite the vigorous efforts of the LSAP to attack the outgoing CSV–DP coalition on the issue.

Otherwise the main thrust of all the parties' campaigns was national in character, concentrating on the comparative records of the outgoing CSV–DP coalition and the DP–LSAP coalition of 1974–79. The greatest attention was paid to the issue of the future coalition, in which the CSV held a key position and sought to keep its options very firmly open. Debate concentrated on the only two realistic possibilities: a continuation of the CSV–DP coalition or a CSV–LSAP coalition. An LSAP–DP coalition on the 1974–79 model could be excluded. European issues were raised by all parties, incidentally or as part of a clear strategy of stressing the linkage between the national and the European dimension. This was particularly true of the DP's approach, although that should not obscure the basically national nature of the campaign.

There was one single election campaign, mainly concerned with national issues, but with some European input.[9] Thus, the CSP Congress was held in Luxembourg. The CSV held a joint meeting with the Belgian PSC and the French CDS in Pétange. The DP did not hold any such 'transnational meetings' or invite foreign Liberal personalities to campaign in Luxembourg, though the German FDP's campaign train did stop at Luxembourg station. The DP leadership felt that such meetings would not be effective, but the party was actively involved in ELD activities, sending large delegations (who later acted as 'multipliers') to ELD events. The parties invented posters which advertised both elections at the same time. The DP and some of the other parties organised their teams of speakers which went round from place to place holding meetings in such a way as to include a European expert in each team, who would either give a short speech on Europe, or field 'European' questions from the audience.

Analysis of the Luxembourg press over a six week period before the poll shows frequent reference to the EC and events in the EC, but not much more than usual and little specific reference either to a specific Luxembourg viewpoint on these matters, or to the EP elections. Nor was there much direct coverage of the 'European dimension' of the election, but articles by the European experts of the various parties did appear. The parties also distributed 'give away' newspapers, which included a page of European news and comment.

The broadcasting authorities provided facilities for party political broadcasts from 27 May 1984, with each party enjoying equal air time, as a result of a law suit brought by the Greng List (the Greens). The content of the broadcasts was mostly national, but the parties included their European 'message'. There were also three round table televised debates between the parties, of which one was devoted to the European campaign.[10]

THE RESULTS[11]

Turnout was 87% in 1984, as compared with 88.9% in 1979 (see Table 8.1).

The LSAP made significant gains in the elections, winning one seat in the EP at the expense of the DP and seriously shaking the CSV–DP coalition's hold on the 65 seat Chamber of Deputies. Its gains were greater than predicted and brought the LSAP closer to the CSV in terms of the popular vote. As in 1979, the LSAP fared perceptibly worse in the EP poll, but the shortfall this time was only 1.2%. The small Greng/Alternativ List made a significant breakthrough at both levels, predictably taking a higher share of the European poll and overtaking the PCL, whose decline continued.

TABLE 8.1   *Results of the 1979 and 1984 (national and European) elections*

| List | 1979 | | | | 1984 | | | |
| | National | | European | | National | | European | |
	%	Seats	%	Seats	%	Seats	%	Seats
CSV	36.4	24	36.2	3	36.5	25	35.6	3
LSAP	22.5	14	21.6	1	31.8	21	30.6	2
DP	21.8	15	28.2	2	20.8	14	20.4	1
PCL	4.9	2	5.0	0	4.4	2	4.2	
IND. SOC.	2.4	1	–	–	2.0	0	2.6	0
GRENG/ ALT.	–	–	–	–	4.2	2	6.2	0
PSD	6.4	2	6.5	0	–	–	–	–
Others	4.5	1	0.5	0	0.4	0	0.4	0
		59		6		64		6

The CSV survived relatively well, despite the wear and tear of power, its vote remaining static, thanks to the 'ralliement' of the PSD under Astrid Lulling, which masked what would otherwise have been a small decline in its share of the vote. The DP was the main loser at both levels. Its European 'premium' which had been some 7% in 1979 fell to an almost insignificant 0.4%. Its new leader, Colette Flesch, had been unable to replace Gaston Thorn as a high profile, charismatic leader. The highest preference vote went to CSV leader Jacques Santer (22 432 votes), closely followed by Colette Flesch (DP). The veteran LSAP MEP Victor Abens won more European preference votes than the LSAP leader Jacques Poos, who headed both LSAP lists, by almost 5000. The members initially elected (order on the list in brackets) were: for the CSV – Jacques Santer (1), Fernand Boden (3) and Jean Spautz (2); for the LSAP – Victor Abens (2) and Jacques Poos (1); and for the DP – Colette Flesch (1).

These results were largely academic in view of the uncertain post-electoral situation. There was uncertainty about the type of coalition (CSV–DP or CSV–LSAP) which would be formed and about individual ministerial appointments. In fact, it soon became evident that few of those actually elected would sit in the EP. Indeed the CSV, virtually certain to remain in power, pre-arranged this. Santer was certain to become Prime Minister and the two others, ministers. Several other candidates on the CSV European list also preferred national ministerial office. For the LSAP, the situation depended on the type of coalition formed, but in view of the party decision forbidding the dual mandate, it was unlikely that Jacques Poos would sit in the EP. For the DP, Colette Flesch would only sit if the party went into opposition.

When the new CSV–LSAP coalition government was agreed upon, matters clarified somewhat. However, when the EP's inaugural session was held in July 1984, there was still a degree of uncertainty over one seat, simply labelled 'Luxembourg' on the seating plan of the Chamber. In the end none of the CSV elected members served; one LSAP member served and Colette Flesch decided to sit for only six months before returning full-time to national political life. The final delegation was as follows: for the CSV – Nic Estgen, Marcelle Lenz-Cornette and Ernest Muhlen; for the LSAP – Victor Abens and Lydie Schmitt; and for the DP – Colette Flesch.

Thus despite the highly personalised electoral system and Luxembourg's high degree of European commitment, the composition of its delegation depended on national political considerations first and foremost and was determined by the party leaderships rather than by the voters.

NOTES AND REFERENCES

1. For the historical background to Luxembourg in the nineteenth century, see J. Fitzmaurice, *The Politics of Belgium* (London: Hurst, 1983) pp. 24–5; p. 34 and p. 36.
2. Economic statistics taken from Eurostat, *Basic Statistics of the Community*, 1982–83 edn.
3. M. Hirsch, 'Luxembourg' in Henig, S. (ed.), *Political Parties in the European Community* (London: Allen & Unwin, 1979) pp. 170–4 and M. Delvaux, *Structures Socio-politiques du Luxembourg* (Luxembourg: Institut Universitaire International, 1977).
4. D. Nohlen, 'Luxembourg' in Sternberger, D. and Vogel, B. (eds), *Die Wahl der Parlamente* (Berlin: De Gruyter, 1969).
5. M. Hirsch, op. cit., pp. 170–2.
6. Information on the issues supplied to the author by Mario Hirsch, journalist and political analyst.
7. Cases 230/81 and 108/83.
8. *Luxemburger Wort*, 8 Mar. 1984, p. 4.
9. Information on the campaign from interviews with Victor Abens MEP (LSAP), Colette Flesch MEP (DP) and Nic Estgen MEP (CSV).
10. Information on the press and media: study conducted by the author of press and information provided by the Programme Director of RTL.
11. *Luxemburger Wort*, 20 June 1984 and for 1979 see, J. Lodge and V. Herman, *Direct Elections to the European Parliament: A Community Perspective* (London: Macmillan, 1982) pp. 242–3.

9 The Federal Republic of Germany

SIMON BULMER AND WILLIAM E. PATERSON*

The second election to the EP was held in the Federal Republic of Germany (FRG) on 17 June 1984. The date has a political significance in the FRG as the 'day of national unity' although this played no role in the election. As in 1979 the election was only held in the FRG for 78 MEPs, while the remaining one SPD and two CDU MEPs were selected from the Berlin Chamber of Deputies. The main distinction from 1979 lay in the intervening change of power at the federal level. Helmut Schmidt's centre-left SPD/FDP coalition had been replaced in September 1982 by a centre-right CDU/CSU/FDP coalition under Helmut Kohl. This set the scene for what proved to be a nationally-orientated campaign.

PARTIES AND PUBLIC OPINION ON EUROPEAN INTEGRATION

'The main West German parties are all broadly pro-integrationist, first in the sense that they all espouse the further application of integration measures to new and older areas of activity, harbour no ideological reservations about the integration process and advocate a federal Europe, but they reveal all the same differences of emphasis, outlook and priority in the way they interpret the purpose of integration'.[1] This consensus was established by the late 1950s. The SPD had completed its transition from initial harsh opposition to support by mid-1955 and the FDP which had opposed West German membership of the EC had

190

accepted the main lines of the consensus by the late 1950s.[2] The grounds for this consensus are quite well known. The West German political system is one which has been basically consensual and where disagreements over policy alternatives do not loom large.[3] A number of structural factors facilitate consensus and act against any party in government being too partisan. These include the pervasiveness of coalition governments, the German system of co-operative federalism which includes the need for a dual majority in the *Bundestag* and *Bundesrat*, the nature of the *Volkspartei* (Catch-all Party) and the institution of judicial review through the *Bundesverfassungsgericht* (Federal Constitutional Court).

In addition, a number of political and economic considerations made a consensus in favour of European integration extremely likely in the FRG. It became apparent very early in the FRG's history that the attainment of sovereignty depended on accepting integration, and that reunification while remaining an aspiration was not, at least in the short to medium term, a realistic alternative. The economic imperatives were equally strong. It was not just that an export dependent economy like the FRG needed access to markets, there was the prior step of getting the production-ceilings imposed by the western allies in certain key areas lifted. Both these goals involved acceptance of European integration.

The social and political consensus around adherence to liberal capitalism and social market values was reinforced by the complex European structures since they were both based on those values. In the one major area where the EC avoids competition and espouses protection, that is agriculture, the FRG was also not disposed to apply the rigours of economic competition. The last set of factors conducive to a general consensus on European integration was the problematic nature of the political identity of FRG citizens.[4] Counselled by the Basic Law to treat the FRG as 'provisional' and rendered ambivalent towards 'German' symbols by the traumatic recent past, it was hardly surprising that a European identity proved so attractive to West Germans in the 1950s and 1960s. The overwhelmingly consensual nature of party positions on integration has, however, contributed to a situation in which, apart from the exchange of pious rhetoric, debates on Europe often have the character of the participants attempting to pelt each other to death with balls of cotton wool.

THE DIRECT ELECTIONS OF 1979

The problem of lack of debate contributing to declining interest[5] was clear in the 1979 EP election. There was little difference in policy programmes and little public debate. Turnout (65.7%) was 25% lower than in the subsequent 1980 federal election but marginally above the EC average. However, the findings reported by Elizabeth Noelle-Neumann are perhaps of greater long-term significance given the high turnout in all German elections since the last decade of the nineteenth century. 'Although the data indicate support there is the paradox that interest in the EC has steadily decreased as the first direct election for the European approached.'[6]

In terms of support for integration, two problems, one actual, the other potential emerged in 1979. The first and major problem was the difficulty all parties had in mobilising their adherents to take an active part in the campaign and in persuading their electors to vote at all. The potential problem is that if policy-making elites who now support the European consensus become disillusioned with the EC there is no countervailing broad and deep reservoir of positive support: evidence suggests the opposite. Although apparent consensus on the desirability of European integration remains, this masks a number of difficulties: over enlargement of the EC for which the population is not prepared to make sacrifices; over the lack of 'real enthusiasm for [either] the European idea . . . [or] . . . the historical moment';[7] and the fact that 'the preparedness to go supranational decreases as soon as it becomes imaginable and phrased in everyday terms'.[8] In particular the problem of budgetary contributions is one on which West German public opinion is extremely sensitive – a sensitivity that has increased in line with the determination and, to some extent, success of Mrs Thatcher in shifting some of the burden of budgetary contribution away from the United Kingdom.

This dichotomy between generalised support for the idea of integration and a lack of underlying willingness to carry out some of the measures necessary for its achievement helps explain the contradiction between communautaire rhetoric (the Auswärtiges Amt are permanent European finalists in this) and considerable caution in concrete steps. This gap was very marked under Brandt and was sharply reduced by Schmidt who had an austere Popperian distaste for rhetoric. It has reappeared with a vengeance under Kohl, a politician notably fond of rhetoric. Whilst we would not wish to argue that public opinion acted directly on governmental policy, it did have a significant background effect. It helps explain for instance why the Federal Government put so much effort into the Genscher-Colombo plan.[9] It corresponds precisely to a public opinion which, like the British, is against financial sacrifices but, unlike the British, is in favour of rhetorical declarations of support for European integration.

PUBLIC OPINION IN THE RUN-UP TO THE 1984 EP ELECTIONS

In general the above trends continued though opinion is now sharply critical of the EP. Elizabeth Noelle-Neumann, in late summer 1983, pointed to a decline from 53% in 1979 to 32% in 1982 in the number who saw integration as a high priority (besonders wichtig).[10]

Infratest carried out a large-scale survey (2000 sample) for the Konrad Adenauer Stiftung in October 1983. The major positive element from the EC's viewpoint was the scale of support for the EC as a foreign policy actor.[11] Of all the respondents 69% thought it ought to exert a greater global influence; 62% thought Europe should remain a partner of the USA but should pursue a more independent role than hitherto and 19% felt that the Europeans should pursue a quite independent policy. Less hopeful for the EC, given its lack of past and possible future success in the area is the finding that 70% name the combating of unemployment as having a high priority for the EC.[12] On the EP itself, the findings were extremely grim.[13] Those evaluating the EP positively had fallen from 42% in December 1979 to 23% in October 1983.

WEST GERMAN MEMBERS IN THE DIRECTLY ELECTED EP

After the 1980 Federal Election only Willy Brandt (SPD) and Dr van Aerssen (CDU) held dual mandates. Brandt resigned from the EP in 1983 and van Aerssen ceased to be a Bundestag member (MdB) after the March 1983 election. All the parties had to develop special mechanisms for co-ordination. The FDP set up a European Committee to co-ordinate the work of FDP deputies in both parliaments. In the SPD a co-ordination office, located in the Fraktion run by Helga Köhnen links MdBs and MEPs. SPD MEPs meet about ten times a year in Bonn, each *Arbeitskreis* of the *Bundestagsfraktion* has a 'link man' who liaises with the MEPs and the MEPs have an *Obmann* who reports to the *Fraktionsvorstand*. In the CDU/CSU, three MEPs participate in the *Fraktionsvorstand* in Bonn. There is a system of contacts between specialists analogous to arrangements in the SPD. The CDU has a European office and the MdBs and MEPs meet annually for a round table discussion. In general these arrangements seemed to work reasonably well.

From 1979 to 1983 criticism of the CDU/CSU MEPs was rare though they themselves complained of not being taken seriously at home. We encountered a great deal of dissatisfaction with the four FDP MEPs who were invariably referred to as the 'Viererbande' (Gang of Four). The general difficulties of the FDP meant, however, that they were all safely re-selected to contest the 1984 Euro-election.

Most criticism has been levelled against SPD MEPs. This reflects a basically hostile conservative press whose 'European' correspondents as 'verdiente Europaer' are unlikely to be SPD supporters and the fact that the SPD itself, like the Labour Party, is far more critical of its representatives' performances. However, there have also been mini-scandals. The resignation of Karl Hauenschild (*IG Chemie*), Eugen Loderer (*IG Metall*) and the lesser known Heinz Schmitt, after six months exposed the SPD to the charge (not entirely unfounded) that their candidatures had been a cynical electoral ploy. Mid-way through the session Erdmann Linde (Bochum) resigned claiming to be disillusioned with the EP and the opportunities it offered for political action. He was also extremely critical of the habits and life-styles of his colleagues. Throughout 1979–82 there was a lot of criticism of Brandt's performance as MEP, which focussed on his failure to appear often enough in Strasbourg. He appeared on eighteen days in all. To some extent this criticism was exaggerated, but Brandt's multiple office holding certainly raised problems. The fall of the Schmidt government meant that the whole burden of representing the SPD fell on Brandt who announced that he would resign in October 1982 and did in fact resign in early 1983. Thus the SPD was in a more defensive position about its record than the other parties.

NOMINATION PROCEDURES AND PARTY CANDIDATES

Unlike the other parties the CDU/CSU did not contest the 1984 EP election on the basis of one *Bundesliste* but as in 1979 under separate *Landeslisten*. There had been some indecision about this throughout

1983. Although most statements indicated that the election would be fought on the basis of *Landeslisten*, the CDU Party Conference at the end of May 1983 in Cologne passed a resolution allowing for a *Bundesliste*. The CSU saw such a procedure as inimical to its interests. Kohl justified a *Bundesliste* publicly on the grounds that the *Landeslisten* system was problematic as it meant that candidates from the small states of Bremen, Hamburg and Saarland had to be accommodated on the larger states' lists whereas a *Bundesliste* allowed even the smallest normally to have one representative with a *Grundmandat*.

The nomination process in the CDU caused few surprises though some resented senior MEPs seeking re-election. A number of well-known MEPs did not seek re-election: Hans Katzer, Ernst Müller-Hermann and Ernst Majonica. Kai-Uwe von Hassel dithered for some time when he encountered some opposition in Schleswig-Holstein and decided not to stand though he did speak for the CDU in the campaign. Three prominent MEPs were given surprisingly low places on their respective lists. Dr Philipp von Bismarck and Wilhelm Helms, a former FDP member who has had a somewhat chequered career, were given sixth and eighth place on the Lower Saxony list respectively. Professor Wilhelm Hahn, a former minister in Baden-Würrtemberg, was only placed seventh on the Baden-Würrtemberg list. The CDU's *Spitzenkandidat* was Egon Klepsch.

The CSU list was headed by Dr Fritz Pirkl, formerly Minister for Social Affairs in Bavaria. Hans-August Lücke was not re-selected. The most interesting newcomer at number seven in a safe position on the list was Graf Stauffenberg, former CSU foreign policy spokesman and sharp critic both of the *Bundestag* and the CSU's role in it.

FDP candidates were nominated at a special conference of 400 delegates in Leverküsen on 21–22 January 1984. Three sitting-MEPs – Martin Bangemann, Mechthild von Alemann and Ulrich Irmer – were readily adopted to fill places one, two and four. There was a struggle for place three between the sitting-MEP Heinrich Jurgens and Kurt Jung who failed decisively. The FDP filled the top ten places with one representative from each *Land*. Bangemann was elected *Spitzenkandidat* by 337 votes to nine votes with six abstentions.

The task of replacing Brandt as the SPD *Spitzenkandidat* proved very difficult. The initial choice of the party leadership, Hans Matthöfer, proved unacceptable to SPD MEPs because of his attitudes towards Europe while in office. After prolonged negotiation Katherina Focke was nominated by the SPD Party Executive to succeed Brandt on 27 June 1983. She has long been identified with the European Movement and played a very important role in the Chancellor's Office when Brandt was Chancellor. She quarrelled with Schmidt and was dropped from the government in 1976.

The SPD fought the election on a unified *Bundesliste* of 78 candidates drawn up at a Federal Delegates Conference in Cologne on 18 November 1983. One MEP Helmut Rieger was given the hopeless 52nd place and Rudi Schieler (Freiburg) would have run had he not been offered a hopeless place. Dieter Rogallo who came in to replace Erdmann Linde (placed 25th in 1979) was reported to be very disappointed with his insecure position at thirty-one. Twenty-two candidates were women and the SPD made a major feature of this in the campaign.

The Greens selected their candidates at their *Bundesversammlung* in Karlsruhe on 3–4 March 1984. Most press and public attention focussed on the selection of Brigitte Heinrich, Benni Harlin and Michael Klockner for places 2, 3 and 6 on the list. All have been convicted and sentenced to terms of imprisonment for involvement in terrorist activities, but only Heinrich actually served a term of imprisonment. The Greens chose as their *Spitzenkandidat* Friedrich Wilhelm Gräfe zu Baringdorf. Gräfe was a farmer active in the initiative 'Bauernblatt' but was surprisingly not himself a member of the Greens. At the same conference the principle of rotation (a constant source of tension in the various Green *Fraktionen*) was adopted by 437 votes to 347 votes. Taken at face value this meant that any Green MEPs would serve only half the EP's five-year term and then be replaced by Nachrücker (alternates). Experience of the *Bundestagsfraktion* cautions scepticism as to whether or not this will actually happen.

THE CAMPAIGN

The principal aim of all the parties was to mobilise voters in the face of a pervasive popular feeling of weariness regarding the EC (*Europamüdigkeit*).

The EP campaigned alongside the parties. Unlike in the United Kingdom, the EP was unable to use television in its information campaign due to the legal position in the FRG. So it placed advertisements in magazines or newspapers of a similar type to those elsewhere in the EC. The three basic double-page spreads used in magazines revolved around three key words: 'responsibility' (referring to the cross-border nature of environmental problems), 'solidarity' (dealing with the EP's wish to see increased measures against unemployment) and 'partnership' (with the Third World). The environmental issue featured in the main parties' campaigns although the employment policy area was perhaps a curious choice since it was particularly associated with the SPD's campaign. Furthermore, the issue area demonstrates the EP's weakness in making its activities have an impact on the Council of Ministers. Other publicity materials were made available to candidates and to various public authorities for distribution but the overall impact of the EP's campaign was very small due.

This contrasted strongly with the parties' extensive publicity campaigns. The publicity materials and slogans were dominated by national considerations but made some reference to an EC-wide campaign notably in the (variable as it proved) co-operation of the main German parties in some transnational campaign discussions. In addition, several prominent issues had clear European dimensions. (For example, the wish to reduce customs formalities at the internal frontiers of the EC and the recognition that environmental pollution would require European rather than national measures were issues that were not purely national.) Yet, the broad consensus on integration meant both themes were taken up by all the main parties and were not the subject of any disagreement. Thus 'European' issues tended not to enliven the campaign.

Another aspect of the campaign that deserves mention at this introductory stage concerns the proliferation of parties or 'other political groupings' that put up lists of candidates at the federal or state levels. The main incentive for them was the chance to gain cheap, free or even subsidised publicity. Each party or group was granted a $2\frac{1}{2}$-minute 'spot' during prime viewing time free of charge on both television networks. Moreover, if any won more than 0.5% of the federal vote, they were entitled to a flat-rate, per vote, contribution to their election expenditure. Given that no deposit was required – merely a large number of signatures – it is not surprising that nine groupings[14] not in the *Bundestag* took advantage of these facilities for self-publicity, though their impact was minimal.

THE CDU/CSU

As in federal elections the CDU and the CSU had independent campaigns. However, some features emphasised commonalities between them. As both parties are EPP members some emphasis on shared themes was assured though reference to the EPP was limited.

Indeed, the CSU adopted its electoral programme, the so-called Augsburg Declaration, on 11–12 February 1984 at its European conference: some six weeks before the EPP launched its programme in Rome. Yet this should not be interpreted as disregard for the EPP's activities since this transnational party is pretty cohesive, and the CDU/CSU played a key role in shaping the manifesto. The CDU held its party conference rather later, 9–11 May 1984, so that it could build upon decisions (it had influenced) reached in Rome by the EPP on 2–4 April 1984. To put this into proper perspective, however, we must note that much of the CDU's electoral material had been prepared before the Rome conference so that one should not attribute too much importance to the EPP's role in the CDU campaign on this account.

The CDU's campaign originally centred on presenting itself as 'the European party in Germany'. The early phase of the campaign, until Easter, was fairly low-key with the objective of reviving interest in the EP and mobilising the party itself through regional conferences and by discussing European themes in the party's various internal associations, such as women's and farmers' groups.

Among the European issues in the CDU campaign were environmental protection, completion of the internal market, peace in Europe, calls for 'political union', sexual equality and the importance of the EC to the FRG's reviving economy. All mixed European and national dimensions and had more than a touch of rhetoric. In sum, the campaign was in keeping with the party's slogan of 'Aufwärts mit Deutschland – Mit uns für Europa' (Germany's getting better – with us for Europe). Kohl's prominence in the CDU strategy caused some problems for its campaign. The revelation in 1982 that the Flick concern had been in the habit of making major donations to individual politicians through its manager von Brauchitsch led to the drawing up of legal charges against various politicians of whom Count Lambsdorff, the FDP Economics Minister, was by far the best known. In May 1984, a proposed amnesty for those involved in the illegal payments was closely identified with Kohl. The proposals created major public controversy and were eventually defeated in the *Bundestag*.[15] The affair embarrassed the CDU and made its Kohl-centred campaign correspondingly more difficult. The CDU retorted to media preoccupation with the amnesty issue by playing upon the unpopularity of the metalworkers' proposed 35-hour week and the associated strike, claiming that the trade unions and the SPD were trying to undermine the economic recovery.

The CDU campaign was in keeping with the general razzamatazz of German elections; a CDU ship on the Rhine was a focal point and two low-loaders, decorated as ships, cruised the motorways. Much attention was drawn to the CDU ship when it ran aground near Mannheim at a late stage of the campaign: a fate which the other parties found to be very appropriate.

The CSU's campaign, though similar to the CDU's, differed in four ways. Firstly, the CSU was not affected by the amnesty controversy. Indeed, Strauss would hardly be too bothered about the connected issue of Lambsdorff's fate as his dislike of the FDP is well-known. Another distinction derives from Strauss' major role in the campaign. He was particularly concerned about turnout given a limited degree of dissent within the CSU, and his worry that any fall in the CSU vote might weaken his and the party's position in the Bonn coalition. The result was that his own ideas on integration were aired. He had a more 'Gaullist' view of the EC, reflected in his references to the EC as a power in international politics, to the EC in a security policy context and to pan-Europeanism.[16] His is a much more 'power politics' approach to the EC than Kohl's functionalism.

A third distinction lay in the CSU's programme which emphasised Bavaria's special role in the EC and called for greater involvement of the Länder in EC policy-making.

Finally, the CSU was much more strongly affected by the situation in agriculture. Farmers represent a much greater proportion of the CSU's core support (*Stammwählerschaft*). The CSU was itself under attack through holding the agricultural portfolio in the Bonn cabinet. The farmers' response to a potential fall in income of up to 30% was to mount a vigorous campaign. In some rural areas electoral meetings were heavily attended by farmers prompted by the Bavarian Farmers' Union. There were reports of farmers spontaneously resigning from the CSU at such meetings. In all, these were scenes of substantive policy controversiality unparalleled elsewhere in the campaign.

The CSU tried to mobilise its organisations against a threatened boycott of the EP elections by farmers.[17] It put pressure on and in the Bonn coalition to pass a package of national measures to alleviate the hardship farmers would face. After the election Strauss claimed that the CSU would have performed much worse but for his 'massive intervention in Bonn' for these measures.

THE FDP

The FDP's campaign was hampered by financial constraints. The main focus of attention was a train which traversed the FRG and neighbouring countries, calling in Münster for the party conference on 2–3 June 1984. The lack of interest in this train reflected the FDP's difficulties. Its campaign was based around that of the ELD and much greater attention was paid to the transnational campaign than for the other parties.[18] The FDP has been influential both in the ELD and in the EP Liberal Group, partly because of the importance of Martin Bangemann.[19] The FDP's change of coalition allegiance in 1982 and the amnesty issue undermined its campaign. As a result of 'the change' the FDP has become rather introspective. In particular, the criticism of the way that party leader and Foreign Minister, Hans-Dietrich Genscher, personally pushed through 'the change' led to the exodus of some left-wing Liberals and it caused concern also about the party's internal decision-making procedures. With Genscher's announcement before the Münster conference that he would stand down as party leader in 1986 (subsequently brought forward to early 1985), further speculation over the leadership emerged. Another impact of the change of government was to render the FDP's pro-European stance less distinctive. Genscher could not demonstrate through his 'European Act' initiative[20] that his party was 'the' European party in government as this standpoint was less credible than in the Schmidt coalition, especially since this was precisely the basis of the CDU's strategy. Thus the FDP could not capitalise effectively on Genscher's European reputation. His calls for voters to rally around the FDP to avoid a socialist-communist majority in the EP and criticism of the SPD as the 'Streikpartei' (because of the metalworkers' strike for a 35-hour week) hardly did justice to the party's governmental record on EC affairs. Only the slogan 'Wir brechen Bahn für Europa' – We are pioneering for Europe – remained and the half-empty train.

THE SPD

The SPD campaigned on national issues as it felt it could win voters from disillusioned supporters of the Bonn coalition. The EC dimension was played down and thus links with the CSP-Manifesto. EP President Dankert appeared on an SPD platform but there was little other transnational campaigning. Nevertheless, the SPD did present itself as a pro-European party through its main slogan 'Macht Europa stark' (Make Europe strong). The triumvirate of party chairman, Willy Brandt, parliamentary leader Hans-Jochen Vogel and the Prime Minister of North Rhine-Westphalia, Johannes Rau spoke against the coalition's record in government; and notably the 'amnesty' proposals, the failure of the coalition to secure any improvement in the economy and on social policy cuts. They saw the EP election as one of three chances to oppose the centre-right coalition.[21]

The SPD's programme was agreed in Cologne in November 1983. The campaign focused rather more on European issues until May 1984 when several key themes were stressed and Katharina Focke played a relatively important role. The first main area emphasised was the wish to see a common employment and industrial policy in the EC: something which the SPD had supported in the EP but which Schmidt had shown no sympathy towards during his chancellorship. A second area was a strengthening of Europe's independent identity in international relations. This policy was brought out in a discussion document by Horst Ehmke: 'Programm für eine Selbstbehauptung Europas'. This foresaw employing the Franco–German friendship as the basis for a strengthened European role in foreign affairs. It also envisaged a strengthened European arm of the Atlantic Alliance and was presumably aimed at those disenchanted with American defence policy and its European implications. This theme continued during the later stages of the campaign and was positively received.

Another theme taken up early on was women's rights. Photographs of the SPD candidates showed all the women candidates in the front rows even though many of them were in hopeless places on the party list. When the campaign started in May 1984, Focke led a 'Frauen-Tournee für die Europawahl' with a view to enlivening women voters. However, the team of eight EP candidates found the greatest response when criticising the Kohl government's cuts in maternity grant rather than when discussing EC themes.

This tour was one of the many side-shows orchestrated by SPD General Secretary, Peter Glotz. Perhaps the most novel was 'Katharina's Circus': a real circus with European themes brought up in various parts of the programme. From mid-May to mid-June 1984 the circus toured 31 cities and was well-received, although it is unclear whether it had the desired political effect. The launching of the campaign in Essen introduced two slogans which overshadowed 'Macht Europa stark'. These were 'Lasst die Wende wackeln' and 'Der Stimmzettel muss zum Denkzettel für die Rechtswende werden'. Both refer to the change of government, 'die Wende', and mean approximately: 'make "the change" totter' and 'the ballot paper must be used as a warning about the change to the right'.

There were many reasons why the European accents were put into the background during the campaign proper. The SPD leadership was even more worried than other party leaders about the extent to which its supporters could be mobilised by European issues. A number of surveys indicated that up to 25% of the party's core voters would not vote and the SPD could not rely on Brandt's effect as *Spitzenkandidat*. The resignation of the three trade union leaders reduced the trade union nexus as a mobilising agent. Only Heinz-Oskar Vetter, former secretary of the German trade union confederation and an MEP seeking re-election, was left to mobilise the trade unionist vote. These factors would always have been likely to persuade the SPD to run a campaign based on domestic issues. The amnesty merely strengthened this inclination. The metalworkers' strike for a 35-hour week was unpopular but it would have been impossible for the SPD not to identify itself with the aims. This issue thus further emphasised domestic politics, although not particularly to the SPD's benefit. Thus campaign controversy focused on domestic politics.

THE GREENS

The Greens' campaign introduced a rather more critical perspective on the EC and enlivened the campaign somewhat. No transnational party grouping of ecologists had existed in the past but co-operation did take place prior to the 1984 elections, notably at a conference in Liège, 31 March–1 April 1984. The German party found itself at odds with some rather more strictly ecological parties in the Low Countries due to its espousal of radical policies on non-environmental matters, such as disarmament. The Dutch ecologists, De Groenen (European Greens), were unhappy at its wish to allow a radical left-wing Dutch grouping to participate in such transnational co-operation. However, the real significance of transnational ecological parties remains for the future because the German party did not play up this dimension in its campaign. The broad transnational manifesto called for a Europe of the peoples and the regions. But virtually all themes were covered in the Greens' national electoral programme which added radical policies regarding US missiles.

Like the SPD, the Greens criticised the CAP, although not purely on the grounds of its cost but also for its encouragement of mass techniques (to the cost of the smallholder) and of pesticide use. The Greens opposed the EC's development into a superpower. Like other parties they stressed the need for equal opportunities for women and committed the party to defending the consumer in the CAP. Thus the Greens introduced some new themes into the debate. Their strategy was encapsulated in the title of their campaign booklet: 'Think globally; act locally!' Whilst criticising all the other parties for their various involvements in the Flick party finance affair, the Greens ran a very cheap and disorganised campaign having agreed their programme at a special conference in March 1984.

SUMMARY

The European themes of the election campaign played a secondary role in proceedings. The 'amnesty' proposal dominated the campaign in its later stages both in terms of debate and of media coverage. Newspapers covered rather less of the campaign than anticipated due to a printers' strike which led to the irregular appearance of some major newspapers or short editions of only eight pages. However, it is unlikely that this contributed to the lack of public interest which is a longer term phenomenon. Finally, it is worth mentioning three calls for a boycott of the EP elections. One came in a full-page article in *Stern* magazine where Rolf Winter argued that a low turnout would be the best way of signalling that a real Europe should not consist of national self-interest, bureaucracy in Brussels and a powerless EP. The two others were in the form of threats: by farmers in Bavaria and by wine-growers in the Rhineland-Palatinate.[22]

THE RESULTS

The outcome of the elections broadly confirmed expectations.[23] The most significant features were: the much lower turnout compared to the first EP elections; the FDP's failure to surmount the 5% barrier; the Greens continuing electoral success; and the SPD's inability to capitalise on the centre-right coalition's indifferent performance since taking office in Autumn 1982.

The decline in turnout from 65.7% (1979) to 56.8% (1984) confirmed poll predictions. Surveys showed that, between January and June 1984, awareness of the EP elections doubled (from 27% to 52%) but did not help respondents to judge the EP's work. Whilst supporters of the coalition partners had a marginally more positive view than those of the SPD and the Greens, the impression was fundamentally indifferent

TABLE 9.1   *The June 1984 elections results compared with 1979 and 1983*
(% of votes cast)

	EP election 17 June 1984 %	Bundestag election 6 Mar. 1983 %	EP election 10 June 1979 %
CDU	37.5	38.2	39.1
SPD	37.4	38.2	40.8
CSU	8.5	10.6	10.1
FDP	4.8	7.0	6.0
Greens	8.2	5.6	3.2
Others	3.7	0.5	0.8
Turnout:	56.8	89.1	65.7

SOURCE   West German Embassy, London (official results).

or negative. All agreed that the EC had suffered setbacks since 1979. Hence the fall in turnout must be interpreted first and foremost as a decline in interest in EC (and EP) affairs. The differential turnout between the 1983 federal elections and the 1984 Euro-elections amounted to no less than 32.3%. This is not the full picture. The Rhineland-Palatinate (76.4%) and the Saarland (78.5%) had turnout levels some 20% above the federal average (56.8%) due to the simultaneous holding of local elections.

Three other less important factors influenced turnout. One concerns the CSU Bavarian government's decision to hold a referendum on whether environmental objectives should be included in the state's constitution by amendment. Although there was a view that this step was taken in order to get voters to the polls for the simultaneous *European* elections, its impact was minimal. Not only did Bavaria still manage to achieve the lowest state turnout but the total absence of controversy over incorporating the proposed measures into the constitution rendered the referendum rather irrelevant.[24] A second aspect concerning turnout was the increase in invalid votes. Although the total represented only 1.6% (1979: 0.9%), the figures for Saarland (4%) and the Rhineland-Palatinate (3.9%) were conspicuous. In the former case, the array of simultaneous elections to three tiers of local government evidently confused some voters. In the latter case, many votes were spoilt deliberately in connection with wine-growers' protests.[25]

A final specific point to be noted in connection with the low turnout is that it did have a small discriminatory effect between the parties. The

Forschungsgruppe Wahlen survey judged that the Greens, CDU and the CSU performed marginally better because their voters are mobilised easily, whilst the low turnout was to the SPD's disadvantage.

To conclude on the turnout in June 1984 some more general explanations are also in order. Some voters are clearly reluctant to participate in the election of what they judge to be a powerless institution. The absence of constituencies (unlike in federal elections) makes the candidates much more remote and this is a small contributory factor to the low turnout. The remoteness of the next federal election (March 1987) lowered the national stakes. And, finally, the absence of major conflict between the parties over the desirability of integration (excepting perhaps the Greens) reduced the competitive nature of the Euro-election.[26]

Euro-elections have been incorporated into the national electoral cycle.[27] Themes are integrated into national party strategies or the national political 'game'. These developments are by no means exclusive to the FRG; Pridham explains similar developments in Italy elsewhere in this volume.

Certain features about the result are common to the CDU and CSU: both suffered losses compared to 1979. At the same time it is important not to see the 1984 result as a true test of the national political balance. On behalf of the CSU, Strauss saw the result explained primarily by farmers' disaffection with the party and re-emphasised his criticism of the Greens since three of their seven MEPs have 'criminal' records. About a month after the EP election he was reported to be pressing his claims for a cabinet portfolio in Bonn again. The resignation of Lambsdorff and the FDP's failure to win EP seats lay behind his call.

The FDP's failure to achieve 5% of the vote – the first time that this has happened in an election conducted throughout the FRG – had a dramatic impact. The absence of FDP MEPs in Strasbourg makes the EP Liberal Group a mockery given the absence of British Liberals. It must be unique that an important governing party is not in the EP.

We have noted already factors that de-railed the FDP's campaign. Also critical was the FDP's inability to play its 'moderation card' by calling for support (second votes) in order to restrict coalition partners' 'extremes'. Since the EP elections do not lead to the formation of a government and since vote-splitting cannot exist in these elections, the FDP's ability to pick up floating voters was severely hampered as in state elections.

With Lambsdorff's eventual replacement as Economics Minister by Bangemann a week after the elections only a temporary halt has been

TABLE 9.2   *The distribution of seats in the EP, 1979 and 1984*

	1984	1979
CDU	34	34
SPD	33	35
CSU	7	8
FDP	–	4
Greens	7	–
Total*	81	81

*Only 78 MEPs are directly elected; 3 are nominated by the Berlin Chamber of Deputies (CDU = 2; SPD = 1).
SOURCE   West German Embassy, London.

made regarding the FDP's turmoil. If Bangemann is to lead the FDP out of this crisis – he is the most likely successor to Genscher as party leader – he will have to make a rapid impression on the public for whom he is little known. The national impact of the FDP's performance in the EP elections was substantial but before writing off the FDP we must remember that it has recovered in the past. However, this defeat may be the most significant as it followed a succession of defeats in state elections.

The SPD vote fell relative to the 1983 federal election. Yet, the SPD's performance in June 1984 confirms existing trends but its failure to stage a come-back, despite the coalition's problems, causes concern at SPD headquarters. The SPD's attempt to make the elections a 'Testwahl' failed.

The EP elections confirmed that the Greens will have a lasting impact on German politics. In the new EP they will be in the vanguard of a transnational ecological group's attempts to change the EC's agenda. Whilst it is unlikely to succeed in getting action on disarmament it may inject a new urgency into the EC's environmental policy. It will also be interesting to see whether the Greens can successfully defend consumers *vis-à-vis* the CAP. One final point worth mentioning in order to underline the Greens' good performance is that they were confronted with several other challengers for the protest vote, especially the 'peace list'. To achieve their best vote at the federal level – up from 5.6% in the 1983 federal election to 8.2% in the 1984 EP election – under such circumstances shows depth in the party's support.

The minor parties achieved a result not in line with other federal or *Land* elections. The unprecedented size of the collective vote can be explained, first, as a protest vote against the EP elections and, second, in terms of what voters perceived as the irrelevance of the elections. This implies positive support for a particular minor party under circumstances where the stakes are low.

ELECTORAL FINANCE

The performance of the minor parties leads us to the role of electoral finance in the EP election campaign. There is no doubt that the availability of a public platform – in the form of television 'spots' – was an encouragement to minor parties. Further assistance came from the looser qualifications necessary for eligibility as candidate-parties by comparison with those prevailing for federal elections. These factors led to the submission and acceptance of nine lists from minor parties and other electoral groupings. Moreover, upon exceeding the magic figure of 0.5% of the vote, parties receive from the public purse a contribution to their campaign expenditure. Prospects of exceeding this figure may be greater in an EP election where the stakes are lower. The fact that 'other parties' secured 3.7% of the vote appears to bear this out. In 1984 two lists – the 'peace list' (with 1.3% of the vote) and the right-wing NPD (with 0.8% of the vote) – qualified for such financial aid. Two others with 0.4% of the vote each came close: the *Zentrum* (anti-abortion law) and the *Frauenpartei* (pro-women's rights). Of the four, only the NPD is a party in the sense of the legal position which prevails for federal elections. It is open to question whether the electoral law should allow Euro-elections to be used in this manner. The reason for the looser provisions was to facilitate the direct participation of transnational parties.

Other serious questions emerge from the party finance system and apply to all parties. Prior to the 1984 Euro-elections the *Bundestag* decided to increase the sum payable per vote for qualifying parties from DM3.50 to DM5.00. A further measure was taken specifically for the Euro-election. This was the decision to desist from the normal practice of paying this sum per vote cast. Instead each party's performance is re-calculated to a notional figure based on the electorate as a whole. It does not require too much ability at mental arithmetic to establish that parties receive much more money if the turnout is assumed to have been 100% rather than the actual figure of 56.8%. The net effect was to give each qualifying party about DM8.81 per vote cast. The combined effect of these two decisions was to increase party finance to over twice

TABLE 9.3   *Party finance and the 1984 European elections*

Party/group	Estimated expenditure (million DM)	Aid available (million DM)	Profit (million DM)
CDU	50.0	82.0	32.0
SPD	27.0	81.9	54.9
CSU	6.6	18.6	12.0
Greens	1.0	17.8	16.8
FDP	6.7	10.5	3.8
Total Major Parties	91.3	210.8	119.5
Peace List	n.a.	2.8	n.a.
NPD	n.a.	1.7	n.a.

SOURCES   Estimated expenditure from *Wirtschaftswoche*, 25 May 1984 and *Handelsblatt* 5 June 1984; aid available is based on the authors' calculations.

as much as what would have been payable previously. Party treasurers are not happy with this situation. They justified the decision – voted for by the parties themselves(!) – on the basis that greater expenditure would be needed to mobilise voters in Euro-elections. Of that there is little doubt. However, equally surely, some parties have managed to make a healthy profit on Euro-elections. There is also the rather dubious situation where each of the parties would have got the same sum of money provided that their share of the vote remained the same but regardless of whether the turnout was 80% or 20% or any other figure. The position hardly seems conducive to ensuring that the parties carry out their campaigns in the most cost-effective manner. It is perhaps not too surprising that a 'showy' campaign was run by some parties.

All the parties represented in the 1979–84 EP had other sources of public financial support – 43 million ECUs (about £24.8 million) were allocated to the EP party groups and 69% went to the groups existing prior to the elections, the remainder being shared out on the basis of the new EP party groups from all member states. The availability of European money over and above German electoral finance raises further questions about how this situation can be justified. Indeed, a complaint has been lodged with the Federal Constitutional Court over the constitutionality of giving financial aid for expenditure which has not been incurred. At the time of writing the court's decision is still awaited.

CONCLUSION

The 1984 EP election was clearly regarded by the major and minor parties as primarily an extension of the national political struggle, and as a means of subsidising their primary goal: national political power. The election was in line with a gradual weakening in public and elite attitudes. An internal paper of the Federal Government, commenting on a public opinion poll conducted during the campaign by EMNID, referred to West Germans' feelings towards the EC as being 'characterised by considerable inner distance'.[28] The same survey indicated also that, although West Germans still gave formal priority to European integration and the majority were in favour of faster progress, they were against any further loss of national independence.

NOTES AND REFERENCES

*The authors are grateful to Inter Nationes, Meyer zu Nattrup, Oskar Niedermayer, Otto Schmuck and Wulf Schönbohm. The usual disclaimer applies.

1. G. Pridham, 'The European Policy of Franz Josef Strauss and its Implications for the Community', *Journal of Common Market Studies*, 18 (1980) 314.
2. W. E. Paterson, *The SPD and European Integration* (Farnborough: Saxon House, 1974).
3. W. E. Paterson, 'Problems of Party Government in a British Perspective' in H. Döring and G. Smith (eds), *Party Government and Political Culture in Britain and West Germany* (London: Macmillan, 1981) pp. 101–15.
4. W. E. Paterson, 'Foreign Policy and Regime Stability – the case of the Federal Republic', in R. Tilford (ed.), *The Ostpolitik and Political Change* (Farnborough: Saxon House, 1975) pp. 23–44.
5. E. Noelle-Neumann, 'Phantom Europe: Thirty Years of Survey Research on German Attitudes towards European Integration', in L. Hurwitz (ed.), *Contemporary Perspectives on European Integration* (London: Aldwych Press, 1980) pp. 53–74.
6. Ibid., p. 58.
7. Ibid., p. 55.
8. Ibid., p. 60.
9. The lack of cost and the nature of German public opinion help explain the general popularity of European Political Cooperation (EPC) with West German decision-makers.
10. E. Noelle-Neumann and G. Herdegen, 'Die Europäische Gemeinschaft in der öffentlichen Meinung: Informationsdefizite und enttäuschte Erwartungen', *Integration*, 6 (1983) 95–105.
11. Konrad-Adenauer-Stiftung, 'Europa im Spiegel der Umfrageforschung', Bonn, 1983, 12.
12. Ibid., p. 41.

13. Ibid., p. 23.
14. These were die *Friedensliste* (peace list), *Europäische Arbeitspartei* (European Workers' Party), *Zentrum* (campaigning against the abortion law), *Bayern Partei* (Bavarian Party), the *Europäische Föderalistische Partei* (European Federalist Party), *Frauenpartei* (Women's party), the rightwing *Nationaldemokratische Partei Deutschlands* (NPD), *Ökologisch-Demokratische Partei* (Ecological Democratic Party) and the *Wählergemeinschaft mündiger Bürger* (the so-called electoral group of responsible citizens).
15. For details of the Bundestag amnesty debate see *Das Parlament*, 9/16 June 1984.
16. Pridham, op. cit., pp. 312–32.
17. For example, the *Arbeitsgemeinschaft Landwirtschaft* of the CSU's 'Aufruf zur Europawahl', *Bayern-Kurier*, 9 June 1984.
18. The ELD programme was agreed in December 1983 in Athens. The 1982 ELD statutes committed member parties to campaign on a joint programme.
19. Genscher's international standing and the FDP's domestic strength (in governmental terms) gave Bangemann a key role in the EP's Liberal Group.
20. Eventually adopted in watered-down form as the 'Solemn Declaration on European Union', June 1983.
21. The other opportunities were the local elections in September 1984 and 1985 state elections, both in North-Rhine Westphalia.
22. *Stern*, 14 June 1984. The wine-growers boycott threat was aimed at the local elections as specific issues were but marginally connected to the EC.
23. This section draws on the survey results done by the Mannheim University Forschungsgruppe Wahlen, 'Europawahl: eine Analyse der 2. Direktwahl zum Europaparlament am 17 Juni 1984', Mannheim, 20 June 1984.
24. Six per cent voted against the proposals with 4.2% spoilt ballot papers presumed to have been Green supporters who felt the changes would be inadequate.
25. The year 1926 was written on many spoilt ballot slips to refer to the year when enraged wine growers set fire to a tax office at Bernkastel.
26. On the cross-party consensus, see S. Bulmer, 'West German Political Parties and the European Community: Structures without function?' *Political Studies* 31 (1983) 566–83.
27. On the 1983 election see R. Irving and W. Paterson, 'West Germany: the Machtwechsel of 1982–83', *Parliamentary Affairs* 36 (1983) 417–35.
28. *Tagesspiegel* (Berlin), 22 April 1984.

10 The Netherlands

ISAAC LIPSCHITS

By Dutch standards turnout on 14 June 1984 to elect the 25 Dutch MEPs was unusually low. Admittedly, since the repeal of compulsory voting in 1970, the Dutch have become used to turnouts below 90%. Yet the 1984 turnout of 50.5% was below that of any other post-1970 election, whether European, national, provincial or local. This low turnout was one of the most notable features of the 1984 Dutch EP elections.

THE PARTY SYSTEM

In 1982, in the last national election before the 1984 EP election, twenty parties took part: twelve won seats in the Second Chamber,[1] and the three major parties, the Dutch Labour Party (PvdA), Christian Democratic Appeal (CDA) and the Dutch Liberal Party (VVD) won 47, 45 and 36 seats respectively.

Dutch parties belong essentially to four political families: the socialist/communist, the protestant–Christian, the Catholic and the liberal family. The socialist/communist family includes the PvdA, the Pacifist Socialist Party (PSP) and the Communist Party of the Netherlands (CPN). In 1946 the pre-war Social Democratic Labour Party (SDAP) joined several small protestant–Christian, Catholic and liberal groups to form the PvdA. The CPN can be traced back to 1909 when the SDAP split over the controversy caused by the revisionist movement and a small group of party members seceded to form a separate party, which after the Russian Revolution of 1917 called itself the Communist Party. The PSP started in 1957 with the fusion of radical elements from the PvdA, some dissatisfied CPN members and a pre-war group of revolutionary socialists.

The Christian Democratic Appeal (CDA) is the outgrowth of a federation of three religious parties which hitherto belonged to either the protestant–Christian or the Catholic family. The CDA was organised as a federation in 1975. In 1980 the three component parties merged. Such close and organised co-operation between protestant–Christians and Catholics is a new and remarkable development in Dutch politics. Two of the three parties forming the CDA previously belonged to the protestant–Christian family: the Anti-Revolutionary Party (ARP) and the Christian Historical Union (CHU). Founded in 1879, the ARP was the oldest political party. In the 1890s, controversy arose over the issues of suffrage expansion and political co-operation with Catholics; several groups left the ARP and formed the CHU in 1908. Ten years later another group broke away from the ARP and formed the Political Calvinist Party (SGP). This group rejected separation of church and state, wished to subordinate the state to the church and opposed any co-operation with Catholics. Directly after World War II another group left the ARP for theological reasons; in 1948 it set up its own party: the National Reformed Political Association (GPV). Finally, in 1975, a group opposed to the ARP's radical–Evangelic policy and to fusion with the CDA, left the ARP and formed the Reformed Political Federation (RPF).

The Catholic political family has been dominated by one big party since the turn of the century. After World War II that party changed its name to Catholic People's Party (KVP). In 1980 the KVP merged with the ARP and the CHU into the CDA. During the KVP's existence, the Political Party of Radicals (PPR) split off in 1968; its development was such, however, that it cannot be included in the Catholic political family. If anything, given both the lack of religious appeals in its programmes or policy and its critique of contemporary socio-economic structures, it is closer to the socialist/communist family. Soon after the CDA's founding, a group of members who felt that its policy was too conservative split off in 1981 and formed the Evangelic People's Party (EVP).[2]

Finally, the liberal political family embraced a number of parties before World War II. One helped set up the PvdA and another re-established a separate party in 1946. Several pre-war liberals who joined the PvdA soon discovered their folly and left in 1948 to set up with the liberal party a new Dutch Liberal Party (VVD).

Related, but not clearly a member of the liberal family, the Democrats '66 (D'66) are hard to fix in the political spectrum. The leaders who set up the D'66 were largely former PvdA or VVD members aiming to advance a new type of progressive liberalism as a viable alternative to the PvdA's socialism, the VVD's liberalism and the CDA's christian democracy. Still, more difficult to place is the Centre Party (CP), founded in 1980, that bases its policy on aversion to foreign elements in Dutch society. Foreign workers are seen as a threat to the purity of the white Dutch population. The CP is deemed to have fascist elements, and to be a racist, extreme right party.[3]

The multiplicity of Dutch parties is not without its rationale. In the past, four warring and internally divided ideological families dominated Dutch politics. They still do but significant changes are occurring: the CDA, D'66 and CP are perhaps the best examples of new parties trying to transcend old political relationships.

THE 1979 EUROPEAN ELECTIONS

By Dutch standards, an unusually small number of voters turned out for the first Euro-election: 58.1%. Some four million citizens abstained with a 'Euro-Hangover', as one of the newspapers called it. Several explanations were offered for the low turnout: unfamiliarity with the activities of European politicians, criticism against EC policy and especially against the EP's limited powers, nationalist feelings against the idea of a united Europe, and extensive media coverage of the activities of outspoken opponents of the Euro-election.

Compared to the 1977 national election, the 1979 election results had striking features. First, two parties – CDA and D'66 – were big winners in that they improved their positions. Second, the PvdA suffered a serious setback and the VVD also suffered losses. Finally, despite the fact that small parties stood no chance of winning a seat in the EP (because of the electoral quota), they either maintained or strengthened their electoral positions. Remarkably, compared to the 1977 national election, of the two governing parties one (CDA) was winning and the other (VVD) losing votes, while of the two main opposition parties also one (D'66) was winning and the other (PvdA) was losing votes.

The PvdA is a CSP member. PvdA leaders were disappointed with the 1979 election outcome as their party ceased to be the most popular party in the country. This hit the leaders hard because the PvdA had placed such emphasis in the campaign on replacing the CDA–VVD coalition cabinet. Low turnout was blamed for the party's poor showing. But important also was dissent in the PvdA over the issue of holding Euro-elections.

The leaders of the CDA – aligned with the EPP – were pleased with the election outcome. The CDA became the largest party in the country. The party had conducted a vigorous campaign with a consistent emphasis on the European dimension of the election. The leaders of the VVD – aligned with the ELD – also were satisfied with the outcome, although their party had lost votes, but fewer than public opinion polls had predicted. Yet, D'66 with no Euro-party alignment was the true victor.

Three Dutch MEPs did not serve the whole EP term. Dr Anne Vondeling, PvdA list leader, was killed in a car crash in November 1979, and succeeded by Mrs Phili Viehoff-Maag. The two D'66 MEPs did not get on with each other: one, Mrs Suzanne Dekker, stood for and was elected to the Second Chamber in May 1981. She was succeeded by Mr Doeke Eisma. Due to ill-health, Mr Frans van der Gun (CDA) gave up his Euro-seat in December 1981. Mr Joep Mommersteeg succeeded him. There were no problems in filling the vacancies in the EP. Voting is based on party lists and if a vacancy arises, it goes to the next on the list.

THE ELECTORAL SYSTEM

For the 1984 election, the 1979 electoral system was amended. Whereas for the 1979 election Dutch citizens living in another EC member state were allowed to vote via embassies and consulates, in 1984 they could have a postal vote if they applied for it no later than 28 days before the election. 17 149 made use of this provision.

The 1984 election took place on Thursday 14 June: in view of the religious composition of the population, a Sunday election having been ruled out along with Saturday (the weekend) and Friday (leading up to the weekend) both thought likely to deter turnout.

According to electoral law counting ballots is public: in every polling station the count is open to the public. But the election outcome had to be kept secret until Sunday evening when the elections would be completed throughout the EC: from a European perspective it was feared that earlier publication of the Dutch outcome would influence the results in other member states. For the 1979 election the government got the Second Chamber, on the smallest possible majority, to agree that ballot boxes would be sealed on Thursday evening (7 June 1979) and the ballots counted on Monday (11 June 1979). There was a great deal of opposition to this as the Netherlands would be one of the first countries to vote and the very last to announce the election results, since in most other states the count was on Sunday evening. In 1984 another solution was adopted. In every polling station the ballots were counted in public on Thursday evening (14 June 1984), but the results for the Netherlands as a whole were kept secret until Sunday evening (17 June 1984).

The Dutch electoral system is based on proportional representation without an electoral threshold. In the case of the Second Chamber with its 150 seats, the electoral quota is 0.67% (1/150) of the valid votes cast. A party that does not win 0.67% of the valid votes is not eligible to participate in the distribution of seats.

For the Euro-elections, the quota is at 4% six times higher. For the majority of parties in the Second Chamber this quota is too high. Eight of the 12 parties that won one or more seats in the 1982 national election did so with less than 4% of the valid votes. The 4% quota places an insurmountable obstacle to small parties unless they find a way to combine their strengths.

THE NATIONAL POLITICAL SETTING

According to an unwritten rule of constitutional law, any cabinet must have the support of a majority in the Second Chamber. In 1982, the CDA, PvdA and VVD accounted for 82.8% of the vote.[4] This, plus the above rule, makes it inevitable that at least two of the three big parties form a coalition cabinet. However, since the 1950s, the PvdA and the VVD have excluded one another from coalition cabinets. This augments the CDA's position: it can opt to form a cabinet with either the PvdA or the VVD as long as it has a majority in the Second Chamber with either the PvdA or the VVD.[5] The PvdA especially dislikes this situation and has consistently tried to force the CDA to say before the national election with whom it wanted to govern.

In the 1977 national election the PvdA increased its seats from 43 to 53 in the Second Chamber. With 33.8% of the valid votes it became the party with the largest electoral support in the country. This victory was particularly noteworthy in as much as the PvdA had been the major party of the governing coalition with its leader, Mr Joop den Uyl, serving as Prime Minister. It was expected that he would continue in this role in a new coalition but the PvdA put such tough demands to the CDA that after 170 days of negotiations the attempt to reconstruct a den Uyl-cabinet failed. The CDA then undertook negotiations with the

VVD and within two weeks formed a cabinet. This led to bad feeling between the PvdA and the CDA. The CDA–VVD cabinet served its full four year term. The 1981 national election result left the CDA and the VVD without a majority in the Second Chamber.[6] After 108 days of negotiations a CDA–PvdA–D'66 cabinet was formed, with the CDA leader as prime minister. Within a year, new elections had to be held. The CDA–VVD combination recovered the majority in the Second Chamber and formed a government with CDA leader Ruud Lubbers as prime minister which was still in office come the 1984 EP elections. The PvdA, still led by den Uyl, was the main opposition party, particularly opposed to the government's socio-economic policy and the deployment of cruise missiles in the Netherlands. The PvdA rejected the government's policy of retrenchment with its direct consequences for public expenditure, unemployment and cuts in social welfare allowances. Shortly before the 1984 elections, the PvdA announced a plan for more public expenditure, increased employment and less sharp cuts in the social welfare allowances that was to feature in the 1984 election campaign, though rejected by the government. The problem of deploying cruise missiles played a still greater role. According to NATO plans, the Netherlands was to deploy 48 cruise missiles. The PvdA opposed deployment under any circumstances. The VVD favoured deploying all 48 cruise missiles. The CDA hesitated over whether accepting or rejecting deployment, and if the former, whether to deploy 16, 32 or all 48 cruise missiles.

On 1 June 1984, two weeks before Euro-election day, the government announced its decision to deploy cruise missiles at a later date.[7] The CDA's and VVD's parliamentary wings insisted that this decision be debated by the Second Chamber before the EP elections. That debate took place the day before those elections. It was broadcast by television from the morning of 13 June until the early hours of 14 June, election day. The government narrowly won the vote but the debate influenced the EP elections.

PARTIES AND THE 1984 ELECTION

There was never any doubt that the four largest parties, the CDA, PvdA, VVD and D'66, would take part in the EP elections. Given the 4% electoral quota, the other parties prospects were hopeless unless they formed joint lists. In 1979 such attempts had failed. The three small protestant-Christian parties (GPV, RPF and SGP) feared that forming a joint list would cause a loss of their separate identities. This was especially true for the GPV and the SGP, and to a lesser degree for the RPF which was the first to agree to a joint list. The GPV devoted a party congress to this problem in December 1983. The executive's proposal for an individual GPV list was voted down by the congress which opted by 108 to 68 votes for a joint list with the RPF and the SGP[8] under certain conditions. To safeguard their identities, the three parties had to campaign individually on their own manifestos; and the manifestos of the RPF and of the SGP had to be acceptable to the GPV. Finally and most importantly, despite the joint list, it had to be clear that unbridgeable gaps in theological conceptions between them remained. The SGP accepted these conditions, albeit under strong protest from some of its members.[9]

The small left of centre parties (PSP, CPN, PPR and EVP) faced a similar problem over a joint list but one complicated by the 'green movement'. Since the 1970s numerous small national, regional and local green organisations had been founded. Under the leadership of Mr Bas de Gaay Fortman, one of the PPR leaders, a form of co-operation between these organisations was effected in the so-called Green Platform. During 1983 negotiations were held between it and the four small left parties with a view to forming a joint list for the 1984 EP elections but not all members of the Green Platform were leftists.

A PPR congress in November 1983 opted for a joint list, opposed by a minority who were not convinced of the leftists' feelings of the Green Platform. As one put it: 'If green is not left, I will not be green'. A week later the CPN accepted the idea of a joint list against a minority opposition that disliked the Green Platform. The same day a PSP congress sanctioned the joint list though again many disliked the Green Platform and the PSP congress even voted for a resolution deploring the participation of the Green Platform. The EVP congress in December 1983 opposed a joint list not because it disliked the Green Platform but because, as a split-off from the CDA, it hoped to gain votes from the CDA in national elections. If it co-operated in a joint list with left parties, especially with the communists, it would have to have given up hope of ever winning over CDA-followers. The EVP decided not to take part in the 1984 EP elections.

So, the PPR, the CPN and the PSP accepted a joint list with the Green Platform. However, in December 1983, the latter divided over those favouring and those opposing a joint list with small left parties. Those in favour called themselves the Green Party Netherlands (GPN) and joined the small left parties. Those against a joint list called themselves the European Greens and devised their own list. Further-more the Centre Party (see above) and 'God be with Us' (see note 3) entered the electoral race. So there were nine lists, which were num-bered by the Electoral Council as follows: (1) Christian Democratic Appeal/EPP; (2) Dutch Labour Party/CSP; (3) Dutch Liberal Party/ ELD; (4) Democrats '66; (5) SGP, RPF, GPV; (6) CPN, Green Party Netherlands, PPR, PSP; (7) European Greens; (8) Centre Party; and (9) 'God be with Us'.[10]

ELECTION PROGRAMMES[11]

The CDA campaigned on the EPP manifesto which called for a greater unity in Europe. The Christian Democrats call themselves convinced federalists. In the economic field, they advocated measures to increase employment on the basis of an economic recovery arguing that full-employment was impossible in the short-run and that present employ-ment should be redistributed among more people. They were for keeping but adjusting the CAP, common measures to protect the environment, greater co-operation in security matters and more co-operation within NATO, the EC's further democratisation, strengthen-ing the EP, and better co-ordination of aid to developing countries.

The PvdA campaigned on the CSP manifesto and on its own national election programme calling for economic recovery, with selective economic growth, more employment and a cut in the working week to thirty-five hours. It was argued that economic recovery may not jeopardise protection of the environment. The use of nuclear energy was rejected. The CAP's reform to cut surpluses and enable small farmers to earn a reasonable income was called for along with democratising EC institutions, and increasing the EP's legislative powers. The PvdA spoke out against the deployment of middle-range missiles in Europe, arguing for the removal of the SS-20, Pershing II and cruise missiles already deployed.

The ELD manifesto was accepted by the VVD as its election programme. More European co-operation and unity was argued for, based upon the principles of freedom, individual responsibility and tolerance. The functioning of EC institutions was criticised, majority voting in the Council and increasing the EP's powers advocated. The ELD and VVD argued that the social market economy should be strengthened, with less government interference and less protectionism; the environment protected and the principle of the polluter paying for damage adopted. Much attention was paid to peace, security and development aid. NATO was seen as fundamental to peace and security.

Each of the SGP/RPF/GPV joint list had its own manifesto. However, common points were assembled in a Euro-manifesto where they opposed a united or supranational Europe and favoured co-operation based on the independence of member states: an idea clearly from the titles of the party manifestos – 'Unity in Diversity' (SGP) and 'For National Independence in the European Co-operation' (GPV). They fear a Europe dominated by humanism and Catholicism; want EC institutions to be as national as possible with the EP, for instance, being composed of national delegations with a power of veto in important questions, and the EP deprived of legislative powers, and having only an advisory role. They insist on EC policies according with biblical norms, which means, among other things, acknowledging God as the origin of all public authority.

Finally, the common manifesto of the joint list of the small left parties and the Green Party Netherlands stressed environmental protection. Titled 'Chances for Survival', it was highly critical of the present EC, which it saw as dominated by capital and multinationals instead of the ideal of a Europe without nuclear weapons, without dominating capitalist interests, without a dominating technology and with more small-scale industry: a Europe of regions not of national states, and with EC institutions whose powers have been drastically cut. The PSP had its own manifesto that was even more critical of the EC, proposing to abolish it altogether. It argued that the EP existed only to give the EC a democratic appearance in order to disguise the fact that the EC is the servant of international industry.

CANDIDATE SELECTION[12]

No legal provisions define how parties may nominate their candidates, so they set their own procedures. In the 1979 Euro-election, the CDA won ten seats. In 1984, two MEPs – Mr Joep Mommersteeg and Mr Harry Notenboom – did not seek re-election. The CDA had to reckon on losing up to three seats, so the first seven places on the list were safe: six went to sitting MEPs but Mr Jim Janssen van Raaij (MEP) was placed ninth and Mr Sjouke Jonker eleventh which meant that he would not be re-elected. As in 1979, Mr Bouke Beumer led the CDA list.

The PvdA won nine seats in the first EP elections. Mr Willem Albers was the only MEP not seeking re-election. Nine and possibly ten seats were deemed safe. A specially established party committee chaired by Mr Relus ter Beek, a leading member of the Second Chamber, had the task of advising the Party Council on candidates to be nominated and on the sequence of their names on the list.[13] An important question for this committee was who was going to head the PvdA list. The two candidates for this position were Mr Piet Dankert, EP President, and Mrs Ien van den Heuvel, leader of the Dutch group in the EP Socialist group. In an interview in a Dutch weekly, Dankert had been vague about deploying cruise missiles in Holland although the party manifesto stipulated that under no circumstances whatsoever could missiles be deployed. Mrs van den Heuvel fully agreed with this and enjoyed the support of the party's left-wing, its feminist group and a small majority in the party executive. In the end, the special party committee recommended Dankert to head the list, followed by van den Heuvel. The Party Council endorsed this by 99 votes to 23 votes.

Of the six remaining sitting MEPs, four got safe places (the numbers 3, 5, 6 and 7 on the list) and one was placed at number ten, an uncertain position, but Mr Johan van Minnen was placed fifteenth, a hopeless place, as the special committee felt he had failed as an MEP: lacked results, dedication and co-operation.

The VVD won four seats in 1979 with a list headed by Mr Cees Berkhouwer, a striking controversial personality, well-known in EP circles.[14] The VVD, sometimes embarrassed by him, in summer 1983 put pressure on him not to seek re-election. In August 1983 he announced, given his age (64), that he, like Mr Aart Geurtsen, would not seek re-election. Mr Hans Nord and Mr Hendrik Louwes had no difficulties in being re-selected and placed first and second on the VVD list.

The two joint lists, small right and small left, faced the problem of the sequence of the parties on their lists of candidates. The small right solved this in accordance with party strength in the Second Chamber: SGP, RPF and GPV. The small left had difficulties. After negotiations it was decided that the list would be headed by a member of the PSP – the small left party with the greatest electoral support in the 1982 national election. Number two was a PPR member active in the GPN. Third and fourth places went to the CPN and the GPN.

THE ELECTION CAMPAIGN

The election campaign got underway slowly and by comparison with a campaign for a national election was exceedingly dull. The major parties failed to get across clearly to the voters their differences of opinion and outlook on European affairs. Yet in January 1983 members of the Second Chamber had asked the government to do something about the lack of public interest in the Euro-election. The government declined to provide funds. A special Euro-election stamp was issued in March 1984. The government provided two television spots regularly broadcast, urging citizens to vote.[15] As usual at election time, the government provided political parties with time on radio and television to broadcast their ideas.

Party campaign leaders complained about citizens' lack of knowledge about European affairs and EC institutions. The Dutch European Movement made a great effort to enlighten the public. Starting in September 1983 until a week before election day, it held countless meetings all over the country. In general, the audiences were small. A special 'Europe Week' (2–6 April 1984) was organised at Erasmus University, Rotterdam. Leading people from national and European politics, universities, the civil service, trade unions and employers' associations spoke. Some of the media tried to arouse interest in the general problems and policies of Europe.[16] However, public apathy remained. Campaign meetings, which in national elections attract hundreds, were attended by scores: one week before election day, the PvdA held a meeting in Breda, a city with more than 100 000 inhabitants. Speeches were delivered by party leader Mr Joop den Uyl, by party chairman Mr Max van den Berg and by Mr Piet Dankert. When the meeting started – 8.00 p.m. – seven people were present. At 8.30 p.m. the audience reached its maximum: sixty.

The campaign was not even enlivened when national issues were broached. The PvdA, the main opposition party, took up the government's socio-economic policy and the question of cruise missiles. The party 'nationalised' the EP campaign openly with advertisements in daily newspapers with texts like: 'Thursday 14 June: demonstrate with your vote against the deployment of Cruise Missiles. Vote PvdA. List 2' (and with smaller sized letters at the bottom) 'also for Europe'. Or, as in another advertisement, the outcome of the election should be 'a signal' against 'the socially unjust policy of the CDA and the VVD', a 'warning shot across the bows' of the CDA–VVD cabinet.

At first the CDA and the VVD did not take up national issues. They stressed the idea of a *European* election. They did not deny the national significance of the election, but said the campaign should be about European affairs, and the EP had no say whatsoever in the deployment of cruise missiles in the Netherlands.

After 1 June 1984 the CDA and VVD tactics changed. That day the government took a decision on the deployment of cruise. In the Second Chamber the CDA and the VVD demanded a parliamentary debate over this decision *before* election day. From then on, deployment of cruise became the most important issue in the campaign – but did not enliven it. Asked after election day why the CDA and the VVD had changed their tactics, Mr Bert de Vries, CDA parliamentary party leader, explained that they had to take up the gauntlet thrown down by the PvdA in the election campaign.

The most consistent European campaign was conducted by D'66. Their central slogan was: 'Democrats think European'. As we shall see, it did not win them votes. The main themes of the election campaign of the small left parties were protecting the environment and opposing the deployment of cruise. The Young PSP called for a boycott of the European election, and published a brochure arguing that 'opting for the EC is to opt for police violence, neo-colonialism, European nuclear power and tutelage. Therefore: do not vote'. The small parties conducted a very low key campaign.

Many parties tried to put the campaign on a Euro-level by seeking contacts and co-operation with corresponding parties in other member states. These efforts had little or no impact on the campaign. Small left parties attended an international congress of green parties in Liège in April 1984. They closed their campaign with a speech from Mr Roland Vogt of the German Grünen. D'66 invited Mrs Shirley Williams, chairwoman of the British Social Democratic Party (SDP), to attend its opening campaign meeting. It negotiated with the SDP and French Radicals to form one group in the EP after the elections, if possible with Italian Radicals, the Danish Venstre and the British Young Liberals. But D'66 like the SDP failed to win any seats in the EP.

The VVD started its campaign in the presence of Mr David Steel, leader of the British Liberals. The PvdA invited Mr Neil Kinnock, leader of the British Labour Party, who gave a speech at a meeting but the media virtually ignored both of them. More attention was paid to the CDA's announcement that it would start its campaign with a big meeting for the European Christian-democratic youth in the presence of Kohl (FRG), Martens (Belgium), FitzGerald (Ireland), Andreotti (Italy), Tindemans (Belgium) and Werner (Luxembourg). It took place at the end of May 1984 in Maastricht but was an anti-climax as none of the above showed up. The audience was told that they had other, more important, business to attend to. Instead they got speeches from Klepsch (CDU) and Croux (list leader for the Belgian CVP).

TURNOUT AND RESULTS

Since 1970 turnout has been in decline: for municipal councils turnout ranged from 61.2% (1970) to 73.3% (1978); for provincial assemblies from 67.9% (1982) to 79.1% (1978); and for the Second Chamber from 78.5% (1971) to 87.6% (1977). Previously the electoral law had ensured turnout of over 90%. Turnout fell to 58.1% in the first EP elections and to 50.5% in 1984. But polls had predicted a higher turnout in the region of 66%.[17] According to *Eurobarometer*, 64% of Dutch respondents were certain to vote and 19% would probably do so: an expected turnout of 83%.

Politicians and the media deplored the extremely low turnout. One in two voters abstained. Questions were asked about the EP's democratic value and validity given the low turnout.

The media variously explained the low turnout thus:

1. Voters are unfamiliar with MEPs' activities. They think the EP is only concerned with the CAP, do not see themselves as EC citizens and do not feel responsible for EC policy.
2. The idea of a united Europe has not caught on with the voters. For many, Europe is a collection of nation states: differences are too great and nationalism too intense for unity ever to be more than a facade.
3. Criticism was directed against EC policy made by specialists and excluding citizens. Disparaging remarks were often made about the waste of time and of money.
4. During the campaign the EP's limited power was criticised frequently. As long as the EP has restricted functions and no real legislative powers, it will not be taken seriously and high turnout cannot be expected.
5. Europe is in crisis. The idea of unity is stagnant. EC summits are a failure. The EP is powerless to improve the situation. Voters are disheartened.
6. Political parties failed to perform their campaign functions properly. Differences in policy were not presented clearly, manifestos were vague and not all candidates were known at the national level.
7. PvdA leaders felt the debate on cruise disgusted and de-motivated the electorate to vote. But CDA leaders argued that without the debate turnout would have been even lower.

8. The European football championship influenced turnout. Many Dutch people are football fans. The day before the election, the match between Belgium and Yugoslavia would have been on television, but was replaced by the missile debate. On election day, the match between the FRG and Portugal was televised between 5 p.m. and 7 p.m. when many vote on their return from work before polling stations close at 7 p.m.

On Thursday, 14 June 1984, there was a Euro-election special on television based on a detailed survey by *Intomart* that day. In 38 polling stations more than 18 000 voters filled out questionnaires in which, *inter alia*, questions were asked about the party supported in the 1984 Euro-election and in the 1982 national election. *Intomart* is used to these surveys and its prognosis has always been accurate. That Thursday its prognosis was taken for granted and politicians based their first reactions on it. But this time the prognosis was wrong.

VVD-leader Nijpels and CDA-leader de Vries were delighted that their parties, on the basis of the prognosis, had won a majority of the votes (CDA 31.5%, VVD 18.9%, together 50.4%) and that the coalition was safe. Joop den Uyl said that these had been Euro-elections and no conclusions should be drawn for national politics. On Sunday evening, seventy-two hours later, when the results of the election were televised, the tables were turned. The CDA–VVD no longer commanded a majority (CDA 30%, VVD 18.9%, together 48.9%). The PvdA now argued that people had voted against the CDA–VVD coalition, while the VVD said it was hard to draw national conclusions from the results of an EP election.

The PvdA was the winner. With 33.7% of the votes it became, again, the largest party. It retained its nine EP seats. Joop den Uyl, pleased with the results, attached great significance to the CDA and VVD losing the majority. According to *Intomart*, the PvdA won votes from the CDA, VVD and D'66 but lost many votes to the joint list of the small left parties. Beumer explained away the CDA's considerable losses by saying that he had expected to lose three seats in the EP election. Compared to the 1982 national election, the CDA did well as a governing party in maintaining its position. CDA-leader de Vries said the deployment debate, in which prime minister Lubbers had played a prominent part, had had a good effect on the party's support. In the *Intomart* survey the CDA lost to the PvdA and to the joint list of the small right parties, but won considerably from the VVD. The VVD lost

TABLE 10.1 *Election returns for the European Parliament (1979), the Second Chamber (1982), the Intomart prognosis (1984) and the European Parliament (1984) (in percentages of the valid votes cast)*

Party	EP 1979*	Second Chamber 1982	Intomart 1984	EP 1984*
Turnout	57.8	80.6	52.6	50.5
CDA	35.6 (10)	29.3	31.5	30.0 (8)
PvdA	30.4 (9)	30.4	31.8	33.7 (9)
VVD	16.1 (4)	23.1	18.9	18.9 (5)
D'66	9.0 (2)	4.3	2.2	2.3 (–)
Small right**	3.3 (–)	4.2	5.4	5.2 (1)
Small left**	5.0 (–)	5.7	6.0	5.6 (2)
European Greens	– (–)	–	1.8	1.3 (–)
CP	– (–)	0.8	2.1	2.6 (–)
GMO	– (–)	0.1	0.4	0.4 (–)
Others	0.4 (–)	2.1	–	– (–)

*Seats in brackets.
**Joint list only for the 1984 European election.
SOURCE *Algemeen Dagblad*, 18 June 1984.

heavily compared to the 1982 national election: losing an additional 4.2% of the vote – equivalent to a loss of seven Second Chamber seats. Compared with the 1979 Euro-election, the VVD won an extra 2.8% of the vote and five not four EP seats. The leaders stressed this.

D'66 was the big loser both compared to 1979 and to 1982. It lost its two EP seats and many votes to the PvdA and, to a lesser degree, to the CDA, the VVD, the joint list of small left parties and to the European Greens. The joint list of the small right parties (SGP, RPF and GPV) did well, getting more votes than in 1979 or 1982 and securing one EP seat. The joint list of the small left parties (CPN, Green Party Netherlands, PPR and PSP) did well also, winning more votes than in 1979 and about the same as in 1982. Thanks to the combined list with the PvdA (see note 10 of this chapter), its 5.6% of the vote won it two EP seats. The result for the extreme right Centre Party attracted media attention. With a 2.6% share of the vote, it did not win any EP seats but, in terms of Second Chamber seats, would mean three instead of one MP. As the daily newspaper *Trouw* (15 June 1984) put it: 'The Netherlands has proved once again to be a multiform country'.

NOTES AND REFERENCES

1. The Second Chamber is the directly elected house of the Dutch Parliament. It consists of 150 seats. The First Chamber is elected indirectly via the provincial assemblies; it consists of 75 seats. In 1982, remaining Second Chamber seats were distributed as follows: D'66 (6), PSP (3), SGP (3), CPN (3), PPR (2), RPF (2), CP (1), GPV (1), EVP (1).

2. In 1983, two members of the parliamentary party of the CDA in the Second Chamber seceded from that party while retaining their parliamentary seats. They objected to what was in their view a too conservative policy of the CDA. They have not formed their own political party, at least not yet. They form an independent group in the Second Chamber and they wish to co-operate with the EVP.

3. In Table 10.1 only the parties are mentioned that won at least one seat in the 1982 national election. In addition to those twelve parties another eight parties tried their luck in the elections. One of them also took part in the 1984 election for the European Parliament: God be with Us (GMO), a rather personal list of Mrs H. Cuijpers-Bouman. As far as one can speak of a programme of the GMO, it is based upon orthodox Catholic principles, especially the protection of Catholic morals and morality.

4. These small parties can be divided into small parties left to the centre (D'66, PSP, CPN, PPR, EVP – together 10.7% in the 1982 national election) and small parties right to the centre (SGP, RPF, GPV, CP – together 5% in the 1982 national election).

5. In 1971 the three Christian parties which were later to merge into the CDA did not together with the VVD control the majority in the Second Chamber. As they at that time did not want to govern with the PvdA, they invited one of the small parties into the coalition. That coalition cabinet lasted only for one year and two months.

6. CDA 48 seats, VVD 26 seats and PvdA 44 seats.

7. According to this decision the Netherlands will deploy:
   forty-eight Cruise Missiles if the Soviet Union on 1 November 1985 has deployed more SS-20-missiles than it had on 1 June 1984
   an adequate number of Cruise Missiles if before 1 November 1985 the Soviet Union and the United States by negotiations decide to employ less missiles than foreseen.

8. Some members of the party executive thereupon resigned from their party functions.

9. These members were organised and they gave the advice not to go to the polling station on election day.

10. Next to the possibility to join lists, it is possible to combine lists. After all the votes have been counted, a first allotment of the seats is made on the basis of the *full* electoral quota (in the case of the 1984 European election 4%). Then a second allotment of the 'remainder seats' is made, based on the greatest rest of the votes ('remainder votes') per party after deduction of the votes that were needed for gaining one or more 'full' seats. For this second allotment parties can combine their lists in order to increase the number of 'remainder votes'. For the 1984 European

election the list numbers 2 and 6 were combined. D'66 was asked to enter this combination, but refused to do so.

11. Only for the parties that gained one or more seats in the 1984 European election.
12. Only for the parties that gained one or more seats in the 1984 European election.
13. The Party Council, sometimes referred to as the 'small party congress', decide on the party list of candidates for the election of the European Parliament. This is one of the powers delegated to it by the party congress.
14. He was, for instance, accused of stealing bottles of liquor and of cheeses during parties.
15. One of the TV-spots, showing a windmill with the caption that a united Europe would take care of 'clean' energy, caused the rage of the small left parties. They lodged a formal protest and they demanded its prohibition.
16. A good example is a series of six long articles about the ideologies in Europe, published in the leading quality daily newspaper *NRC-Handelsblad* in June 1984. They were written by Robert Jackson, member of the British Parliament for the Conservative Party.
17. In that same opinion poll only 10% of the respondents said they knew that there would be an election in June; 20% said that they knew that there would be an election in 1984 and 70% did not know anything about an election.

11 The United Kingdom

DEREK HEARL

BACKGROUND

The 1979 Euro-election in the United Kingdom (UK) had been fought in the wake of a national general election held only five weeks previously. In that election the Conservatives had been returned to power under Mrs Margaret Thatcher after some five years in opposition. The new government was only embarking on its 'honeymoon' period. Labour and Liberal activists and supporters alike were demoralised at their general election defeat and consequently seem to have been particularly affected by post-election depression. The Conservatives, in contrast, were cock-a-hoop and the EP election was widely expected to be a walk-over for them. So it proved. Of the 78 seats allocated to Great Britain, the Conservatives won 60 with 50.6% of the Euro-vote. Labour won 33% of the vote and 17 seats, while the Scottish National Party (SNP) with 19.4% of the vote in Scotland (2.6% of the vote in Great Britain as a whole) won one seat. Given the 'first-past-the-post' electoral system and the lesser concentration of its votes, the Liberal Party with 13.1% of the total British vote failed to win a seat.

In Northern Ireland, to which the three remaining EP seats were allocated and which used the Single Transferable Vote (STV) electoral system, seats were more or less accurately distributed in proportion to the votes cast.[1] This gave the Democratic Unionist Party (DUP), the Social Democratic and Labour Party (SDLP) and the Official Unionist Party (OUP) one seat each for 29.8%, 24.6% and 21.9% of the 'first preference' votes respectively. That is two MEPs for the majority or 'Protestant' community and one MEP for the 'Catholic' minority.

The low turnout (only 32.6% in Great Britain although Northern Ireland with its highly personalised electoral system and a plethora of

228

top-line candidates managed to score 55.7%) was generally attributed to lack of knowledge of and interest in the EP, on the one hand, and the widespread expectation that the election result was a foregone conclusion on the other hand. Certainly it was the turnout (low even by British standards, let alone those of the rest of Europe) that attracted most media attention and not, as might have been expected, the Conservatives' remarkable achievement in gaining more than half the popular vote – the first time any party had done so since 1931.[2] Nevertheless, a general shift to the right was noted, especially in Europe as a whole, and commented upon although not much was made of this.

Few newly elected MEPs had any kind of national (or local or regional) reputation and of those who did only Mrs Barbara Castle (LAB: Greater Manchester North) was a senior politician and former Minister. In Scotland, Janey Buchan (LAB: Glasgow) and Winnie Ewing (SNP: Highlands and Islands) were – and are – prominent political figures, while in Northern Ireland, of course, all three MEPs had been leading politicians in the Province for several years past. On the Conservative side, a former chairman of the Confederation of British Industry, Sir Fred Catherwood, was elected for Cambridgeshire as was the then President of the National Farmers' Union, Sir Henry Plumb, for the Cotswolds constituency. Sir Henry Plumb was subsequently elected as Conservative leader in the EP in what was widely seen as a 'wet' (that is, anti-Thatcherite) *coup*. The Conservative delegation also included three former junior ministers among its ranks: Sir James Scott-Hopkins, Sir Basil de Ferranti and Lord Harmar-Nicholls. Of the 81 UK MEPs, four were ex-members of the Parliament of the United Kingdom, and four continued to hold the dual mandate.

There were no surprises when the 81 MEPs arrived in Strasbourg. The Labour MEPs elected Mrs Castle as their leader and she automatically became a Vice-President of the Socialist Group to which all the Labour MEPs affiliated. So did Mr John Hume, the SDLP leader, in accordance with his party's international links. The SDLP is both a full-member of the Socialist International and of the CSP. The Conservatives continued their existing alliance with the Danish Konservative Folkeparti and Centrum-Demokraterne,[3] as well as with the Ulster Unionist MEP, Mr John David Taylor. However, for several reasons, the Conservative Group was re-named the European Democratic Group since it was felt that the word 'Conservative' translated badly into a number of other languages and, in particular, had unattractive connotations for some European political cultures.[4] This left only Mrs Ewing (SNP) and the Reverend Ian Paisley (DUP) 'unattached' to any

EP group. Mrs Ewing subsequently joined the (Gaullist) European Progressive Democrats Group. These allegiances remained unaltered until late-1983 when Mr Michael Gallagher (LAB: Nottingham) left the Socialist Group to join the Technical Co-ordination Group (TCG) following his defection from Labour to the SDP. No vacancies in the UK delegation occurred during the lifetime of the first elected EP (1979-84) and consequently no by-elections were held.[5]

DOMESTIC POLITICS (1979–84)

The 1979-84 period had been one of the most eventful in British politics for a long time. The Conservative government had changed substantially the nature of right-wing politics in Britain; a new political party (SDP) had been born and formed an electoral alliance with the Liberals; and, of course, the country had fought a war in the South Atlantic. Each of these events had a profound effect on the UK political scene. In June 1983, one year before the second Euro-election, the Conservatives were re-elected for a second-term and in the autumn the Labour Party leader, Mr Michael Foot, was replaced by the younger, and considerably more popular, Mr Neil Kinnock who tried to persuade his party to end its internecine struggles not least over its attitude towards the EC.

THE CONSERVATIVES

The second-half of the 1970s, and even more the first-half of the 1980s, have been the 'Thatcher years' in British politics. Ever since she replaced Mr Edward Heath as Conservative Party leader in 1975, Mrs Thatcher had made a virtue out of toughness. Indeed, although it is still probably true to say that, to date at any rate, government rhetoric has generally been tougher than government action, there can now be little doubt that the Prime Minister succeeded in shifting the middle-ground of political debate in Britain significantly to the right. The two Thatcher governments' 'main task has been to reduce inflation and this has determined policy in other areas'.[6] In particular, this has meant continuing cuts in public expenditure and a series of measures aimed at changing the balance of power in industry by the limitation of certain Trade Union rights and privileges. Concerning the EC, this approach has led the Government into conflict with other EC member states over the issue of the EC budget in general and the British contribution in particular.

> However, persistent and tough negotiations by the Conservative Government secured interim arrangements covering the years 1980–3 which reduced the United Kingdom net contribution by two-thirds. ... Although for a time some success was achieved in slowing the rate of growth of agricultural expenditure, by 1983 the production of surpluses and the budgetary costs were running out of control again.[7]

The Government consistently won at home considerable publicity and widespread support for this stand. Thus, it was very hard for the Opposition parties to do more than debate the issue on the Government's own terms. The failures of the Athens and Brussels summits merely accentuated this and the issue came to be widely seen as one on which the Conservatives could lose in terms of domestic politics.

But without doubt the single most significant event in British politics during the 'Thatcher years' was the Falklands War. The crisis first broke in May 1982. The subsequent despatch of the 'Task Force' and the islands' eventual recapture restored the Government's fortunes to an amazing degree.

> It was obvious that an event of the political magnitude of the Falklands War would have an impact over a rather longer period. ... Thus, although it was not widely discussed during the election campaign, the Falklands War still had a very great influence on the outcome of the election.[8]

From an appallingly low opinion poll rating of 23% in December 1981[9] when the newly-founded SDP was at the height of its popularity, support for Mrs Thatcher and her government shot back up first to the low 40s and then, following final victory in the South Atlantic, to 46.5% in July. It remained at this level until the 1983 general election which the Conservatives won handsomely. Nevertheless, after the 1983 election, the second Thatcher government began to appear markedly less successful than its predecessor. While to some extent this was due to a recovery of public confidence in the Labour Party, it was also due largely to a series of unfortunate accidents (or 'banana skins' in British political journalese) which, in the run-up to the 1984 Euro-election, dented popular support for Mrs Thatcher and the Conservative Party.

LABOUR

For the Labour Party too the years between 1979 and 1984 were dramatic ones. Following its 1979 general election defeat, civil war had broken out in the party. The left-wing which had become even more vociferous and influential during the 1970s blamed the defeat on what it saw as the leadership's betrayal of socialist principles and democratically arrived at party policy when in government and determined to do something about this. The strategy the left adopted was that of reform of the Party Constitution to democratise the party and bring its parliamentary leadership into line with activist opinion if not, indeed, under full activist control.[10]

The Labour Party's Annual Conferences in 1979 and 1980 and the Special Conference in January 1981 thus proved bitter and highly divisive. The left won on the issues of mandatory re-selection and the election of the leader but failed to win exclusive control of the manifesto by the National Executive Committee (NEC). Following the right's subsequent capture of the NEC, the left abandoned pressure for the latter reform, at any rate for the time being. In the meantime, former Prime Minister Mr James Callaghan resigned the leadership before the new electoral machinery could be put into effect and was succeeded by Mr Michael Foot. Foot, a veteran rebel with deep roots in the party's so-called 'soft' or traditional left, had for long been one of the Labour Party's (and the country's) most colourful politicians and was almost universally respected – even loved – both inside and outside the Party. But in spite of this his election as leader was to prove a disaster. He failed to capitalise on his widely recognised personal qualities as a force for healing and reconciliation within the party and as a heavyweight politician in his own right. Under Foot's leadership not only did the Labour Party continue with its internal quarrels, particularly on the related issues of 'entryism' and the role of the semi-organised 'hard' left 'Militant' faction within the party,[11] but its alleged slide to the left appeared to continue unchecked. During this period Foot was widely portrayed in the media as an ageing somewhat shambolic, even pathetic, figure who had let the Labour Party get out of his control. During 1983 his personal rating in the opinion polls was the lowest ever recorded for a British party leader. There is little doubt that this poor image of its leader was a major contributory factor to Labour's second defeat in 1983 in spite of the fact that it was widely admitted that Foot had fought an energetic and competent campaign. If the 1979 general election had been a serious defeat for Labour which saw its share of the vote fall to 37%, that of 1983 was an utter disaster. The party only managed to gain 28% of the vote, its lowest since it was founded in its present form in 1918. Indeed, many authorities now doubt whether Labour can *ever* recover from a defeat of this magnitude notwithstanding the 'special factors at work in 1983 which are unlikely to occur in the future'.[12]

After a period of stunned disbelief, the Labour Party began to try to put its house in order. Foot resigned as party leader and the young, charismatic, 'soft' left Neil Kinnock was elected by the new electoral college procedure. Kinnock, who is a consummate media performer, seems to have restored the party's standing in the polls; so much so in fact that, in April 1984, the Labour Party overtook the Conservatives for the first time since the outbreak of the Falklands crisis. Kinnock also patched-up (some would say 'papered-over') the divide between pro- and anti-marketeers in the party with the obvious aim of trying to protect it from attack on what had hitherto been one of its most vulnerable points. Kinnock was clearly anxious for the Labour Party to do well in the 1984 Euro-election. Under his influence, Labour adopted a new, much more 'pragmatic', approach – albeit still a somewhat sceptical one – towards the EC and made a deliberate attempt to avoid the still highly divisive question for the party of British membership as such.

> Britain will remain a member of the EEC for the term of the next European Parliament, and Labour will fight to get the best deal for Britain within it. At the end of that time, Britain will have been a member of the EEC for 15 years – and this will be reflected in our pattern of trade, the way our economy works and our political relations overseas. But we also recognise the fundamental nature of changes we wish to see made in the EEC and that its rules may stand in the way of a Labour Government when it acts to cut unemployment. It is in this context that we believe that Britain, like all Member States, must retain the option of withdrawal from the EEC.[13]

Although there were a few signs that the pro-marketeers in particular were still somewhat dissatisfied at this approach, at long last the Labour Party seemed to have found a position around which it could unite. Indeed, early in 1984, Neil Kinnock went a stage further when, in calling for a 'new Messina', – a concept for which he attracted a lot of continental socialist support – he began to repair the Labour Party's relations with its CSP allies. However, the fact remains that never at any time did he define his 'new Messina' and any attempt to do so would most likely have wrecked these newly improved relations once again.

THE ALLIANCE PARTIES: LIBERALS AND SOCIAL DEMOCRATS

Perhaps the most dramatic event for the Labour Party in the early 1980s was the split between its so-called 'Social Democratic' and pro-European wing and the rest of the party; a split which culminated in the withdrawal of the 'Gang of Four' (Mr Roy Jenkins, Dr David Owen, Mr William Rodgers and Mrs Shirley Williams) to form the Social Democratic Party (SDP) in March 1981. The split had been a long time coming. As early as 1975 following the EEC referendum, a 'Social Democratic Alliance' had been set up within the Labour Party by pro-marketeers, but it was EC Commission President Roy Jenkins' Dimbleby Lecture on BBC Television in November 1979 that was to be the catalyst for a new party. In his lecture Jenkins called among other things for proportional representation and the strengthening of the political centre, suggesting that perhaps the only way to achieve these reforms was through the launch of a new 'Centre Party'. Nevertheless, the ostensible reason for the SDP's formation was the long struggle between the Left and Right within the Labour Party itself over the various constitutional reforms referred to earlier. When the Right lost on the issue of the election of the party leader at the Special Wembley Conference in January 1981, Owen, Rodgers and Williams left the Party and the SDP was launched on 26 March 1981. In one day approximately 8000 members were recruited and £80 000 raised.[14] Within a matter of weeks the new party topped opinion polls and with its Liberal allies with whom it had from the outset concluded an electoral 'Alliance' commanded the support of a majority of the electorate. In a spectacular series of by-election successes during 1981 and 1982, Alliance candidates achieved hitherto unknown 'swings' winning three of the four contests.

Nevertheless, there were problems. The new SDP saw itself originally as some kind of amalgam of all that was good in the 'old' Labour Party together with the intelligent, articulate but hitherto unrepresented centre. Somewhat like D'66 in the Netherlands with which it quickly established friendly relations, it saw itself as 'the reasonable alternative'.[15] The SDP stood for the mixed economy, Keynesianism, Atlanticism and a Western orientation generally, and – above all – it was keenly pro-EC, at any rate at leadership level. In spite of this (or perhaps because of it) relations with its Liberal ally were from the first somewhat strained. Many Liberals, particularly but by no means exclusively, from the party's 'Radical' or 'majoritarian' wing saw SDP as an arrogant and overbearing threat to the Liberal Party's position as the established repository of similar but not identical policies and, of course, as the sitting-tenant, so to speak, of the centre and centre-left ground of British politics. However, this was at no time the view of Mr David Steel, Liberal leader since 1976, who had advanced the 'Pact' of coalition strategy so distrusted by the majoritarians and had taken a very close interest in the SDP's formation, doing what he could to encourage it. He formed a particularly close relationship with Jenkins, following whose election to the SDP leadership relations between the two halves of the Alliance improved.

However, under Britain's 'first-past-the-post' electoral system with its 600-odd single-member constituencies, the two parties needed to agree on a share-out of the available seats in such a way as to ensure that only one of them contested each constituency. This meant of course that the Liberals would have to withdraw from something like half the country and, worse, the SDP expected to get a virtually equal share of good or 'winnable' seats which had been built up largely by Liberal efforts. When negotiations between the two parties began on what were termed 'seat allocations', relations rapidly became acrimonious. Yet, somewhat to the surprise of observers and participants, the negotiations were eventually concluded satisfactorily. The two parties fought the 1983 general election as a more or less united force gaining 26.1% of the vote, just 2.2% behind Labour. Naturally enough, however, given the nature of the 'first-past-the-post' system, the Alliance parties won fewer seats than implied by the percentage of the vote won (only 23 seats in fact).

Since the general election, and especially since the replacement of Jenkins by Owen as SDP leader, cracks in the Alliance re-opened and widened as a consequence of the two parties entering into negotiations for the 'allocation' of Euro-constituencies in preparation for the 1984 Euro-election. However, once these negotiations had been concluded (see below), relations between the Liberals and the SDP improved once more. Following the 1984 Euro-election, the two parties began to reconsider the Westminster allocations for the next general election and relations have cooled-off again. It seems that this pattern of alternating estrangement and reconciliation between the two halves of the Alliance is one that will continue for the foreseeable future.

On the wider issue of the electoral system itself, the Alliance parties remain strong partisans of some form of proportional representation for elections at all levels, including those to the EP. In spite of a recently intensified campaign on this issue however, and notwithstanding the fact that they appear to have high levels of popular support on the question, the bulk of Conservative and even more of Labour opinion remains firmly opposed to any form of proportional representation and there is no immediate prospect of its introduction in Great Britain. Equally, there is no prospect of the STV system being abolished in Northern Ireland.

NORTHERN IRELAND

Compared to the situation in Britain, little in Northern Ireland's party politics changed between 1979 and 1984, with the single important exception of the considerable growth in support for Provisional Sinn Fein at the expense of the SDLP. Sinn Fein is an extreme Republican party closely associated with the illegal Provisional IRA whose political wing it is almost universally alleged to be. Provisional Sinn Fein does not deny this allegation. The party is now locked in what might yet prove to be a life and death struggle with the SDLP to be the representative of the minority 'Catholic' community and, during the early 1980s, seemed to be winning this battle. At the 1983 general election, 42% of the Catholic community voted for Provisional Sinn Fein and there are indications that this level of support increased subsequently. Certainly, in early 1984, there was considerable interest to see whether this increased support would manifest itself at the second Euro-election and, if so, whether it would result in a Sinn Feiner being returned to the EP thereby dislodging the SDLP's leader, Hume. However, on the Protestant side there seems to have been little doubt that both Paisley and Taylor would be re-elected.

PREPARING FOR THE 1984 EP ELECTION

Parliamentary elections in the United Kingdom typically take place rather suddenly and with very little notice either to the public at large or to the various political actors involved, principally of course the parties. Consequently, the country has developed a short, sharp electioneering style in which all activity is concentrated into a period which can be less than three weeks and is almost always less than four weeks. Naturally enough, this tradition spills over into local elections too in spite of the fact that these elections at least are held at fixed intervals. It is understandable therefore that such a recent innovation as Euro-elections, again in spite of their fixed character, should also conform to this pattern.

An integral feature of the British electoral system is that its single member constituencies are subject to regular review aimed at nearly as possible equalising their electorates subject to a number of other criteria of which administrative convenience and geographical compactness are the two main ones. Since the Euro-constituencies are combinations of Westminster ones and since a review of the latter was completed in 1982, the Euro-constituencies had to be reviewed also. However, that review was not completed until shortly before the elections although draft proposals were known by September 1983. The boundary review left only five British Euro-constituencies intact: North Wales, the two constituencies in the far South West and two constituencies in London. Another seven constituencies suffered minor changes, while the remaining 66 constituencies were either re-cast altogether or else drastically revised. Northern Ireland, of course, with its different electoral system was unaffected by these changes. The lateness of the review, quite as much as anything else, accounts for the relative tardiness of British political parties in selecting Euro-candidates. Clearly, the parties needed first the Euro-constituencies' boundaries before they could set up the necessary local organisations. These are not only charged with the planning and administration of the local campaign but, more importantly, are almost always the bodies responsible for the selection of candidates in the first place.

Apart from the boundary review, there were no changes in electoral procedure either in Great Britain or in Northern Ireland although the Government announced increases in candidates' expenditure limits in line with inflation since 1979.[16] Vociferous demands heard in 1979 for the enfranchisement of UK nationals resident abroad (especially, of course, for those employed by the European Communities themselves) seem to have been largely silenced by a Report of the Home Affairs Select Committee which examined this issue along with a number of others. Subsequently the Government announced a number of minor changes in electoral law in general, including the right for UK citizens abroad to vote in elections in the United Kingdom but these changes were not introduced in time for the 1984 EP election.

Neither the Labour Party nor the Liberal Party felt it necessary to adapt national or local procedures in the light of their 1979 experience, though many Labour and Liberal party officials do now regret that their parties did not maintain a nationwide network of Euro-constituency organisations as the Conservatives did. Both parties felt somewhat at a disadvantage in this regard having to start from scratch all over again. This is one mistake at least that seems unlikely to be repeated.

All the principal parties at least have similar structures and procedures at Euro-constituency level and fairly similar selection procedures. None of them has felt it necessary to vary their rules in these respects from those that were in force in 1979 which are generally thought to have been satisfactory. Essentially, each Euro-constituency organisation is a federation of the established Westminster constituency parties. Typically, each such Westminster constituency sends 20 or 25 delegates to a selection conference which actually chooses the party's candidate for the Euro-constituency in question according to procedures which as nearly as possible approximate those used for Westminster selections. These bodies also elect smaller executive committees to raise funds and oversee the election campaign at the local event. In most cases, these selection procedures did not begin until after Christmas 1983 and were not fully completed until Spring 1984. Only the SNP published a full list of adopted candidates before the end of 1983.

Of 60 retiring Conservative MEPs, the majority sought re-selection. However, exact figures are difficult to come by since the party's procedures are shrouded in some secrecy. The names of applicants for particular constituencies are not published and consequently only the list of selected candidates is available. Although re-selection for the EP is said by party officials to have been a good deal less automatic than that for Westminster, few sitting-Conservative MEPs failed to achieve it if they wanted to. Of the 60, 47 were re-selected. Of the 13 who were not, several did not seek re-selection either because they already held a dual mandate and/or had other interests, or because they had been elected to the Westminster Parliament in 1983. Only one Conservative MEP, Mr Tom Normanton, MEP for Cheshire East and MP for Cheadle, sought a dual mandate in 1984.

A similar pattern is evident for the Labour Party. It may well be that the EP now offers a new career-path for aspiring Westminster MPs. The reverse is true also since a number of former MPs who lost their seats in the 1983 general election became candidates for the EP election. Of the 17 Labour MEPs elected in 1979, one defected to the SDP, four were elected to Westminster in June 1983 and opted for national politics. Ten of the twelve MEPs seeking re-selection were re-adopted.

The unlucky two both appear to have lost out for constituency rather than political reasons. It is reported that in at least one case the MEP concerned was too pro-EC and had not paid sufficient attention to powerful trade union forces in his constituency which turned against him. However, again, there is little or no hard information on this point due to the confidential nature of Labour Party selection proceedings.

Insofar as the other parties were concerned, all five sitting-MEPs were re-selected: Mrs Ewing (SNP), the three Northern Ireland MEPs and Mr Gallagher (SDP, though for a different constituency). The Liberals, of course, had no sitting-MEPs as such, although their Foreign Affairs Spokesman, Mr Russell Johnston, MP, had been granted honorary membership of the EP's ELD Group following his narrow defeat in the Highlands and Islands in 1979 and regularly attended its meetings. Since, on the basis of the 1983 general election result, the Liberal/SDP Alliance held a plurality of votes in the Highlands and Islands, Johnston was expected to win the seat from the SNP and was, therefore, re-adopted to fight the seat.

In Northern Ireland the Official Unionist Party decided that it would put forward only one candidate for the Province's three Euro-seats. This was in clear recognition that its 1979 tactic of running two candidates had been a mistake. Then it had been badly shaken when the Reverend Ian Paisley, of the rival Democratic Unionist Party, had topped the poll. The OUP leader, Mr Harry West, had been forced into an embarrassing run-off with his party colleague John Taylor for the Province's third seat, the second seat having gone as expected to the Catholic SDLP. This embarrassment was compounded when Taylor won this secondary contest. This time Taylor was re-adopted as the party's sole candidate, although not without a fight, in tacit recognition of the fact that Paisley could not be stopped.

Each party had a campaign committee topped-off in the case of the Liberal/SDP Alliance by a Joint Campaign Committee under the chairmanship of the Liberal leader, Steel. These committees, typically some 25 strong, comprised politicians and technicians and were responsible for all national aspects of the campaign. These included the preparation and production of radio and television 'Election Broadcasts'; the organisation of national press conferences (in most cases on a twice-weekly basis instead of every day as is the case with general elections), tours by senior party figures from home and abroad, mass rallies and, of course, publications and propaganda. Both the Labour Party and the Conservative Party tried to introduce a degree of 'razzmatazz' which is unusual at British elections. Indeed, the Labour

Party had a fully equipped 'campaign bus' that toured the country. Most party planners seem to have thought that one of the principal issues in the campaign would be the question of the UK contribution to the EC budget and that on this issue the Conservatives were unbeatable. A lot of thought was given by Alliance and especially Labour politicians to this problem and the strategy of both parties was to try to shift the debate away from this issue if possible. Similarly, everyone seemed to accept that the Labour Party would be open to attack on the question of whether it wished to remain in the EC. Both the Conservative Party and the Labour Party planned to attack the Alliance on the grounds of its alleged European federalism – a charge which the Liberals, at least, were happy to accept. There was general agreement that this time the election would be about EC issues as well as about domestic issues: in pre-election interviews party staffs often pointed to institutional reform, frontier controls (the French lorry drivers' blockade had received a great deal of publicity in the UK) and, above all, the UK contribution to the EC budget. Yet, generally, all felt that the election would be predominantly a 'mid-term' one in which the Conservative government would be forced by Opposition parties to defend its domestic policies and record. Thus, it was thought that the 1984 Euro-election in the UK, as in 1979, would be dominated by national and domestic issues although not perhaps to quite the same extent.

Of the various UK political parties, two British and two Northern Irish parties belong to European party federations. The Labour Party and the SDLP, and the Liberal Party have respectively been CSP and ELD members since their inception. Late in 1983, the non-sectarian Alliance Party of Northern Ireland, with the Liberal Party's blessing, also joined the ELD though its rather marginal position, in European terms, meant that it never had any chance of winning one of the Northern Ireland EP seats. None of the other parties has international links of a comparable kind. The Conservatives and the Ulster Unionists, together with the Danish Konservative Folkeparti, form the EP's European Democratic Group. Both the SNP and the Welsh nationalist Plaid Cymru have had occasional contacts with other regionalist and nationalist parties from different parts of Europe but none of these contacts has amounted to anything very significant. Finally, the new Social Democratic Party, in spite of a number of attempts to find allies, has so far remained wholly outside any kind of organised international framework.

Consequently, only the Labour Party and the Liberal Party, together with the SDLP whose role was relatively minor in this respect, had to take serious account of transnational party considerations. In 1979, this had been a relatively easy matter for the Liberal Party and a very difficult one for the Labour Party. At that time, the ELD had agreed a common manifesto which the Liberal Party had had no difficulty in supporting; while the CSP, due as much to Labour's opposition to the entire concept as to the real differences of policy between member parties, had failed to do so. In 1984 both British parties found themselves in much the same boat *vis-à-vis* their respective European party federations: each found itself committed to support a common manifesto much of which it agreed with but much of which it also found impossible to accept.

In some ways, the problem was more severe for the Liberals who, in 1979 and subsequently, had tried to make a virtue of the fact that they, unlike the Conservatives or Labour, were fully integrated into a transnational body. However, at its Munich Congress, the ELD adopted (largely due to a changed orientation on the part of the German FDP) an electoral programme whose energy, foreign affairs and – especially – economics chapters were anathema to many British Liberals. Indeed, under the threat of a total rejection of the entire Programme by the British Liberal delegation at Munich (which might even have cost the ELD the necessary two-thirds majority), the Congress added a preamble to the economics chapter which, by explicitly recognising 'the important differences that still exist between our Member States',[17] went at least part way towards calming British fears. In the event, the Liberal Party delegation split on the issue and the Programme was adopted with the necessary majority leaving party managers with the problem of selling it not only to their own activists at home but also to their SDP allies. The SDP took particular exception to the economics chapter while the Liberals, many of whom have for long been hostile to the Party's membership of the ELD, prepared to challenge the entire Programme at the Liberal Party Council meeting scheduled for February 1984. In the event, the Council was postponed because of the Chesterfield by-election and, by dint of careful compromise and fudging, the two Alliance partners were eventually able to produce a joint-manifesto of their own which the Liberals could claim did not contradict ELD policy. Indeed, those copies of the joint-manifesto circulated by the Liberal Party, although in all other respects identical to those issued by the SDP, actually carried the ELD logo on the back cover. Consequently, of course, it attracted ELD financial support without which the Liberal party would certainly have found it impossible to mount an effective campaign at all.

The Alliance manifesto committed the two parties to working together towards

> ... a concerted Community programme for economic recovery. Particular emphasis should be put upon measures which promote jobs and investment. Finance should also be provided for investment in infrastructure ...[18]

Generally, the Alliance parties favoured increased EC spending in virtually all policy areas except agriculture. In this way the CAP's proportionate share of the EC budget would be cut. This would by itself help solve the problem of the UK net contribution, but the two parties also explicitly demanded a new budget mechanism to transfer funds from richer to poorer regions. On the defence issue. which had also been a bone of contention between the Alliance parties and the ELD, the manifesto called for the suspension of further deployment of cruise and Pershing missiles in Europe even though the ELD congress had voted down a similar British Liberal proposal at Munich. Insofar as the EC's institutional development was concerned, the Alliance demanded severe restrictions on the use of the national veto and the introduction of a system of 'co-decision-making' between the Council and the EP. In this at least, the manifesto fully accorded with the ELD Programme.

If the process of evolving the ELD Programme had resulted in a *distancement* between the Liberal Party and its European allies, its equivalent on the Labour-side had resulted in something of a *rapprochement*. The Labour Party's new and more pragmatic approach to the question of EC membership meant that it approached the issue of a common CSP manifesto more positively than it did in 1978–79. Not only did it accept the principle for the first time but, under the Kinnock leadership, representatives played a full part in the discussions surrounding its elaboration. The inevitable clashes of policy between the Labour Party and its allies were solved by the simple expedient of indicating which sections of the manifesto the Labour Party felt unable to subscribe to. The final document was approved unanimously by the CSP's Luxembourg Congress in March 1984 on this somewhat less than integrated basis. The sections which Labour did not support were indicated clearly in the published text and, predictably, concerned the further development of the European Monetary System (of which the UK is in any case not a member); proposals to increase the EP's influence; and proposals to increase the EC's 'own resources'. Copies of the CSP manifesto circulated in Great Britain also contained a fore-word by Labour Party General Secretary, Mr Jim Mortimer, highlight-ing these and other differences between Labour's own policies and those in the CSP document. Mr Mortimer stressed also areas of agreement, including

> ... the absolute priority that needs to be given, by the [EC] to the issue of jobs – with the Confederation calling on all member states to act together now to create jobs and cut unemployment.[19]

Like the Liberals, the Labour Party also published its own domestic manifesto for the 1984 Euro-election.[20] Labour's manifesto was remar-kably short with but ten pages of widely spaced type, closely based on the NEC's earlier policy statement. Again the Party's overwhelming commitment to job creation was heavily stressed. To this end it demanded new public investment in industry, in training and in depressed regions but specifically opposed any attempt to take the UK into the EMS. It demanded fundamental reform of the CAP; a nuclear weapons freeze; and insisted that EC budget contributions be related to ability to pay. It flatly opposed any extension to the powers either of the EP or of the EC itself, going so far as to demand 'the return to our own parliament [of] the powers so foolishly ceded by the Tories to the EEC in the 1972 European Communities Act'.

As was only to be expected, the Conservative manifesto was princi-pally concerned with the Government's record.[21] It claimed credit, *inter alia*, for 'restoring the economic health of Britain' and 'helping to lead the Community out of recession'. More specifically, it referred to the Government's success in winning agreement on a fairer budget system and on the British rebate; the deals won for farmers and fishermen; and reforms in the Social and Regional Funds. The manifesto offered a large number of quite detailed policies in the economic sphere, gener-ally aiming at extending free trade both within the EC and between it and the outside world; it called for common efforts in research and recognised the need for EC funds for this purpose; and it insisted on an increase in the share of the non-agricultural spending within the context of a system of tight budgetary discipline. The manifesto was very cautious on the question of British membership of the EMS which it said remained under review: 'We should only take that step when the conditions are right, both for us and our partners'. It supported the EP's existing role and functions without proposing any changes in these. It insisted that the national veto be retained, although only as a last resort and concluded by attacking Labour policies in general and the Liberals' federalist ambitions in particular.

THE CAMPAIGN AND ITS OUTCOME

The 1979 Euro-election campaign had been lacklustre. Campaigning had been uninspiring, party workers and voters were election-weary and the result was widely seen as a foregone conclusion. For a number of reasons, it was expected that 1984 would differ. It was true that Mrs Thatcher had won a second term of office with an increased majority in 1983 but that had been as much due to Labour's disarray as to anything else. By spring 1984 when the Euro-campaign finally got underway, it was clear that this time Labour was making a comeback and would fight the campaign wholeheartedly unlike in 1979; that the government was slipping on 'banana skins' and losing support; and that the Alliance was expected to do well given its general election performance. Above all, the Euro-election appeared to many to offer a golden opportunity – almost a kind of by-election on a national scale – for the electorate to pass an interim judgment on the performances of all three main parties a year after the general election. Of one thing all commentators were certain: this time turnout would be markedly higher than in 1979. The mere fact that the Labour Party would go all out to win seats was expected to boost turnout. Considerably more media attention than in 1979 was expected due to the 'mid-term' effect which had been absent then. The relative changes in the various parties' fortunes meant that the outcome of the election was less predictable than in 1979: how many seats would the Tories lose, and to whom? Would the Alliance overtake Labour in terms of votes (they had no hope of doing so in terms of seats)?

Indeed, early indications were that these predictions of increased media and public interest would be borne out. The various parties, as well as the EP's London Office, reported measurable increases in offers of help, requests for information and so on. Opinion polls indicated that more people would vote; politicians of all parties claimed that interest 'on the ground' was much higher than it had been in 1979. Events in Europe too seemed almost to be conspiring to make the election much more interesting and exciting than it might otherwise have been. One can note the French lorry drivers' blockade; the cliff-hanging negotiations about the UK budget contribution; and the agreement on milk quotas which unleashed a stream of protest among the country's dairy farmers who, at one time, appeared likely to turn from the Conservatives to the Alliance in large numbers. Even the anniversary celebrations of the Normandy landings and the London economic summit, both of which showed Mrs Thatcher in the role of world stateswoman, were widely thought to be of electoral advantage to the Government and, hence, as a further encouragement to voters to turn out.

When the campaign proper began, some four or five weeks before polling party managers predicted that the Conservatives would lose some ten seats to Labour and that the Liberals would take the SNP's Highlands and Islands seat. In Northern Ireland, the only questions were whether the OUP candidate would beat Paisley into second place and whether the SDLP could beat Provisional Sinn Fein's challenge. Media interest was muted, but greater than in 1979 and, at the national level at least, the parties tried to create some popular interest both in the elections and in their own policies and arguments. As in 1979, there were a number of publicity stunts designed to catch media attention at both national and local levels. The Alliance leaders travelled down the River Thames on a boat accompanied by scores of journalists and television crews; the Conservatives set up stalls in shopping-centres giving away such things as balloons and paper hats; and a Labour candidate in the West country took a pantomime cow around the markets of his constituency to make a point about milk quotas and so on. But, it was easily the Labour Party itself which took the prize for media events of this kind. Apart from the 'campaign bus', the party arranged a national song competition and, in the words of its European spokesman, Mr Robin Cook, 'even contaminated the platforms of its rallies with people who expressed their support in song or in satire'.[22]

On the more conventional plane, the Conservatives tried hard to attack Labour's commitment or otherwise to EC membership challeng-ing each Labour candidate individually to declare him/herself as a 'pro' or an 'anti'. Labour retaliated by trying to highlight differences among Tory candidates on such issues as the national veto, harmonisation of VAT and immediate repayment of the British budget rebate. On all these issues, it was known that a significant number of Conservative candidates were opposed to Mrs Thatcher's own line. For their part, Alliance leaders, too, concentrated their attack upon the Tories in general and upon the Prime Minister's personal style in particular.

Labour tried to pin the blame for higher food prices in Britain on EC policies in general and on Conservative support for those policies in particular. In spite of these 'European' aspects of the campaign, it was still predominantly a national one, British party elites 'fronted' the campaign, not their EP colleagues and inevitably, therefore, they fought it in domestic terms. The only exception to this rule was Mrs Castle, the Labour leader in the EP, who did play a prominent role in Labour's campaign alongside Neil Kinnock and his colleagues.

The same was generally true in Northern Ireland, although here, of course, the issues were different. The Protestant–Catholic divide in the Province was translated at least partially into the question of EC membership. The two principal Protestant parties both opposed membership, while the SDLP was strongly in favour of membership as was the Alliance Party. Ian Paisley fought the election in his own inimitable style on an uncompromising policy of loyalism and opposition to Irish Republicanism. John Taylor (OUP) was less vehemently opposed to EC membership in principle but hostile to its practical consequences. He concentrated much of his campaign upon the CAP and particularly upon the special deal won by the Irish Republic on milk quotas. On the Catholic-side, the SDLP defended membership of the EC while at the same time attacking the British Government for not having fought more strongly for Ulster's interests within the EC. Provisional Sinn Fein fought the election very largely on a campaign of opposition to the EC on the grounds that in effect it diluted Ireland's own identity and interests. Yet, their candidate, Mr Danny Morrison, undertook to take up an EP seat if elected in contradistinction to his party's long-standing policy in domestic elections.

Polling took place throughout the UK on Thursday, 14 June 1984 but the ballot boxes were not opened until voting had ended throughout the EC on Sunday night, 17 June 1984. However, at the close of poll on 14 June 1984, the turnout was known and published. Against expectations, turnout (32.4%) was even lower than in 1979 (32.6%). The media blamed the parties for the low turnout. *The Times* published a front-page report[23] on the basis of a Harris Poll which showed that only nine per cent of Conservative and Labour voters had been called upon by representatives of the parties. The corresponding figure for the Alliance was 6%. These figures compared with 32% (Conservative), 30 per cent (Labour) and 22% (Liberal) for the 1979 EP election. This proved, said *The Times*, that all three parties could have done better if they had been so minded. However, the low turnout was overshadowed by a much more dramatic event. A British parliamentary by-election had been held on the same day as the EP election for the Portsmouth South constituency and the result was declared later the same night. It proved to be a wholly unexpected and quite stunning victory for the SDP candidate in what had been thought right until the end of the campaign to be a rock-solid Conservative seat. SDP–Liberal Alliance leaders and party managers, most of whom seem to have been as surprised by the result as everybody else, could be forgiven for thinking that their parties were about to see a remarkable series of results when the Euro-ballot boxes were opened. But it was not to be. In Great Britain as a whole the Conservative share of the vote fell from 50.6% in 1979 to 40.8% in 1984, Labour's share of the vote rose from 33% in 1979 to 36.5% in 1984 and the Alliance parties gained 19.5% of the vote in 1984 as opposed to the Liberals' 1979 score of 13%. The Conservatives lost 15 seats to Labour, distributed regionally as follows: three in London, four in the West Midlands, five in the North West and three in Scotland (see Table 11.1). To the Liberals' intense disappointment, Russell Johnston failed to dislodge Winifred Ewing (SNP) so that the net result in terms of seats for Great Britain (1979 result in brackets) was: Conservatives 45 (60), Labour 32 (17) and SNP 1 (1). Naturally, this result gave rise to renewed demands on the part of the two Alliance

TABLE 11.1   *United Kingdom EP seats by region* (1979 EP seats in brackets)*

Region	Conservative	Labour	SNP
London	5 (8)	5 (2)	
South East*	11 (10)		
South West	5 (5)		
East Anglia	6 (6)		
East Midlands*	4 (5)	1 (1)	
West Midlands	4 (8)	4 (0)	
North East	3 (3)	8 (8)	
North West	4 (9)	6 (1)	
Scotland	2 (5)	5 (2)	1 (1)
Wales	1 (1)	3 (3)	
Great Britain	45 (60)	32 (17)	1 (1)

**Regions:* 1979 taken from Butler and Marquand, op. cit.; 1984 adapted from same. South East gains one seat on redistribution and East Midlands loses one seat.
Northern Ireland:
  DUP 1 (1)
  OUP 1 (1)
  SDLP 1 (1)

parties for a change to a proportional representation system but these demands are likely to be in vain.

Of the MEPs who sought re-election in Great Britain, 37 of 47 Conservatives and 10 of 11 Labour candidates were successful. Mr Gallagher (SDP) was defeated in Lancashire Central but Mrs Ewing (SNP) held her Highlands and Islands seat. In Northern Ireland, all three MEPs were re-elected. To the surprise of many and the relief of others, Ian Paisley increased his share of first preference votes to 33.6% (29.8% in 1979) and John Hume defeated the Provisional Sinn Fein candidate with a first preference vote share of 22.1% (24.6% in 1979) as opposed to Provisional Sinn Fein's 13.3% share of the vote. John Taylor's (OUP) vote held steady at 21.5% (21.9% in 1979). In Great Britain only one MEP, Tom Normanton (Cheshire East and Cheadle) now holds a dual mandate, while in Northern Ireland Ian Paisley continues to hold his dual mandate.

In conclusion, it is clear that national considerations dominated the campaign. As one observer noted, this was at least partly due to the invisibility of Euro-issues and MEPs; to the inability of the Opposition to draw the Prime Minister or key cabinet ministers into any campaign confrontations; and to the sporadic media coverage of EC and EP affairs as opposed to Westminster's business.[24]

NOTES AND REFERENCES

1. Technically, STV is not a *party*-proportional system at all since all voting is for named candidates. However, given that most electors do in practice vote with party considerations uppermost in their minds, its results are usually broadly proportional in party terms.
2. D. Butler and D. Marquand, *European Elections and British Politics* (London: Longman, 1981) p. 136. See also, J. Lodge, 'The European Elections of 1979: A Problem of Turnout', *Parliamentary Affairs*, 32 (1979) 448–58.
3. The Centrum-Demokraterne MEP, of course, subsequently left the European Democratic Group to sit with the European People's Party Group.
4. See J. Lodge and V. Herman, *Direct Elections to the European Parliament: A Community Perspective* (London: Macmillan, 1982) p. 183.
5. Technically, there was one by-election occasioned by a highly technical breach of the incompatibility rules as a result of which the elected MEP for London South West was disqualified. However, since all that happened was the election was simply held again a few weeks later and Dame Shelagh Roberts, the disaqualified Conservative MEP, was re-elected, it hardly counts as a by-election in the usual sense.

6. P. Norton and A. Aughey, *Conservatives and Conservatism* (London: Temple Smith, 1981) pp. 162–5.
7. Conservative Research Department/EDG Secretariat, *Handbook for Europe 1984* (London: 1984) p. 258.
8. P. Whiteley, *The Labour Party in Crisis* (London: Methuen, 1983) pp. 210–11.
9. *Ibid.* pp. 210–11.
10. 'The campaign for Labour Party Democracy pursued three aims: the mandatory reselection of MPs by constituency parties during the lifetime of each parliament; the introduction of an electoral college for the appointment of the party leader, containing representatives from the unions, constituencies and the parliamentary party; and, thirdly, the vesting of the right to draw up the Manifesto in the National Executive Committee, and the removal of the veto on the contents of the Manifesto of the leadership'. *Ibid.*, p. 3.
11. Although 'Militant' always denied that it was an organised group, of course.
12. Whiteley, op. cit., p. 209.
13. Labour Party, *Campaigning for a Fairer Britain* (London: 1983).
14. J. Josephs, *Inside the Alliance* (London: John Martin, 1983) p. 30.
15. Although there have been several instances where D'66, which has had close links with the Liberal Party for many years, has fought shy of too close an involvement with the SDP for fear of offending the Liberal Party.
16. The limit was raised to £8 000 plus 3.5 pence per elector. This works out at around £26 000 for the average Euro-constituency.
17. ELD Secretariat, *For a Liberal and Democratic Europe* (Brussels: 1984).
18. Liberal–SDP Alliance, *Let's Get Europe Working Together* (London: 1984).
19. Confederation of Socialist Parties of the European Community, *Manifesto* (Luxembourg: 1984).
20. Labour Party, *Labour's Manifesto for the European Elections* (London: 1984).
21. Conservative Party, *The Strong Voice in Europe* (London: 1984).
22 *The Times*, 20 June 1984.
23 *Ibid.*, 18 June 1984.
24. See J. Lodge, 'The 1984 Euro-elections: a damp squib?', *The World Today*, 40 (1984) 333–40; and J. Lodge, 'Euro-elections and the European Parliament: the dilemma over turnout and powers', *Parliamentary Affairs*, 38 (1984) 40–55.

12   Conclusion

JULIET LODGE

As the results of the second EP elections began to come in, EC
Commission President Gaston Thorn pronounced them a catastrophe:
for the EP's aspirations; for the fate of the draft treaty on European
Union (EUT);[1] and for all those who had hoped that the EP would gain
extra democratic legitimacy from its direct election, and that thus its
repeated claims for an increase in its powers would be vindicated.
Thorn's view that turnout was disappointingly low, having fallen from
62% in 1979 to 60% in 1984, was echoed in the inaugural speech of
Pierre Pflimlin upon his election as the new EP's first President on 24
July 1984. He commented upon the 'abysses of ignorance' among EC
peoples over the EP. Here is a clue to the real origin of the disappointment over the elections. It was not simply the actual level of EC turnout
that gave rise to concern. Rather, what was worrying was that public
knowledge about the EP and the point of the elections was so low: in
some cases, as successive *Eurobarometer* polls revealed, lower than at
equivalent junctures in the pre-1979 election period. This was a severe
blow to all those who, like outgoing EP President Piet Dankert, had
been campaigning since 1982 for a higher turnout in 1984. They had
argued convincingly that the EP's credibility and its claim for an
increase in its powers would be undermined by a poor turnout. Yet at
no point was a figure placed on what would constitute a satisfactory
level of turnout. It was hoped simply that between the first and second
direct elections the EP's visibility and intelligibility to the electorate
would increase sufficiently to persuade voters of the usefulness of
turning out to vote.

But this hope rested upon a number of presuppositions that were not
met. Most of these were based on the assumption that more people
would turn out if there was greater media coverage of the EP. The
expectation was that media coverage of elected MEPs' activities would

increase; that people would begin to associate positive developments in the EC and benefits derived from it with their elected representatives;[2] and that the latter would themselves develop a career-ladder in the EP,[3] seek re-election and campaign on a record of achievement that meant something to the voters. All this presupposed that the EP's image would improve and that public awareness of and support for it would increase rather than remain static or fall after the first elections in 1979.

The problems of improving interest in the EP, dispelling myths about it and combating its poor image, as well as mobilising a largely apathetic or ignorant electorate, proved formidable. Indeed, polls suggested that the 1984 turnout could be lower than in 1979.[4] In some countries traditionally regarded as among the most pro-European of the Ten, such as the FRG and the Netherlands, there was both public condemnation of MEPs' remoteness and above all frustration at the EP's limited powers. Thus, even where the EP's role was understood, the public were aware of what was at stake in the elections and abstained accordingly. This compares with the general finding of ignorance about what was at stake, and how the election results would influence policy initiatives and outcomes. Widespread media characterisation of the EP as an impotent talking-shop was hardly likely to overcome public indifference. The overall effect was to undermine

TABLE 12.1   *Turnout in European elections (in million voters and in %)*

| Member state | 1984 | | 1979 | | Number of seats |
	Registered voters	Turnout	Registered voters	Turnout	
Belgium*	6.97	92.2	6.80	91.4	24
Denmark	3.80	52.2	3.72	47.8	16
Germany	44.45	56.8	42.75	65.7	81
Greece*	7.79	77.2	6.80**	78.6**	24
France	36.83	56.7	35.18	60.7	81
Ireland	2.41	47.6	2.18	63.6	15
Italy	44.44	83.9	42.20	85.5	81
Luxembourg*	0.21	87.0	0.21	88.9	6
The Netherlands	10.70	50.5	9.81	58.1	25
United Kingdom	41.92	32.4	40.53	32.6	81
Total:	199.52	60	190.18	62	434

*Voting compulsory.
**Elections of 18 Oct. 1981.
SOURCE   *Bull. EC*, 6-1984.

voters' sense of political efficacy at a time when awareness of the EP and MEPs' records was low and awareness of continual and seemingly insoluble EC crises was high. Given the background to the 1984 elections, it is perhaps surprising that turnout was as high as it was.

PARTIES AND THE CAMPAIGN

EP funds were distributed according to the number of seats won by each party group after the elections, and before then according to the size of the group. Thus, in the first instance, the EP party groups played an important role in allotting funds both within the group and to the transnational federations. But this did not mean that all parties throughout the Ten, or even that all parties represented in the EP, had an equal chance of securing comparable financial aid for their campaigns. Different national rules over party finance, the raising of election campaign funds and other related issues meant that little uniformity was possible. Funds made available from the EP would, therefore, affect the fortunes of parties in the member states differently. Indeed, there were fears, not least within the EP party groups, that EP funds would be used to offset existing deficits in national parties' campaign coffers. Close vigilance over the spending of EP funds was therefore called for. Yet the controversies that ensued over financing of the parties' 1984 election information campaigns simply highlighted but one of the difficulties that must be confronted if a uniform electoral procedure is to be adopted eventually for EP elections.

The EP's failure to persuade EC member governments to adopt a uniform electoral procedure for EP elections, as required by the Rome Treaty, did not mean that the second elections to the EP would simply be a series of more or less simultaneous national elections. The Seitlinger Report[5] on a common electoral procedure was not completely without effect: several member states amended their 1979 Euroelections provisions to accommodate, if only partly, some important principles advanced in the report, especially those concerning the enfranchisement of EC nationals resident in EC member states other than those of which they are nationals. Some amendments were indubitably a reflection of national political expediency. For example, Belgium increased the number of suppléants (elected concurrently with the MEPs) as there had been fears in the first elected EP that Belgium would exhaust its lists as MEPs (for various reasons, including the acceptance of ministerial posts at home, retirement and death) left their seats. Indeed, in Belgium, placement in the suppléant rankings is now an important consideration for the politically ambitious, not least since vacancies are filled by the next on the list and not by by-election as in Britain. In fact, the British delegation to the first elected EP was among the most stable. Turnover was high (and artificially inflated by the legally contested and much reviled DIFE 'tourniquet') in France. Overall of the 434 MEPs initially elected to the EP, 358 remained MEPs at the beginning of 1984. (This figure excludes turnover among any of the 76 original MEPs' successors.) 29 had left the EP to take up ministerial posts at home,[6] 12 to exercise mandates in national parliaments,[7] two to become ambassadors[8] and others had resigned for a variety of reasons.

By state, only the UK could claim, at least until shortly after the 1983 General election, not to have lost MEPs to national politics.[9] The losses for the other states were as follows: Belgium 12, Denmark 2, the FRG 10, France 27, Greece 2, Ireland 4, Italy 12, Luxembourg 5, and the Netherlands 2. Perhaps somewhat surprising, few of those who had resigned their Euro-mandates played active roles in the 1984 campaign, possibly because of the demands of their national posts. In the UK, for example, parliament was in session during the Euro-campaign, a fact that may help to account for the nature of media coverage of political affairs at that time. However, too much cannot be inferred from turnover levels save that high turnover may be symptomatic of low prestige afforded MEPs (to say nothing of their job satisfaction). It may reflect also the demands of coalition government formation in countries where there has been a degree of cabinet instability. Yet, cumulatively, the effect has been to the EP's disadvantage.

It was not obvious that the 1984 EP elections would be less 'European' than the 1979 EP elections. Three levels of political party interaction were involved in 1979 and in 1984: the national, supranational and transnational. The supranational level involved the EP party groups. The transnational level involved the transnational federations: the CSP, EPP and ELD. There were also loose transnational contacts between parties that either eschewed formal transnational links for Euro-elections (for example, the Communists) or that sought such alliances for electoral or financial reasons (for example, the various 'Green' parties). The supranational level was a source of information material and campaign funds in 1979 and in 1984. The transnational level was the forum for co-ordinating campaign activities across the EC where feasible and desirable and for communicating national member parties' transnational – that is, EC-wide – linkages and identities. As in

1979, the 1984 activities of the CSP, EPP and ELD were the most significant, though a number of other parties (including some hitherto not represented in the EP) developed transnational linkages and rudimentary electoral material. The most important of these were the regional alliance comprising the Dutch Demokraten 66 (D'66), the Danish Radikale Venstre, the French Mouvement des Radicaux de Gauche (MRG) and the Greek Komma Dimokratikou Socialismou (KODISO) and the Green alliance that formed after much internal dissent. Divisions over women's and peace issues were at the root of such discord. Yet, whereas in 1979 only in the UK, France, the FRG and Belgium had 'Green' candidates contested the EP elections, in 1984 they were joined by candidates from Ireland, Luxembourg and the Netherlands. In Denmark, Greece and Italy no 'Green' candidates stood for election though some attempt was made to set up 'Green' parties. In terms of the 1984 EP election result, it is noteworthy that Belgium and the FRG (that is, member states where the Greens have had political successes already at the local, regional or national elections and exercised office as a result) fielded successful candidates.

It was to be the transnational federations who, after protracted deliberations in working groups, drafted common manifestos and helped organise electoral events like the EPP's boat that cruised up and down the Rhine and the ELD train that traversed some EC member states. Other political parties tried various devices to arrest media attention and public interest. British and Dutch Labour parties, for instance, held Euro-events with celebrities in attendance. The SPD's campaign, led by Frau Focke, was based on a circus. The circus acts were interspersed with political commentary relating to the election. Frau Focke also led a similar 'Frauentournee (Women's tour) that brought together women entertainers and female candidates and made the SPD's hope of attracting women voters patent. It should be noted that this has to be seen against the background of German parties' quest for women's votes, the fact that since April 1984 the Green's Executive Committee was all-female, and a Frauenpartei (that won 0.4% of the vote) contested the elections. At a more personal level, both the SPD and the German Christian Democrats tried to encourage football fans (that is, mainly men) to turn out. They produced pocket diaries listing international matches in the run-up to 17 June 1984 when the diaries 'reminded' the football fans to vote.

Organisationally and programmatically, the three levels of party activity coalesced and coincided to a small degree in that the national political parties (which had contributed notably to transnational rather than supranational activities) used the limited resources of the other two. There was little contact in many member states between new candidates and national party activists on the one hand, and MEPs seeking re-election on the other hand. The latter had been more or less autonomous and, if not impervious to national party directions, then able to ignore them some of the time. However, as some Labour MEPs found to their cost, the price to be paid for taking a too independent line was de-selection. Yet, it was because of the disjunction in electioneering between the supranational and national levels that the track-record of MEPs, much less of their EP party group as a whole, failed to become apparent. Records are usually important elements in election campaigns because they form a relatively intelligible focal point for the electoral agenda that parties, notably government parties, set.

The problem in the 1984 EP election was that the three levels of party activity and agenda-setting at best only partially coincided and often did not coincide at all. National preoccupations dominated the debate. Its parochial nature was not, however, simply a result of national political and especially governing party elites' ability to manipulate the agenda. Nor can it be explained simply by the content and presentation of the transnational election manifestos. Rather, the lack of a sustained Euro-agenda in party and public debate can be explained also partly by the fact that the agenda was determined elsewhere, without reference to either the transnational manifestos, MEPs or the Euro-aspects of national manifestos for the most part. Furthermore, the fluidity of this agenda and the controversy surrounding it was determined not by the parties so much as by EC member governments – many of whose members were largely absent from the campaign. Their record was a catalogue of failure arising from a sequence of indecision and crises resolved, not as hoped, before the elections but somewhat inconclusively thereafter at the Fontainebleau summit. Yet the fact that the parties did not launch sustained attacks on governments' EC records (possibly out of political expedience) added to the sense of unreality and disjunction in the Euro-election for, in national elections, the government's and parliament's records are usually seen as virtually synonymous. To the extent that in the EC the rather false analogy between the Commission and a government was pursued, the Commission could be derided for policies adopted (after much inter-governmental bargaining) by governments who could then disclaim responsibility for them, if so minded, in the EP election campaign. The campaign was, after all, conducted at a very superficial level. In some member states, the type of televised cross-questioning of politicians that typifies national campaigns was missing largely but not only for want of well-informed interviewers. It is perhaps not surprising that the EP's record as such failed to rise above that of the EC and its many failures. Conceivably, disillusion with the latter was reflected in turnout levels.

Given the lack of sustained debate over the EC and the EP, it was crucial that the parties, notably those linked in EP groups, should agree and campaign on common issues and future policy priorities if they wanted to instill a sense of Europeanism in the minds of the electorate. As shown some efforts were made to do this.

ISSUES

Many MEPs expected there to be some common campaign issues. Indeed, the EP had itself set, in February 1984, the EUT as *the* campaign issue. Many had hoped that this would be the catalyst for a far-reaching debate on the highly controversial and vexed question of institutional reform in the EC. They believed that unless EC decision-making procedures were changed fundamentally, the EC would be unable to pursue effective policies over a range of socio-economic, international, security and defence areas. The institutional changes mooted in the EUT have federal overtones and require an extension of the EP's legislative powers and a curbing of the autonomy of the Council of Ministers. The question, therefore, of whether the EP should be afforded such powers was one that MEPs felt could be an electoral issue throughout the Ten. Far more importantly, however, many felt that the EUT itself could be the key common electoral issue. This was because the EUT confronted the question of the EC's future. It was, therefore, seen as both a focal point for electoral debate and as an important opportunity for the voters to be mobilised over the question of European integration. It was felt also that discussion of contemporary EC problems – such as the perennial agricultural and budgetary crises – could stimulate interest in EUT policy recommendations and *vice versa*. However, this could not happen if both national political elites and the public remained either ignorant of or disinterested in possibly obscure EC questions. Moreover, the prominence given by the media to member governments' repeated failures to solve the EC's difficulties was not likely to inspire faith in any new blueprint for European integration, much less in one espoused by an institution that had failed both to impress itself on the public mind and to induce either the Commission or Council to heed its views.

Immediately before the election, the EC's agenda had been dominated by a set of interrelated issues. All centred on the EC's liquidity crisis and hence more or less directly on the CAP. Farm spending was rising again; and a VAT increase was needed if the EC were to meet its commitments. There was deadlock over how, when and whether to raise the finance needed to meet projected CAP expenditure. Also, the British and German governments had yet to receive their 1983 budget rebates and the British refused steadfastly to entertain more 'own resources' and EC spending (to which they would have to contribute) pending the payment of their rebate. The EP, in its capacity as part of the EC's budgetary authority, became embroiled in this as it then blocked the budget rebates. Ensuing arguments deflected attention from the EP and from the EUT even though the interminable wrangling provided a golden opportunity for a debate over the EC's future. Thus, the EP's positive record – for example, on international affairs and transport – was obscured. Instead, the media focused on budgetary issues and Britain's lack of European commitment. Indeed, a poll revealed that the UK was the least liked state in the EC.[10]

Concurrently, the EUT was presented to several national parliaments as part of the campaign to draw attention to a common electoral issue; and the idea of a two-tier EC was revived discreetly. That the UK would be in a second or third-tier (possibly with two other reluctant member states: Denmark and Greece) was not doubted. While Britain's role in the EC might have been seen as a possible and easy campaign target, it would have been inadvisable politically for parties – notably those in government or coalitions – to have succumbed to temptation. It was safer to call for more 'Europeanism', more co-operation, and less nationalism (that is, as shown by a more limited resort to the veto in the Council of Ministers). But this 'safe' ploy risked being meaningless and tedious for the electorate. While contemporary problems must have influenced national and transnational parties' working groups drafting electoral manifestos, they were not related intelligibly to the issues set before the electorate, even though at an EC-level, some attempt was made to project and relate common election issues on a party-specific and ideological basis. Even so, the most pressing issues failed to surface. Progress between 1979 and 1984 on the situation in a given policy sector was hardly mentioned. This confirmed a negative impression of the EP: had it achieved anything? Nevertheless, it would be wrong to castigate the EPP, ELD and CSP programmes as completely irrelevant since they broached issues that were the stuff of daily politics in the Ten. They raised the very questions that had surfaced in one form or another in the general elections that had taken place in every member state except Luxembourg (where the national election coincides with the EP election) since June 1981. Perhaps one of the problems of persuading the media and the electorate of the programmes' relevance lay not simply with ignorance of what had been advocated but with an ingrained scepticism that any solutions – let alone anything new – were realisable. After all, if the EC had failed to solve CAP-related problems, its credibility in combating unemployment was hardly likely to be high. Furthermore, the very parties recommending the programmes were those that had demonstrably failed to find remedies hitherto at the national level. It is possible, therefore, that manifestos were dismissed as so much rhetoric. This is clearly a general indictment of the parties rather than of the EP alone. Moreover, the campaign dynamics differed from state to state making a sustained Euro-campaign difficult to engineer. The duration and scope of the campaigns varied, the campaigns themselves peaked at varying times, many seemed to be an anti-climax and the issues (despite their obvious European relevance in the sense that questions like unemployment transcended national boundaries) seemed devoid of clear Community policy implications.

THE NATIONAL DIMENSION

It is perhaps not surprising that national issues seemed to eclipse the Euro-dimension to the EP election, and that party elites (because of ignorance or out of desperation) tried to enliven the debate and make it intelligible by putting it in national terms. Inevitably, this gave the appearance of the elections being mid-term referendums on national governments. Even then, the ploy did not always work for parties who deliberately tried to run their campaign to this end. Thus, for example, even while insisting that it must secure far more EP seats than in 1979, the Labour Party in Britain endeavoured unsuccessfully to draw the Conservative government out to defend its record – not on EC matters but on national issues, principally the acute problems resulting from public expenditure cuts in education, social welfare and health. Nor did the Alliance fare much better, despite a telling unmasking of the Conservative government's less than European record that contradicted the Conservative Party's claim of being Britain's 'European' party. The British example in the 1984 EP elections revealed most obviously how non-engagement by the government of the day, and half-hearted engagement by opposition party leaders can (in view of

MEPs' low visibility) exacerbate the problems of mobilising the electorate. One may cynically suggest that governments have a vested interest in ensuring that EP elections do not acquire a status or importance approaching those of national elections; that turnout remains below that for general elections; and that the electorate remains rather docile. Yet some issues were to be sufficiently contentious as to excite some local national interest.

Given the apparent absence of common Euro-election issues throughout the Ten, it is not surprising that the EP election results should be interpreted in national terms, mainly as swings against national governments. For example, the German government appeared to suffer a defeat at the hands of the SPD and the Greens. While the CDU/CSU sustained but marginal losses compared to the previous elections, their FDP coalition partner failed to surmount the 5% hurdle. In Italy, the PCI achieved the 'sorpasso' in winning more votes than the Christian Democrats (DC). But PCI gains were not dramatic and some commentators felt that the party had been able to capitalise on a sympathy vote following the death of Berlinguer. Moreover, DC losses were seen as insufficient to warrant a change in governing coalition. In France, PCF losses were deemed disastrous, and the rise of the National Front (FN) as symptomatic of a protest vote: in 1981, 43.5% of FN supporters had voted for the Gaullist RPR; and 21% for other parties. While British Conservatives maintained quite a lead, this was not seen as significant. Instead, the denial of an EP seat to the Alliance which had won almost 20% of the vote caused a rumpus.

The interpretation of the EP election results in national terms was accentuated by the post-election comments of party spokespersons and media commentators who related the results to the governments' records. But at issue here was not so much the governments' records within the EC. Instead, their records in managing the national economy, curbing unemployment and public expenditure were paraded. Although such themes featured in the elections throughout the Ten, they could not be seen as common issues over which the elections were fought. Instead, the more parochial issue and state-specific questions became themes over which the parties engaged in a contest for votes.

Despite the post-electoral linkage of governments' pre-election records and the votes they won at the polls, the governments' position *vis-à-vis* opposition parties remained more or less intact. The EP elections had few destabilising effects nationally.

The experience of two EP elections has shown the difficulties of mobilising the electorate around common Euro-issues and the potentially damaging consequences of this for the EP's aspirations. Neither transnational parties nor MEPs have been able to assume (either sporadically at elections or continually throughout the EP's term of office) the kind of educative and communication functions performed by national parties in the member states *vis-à-vis* the media, public and party activists. Moreover, it is within the ranks of national parties that scepticism, if not hostility, often lies towards MEPs and the EC. This is a problem as it falls to national parties to mobilise the electorate using, if they so choose, more or less enthusiastically the material and resources of any transnational organisations of which they may be members. They have to bring their sitting and prospective MEPs to the public notice. The problems of the former's visibility is highlighted at election time. Then it becomes patent to the electorate at large (if not to party activists who may have received newsletters from MEPs about their EC work on behalf of the constituency and party in the interim) that national parties' seeming transient interest in MEPs is motivated by political expedience. The electorate may react by a display of indifference or cynicism or both. (The overall effect is a diminished respect for politics.) This is all the more likely if voters sense, on the part of the governing party or parties and other major parties, an absence of genuine commitment to advancing MEPs and/or to working efficiently in an institution whose effectiveness they wish to promote. Derision of the EP is an easy way to sabotage incipient interest in the elections and to undermine the EP's legitimacy.

Parties can hardly expect to mobilise the electorate, even against their domestic opponents, if they do not imbue their activists first with a sense of the EP's importance and legitimacy, and the legitimising role MEPs can play (no matter in how limited a way) in the EC. This is more than a question of countering ignorance of both the EC and the EP's functions, powers and role in it among national parties. It involves persuading them that a Euro-political elite exists and is linked to the national level. As it is, there are fears among many national party activists that such an elite may be a national competitor for higher national *not* EC office. Moreover, it is all too obvious that national governments by and large treat both the EP and the Commission (notably in their nomination of Commissioners) with scarcely concealed contempt. Thus national political elites appear to lack respect for the EC. It is not surprising then that some should make only a token effort to get out the vote in Euro-elections. Nor is it surprising that their campaigns should then come to focus (by design, accident or simple neglect) on highly visible national issues that divide the governing and opposition parties. To view the EP elections as just another of several electoral occasions on which to test the relative popularity of the various parties and particularly that of the government is unremarkable. Moreover, that may seem to be the only way that national parties and commentators can make any political sense of the elections given the fact that they appear devoid of real significance for the EP's future, the formation of a governing majority or an agenda of political priorities.

RESULTS

If the elections had relatively little impact on national political balances, they did have implications for the cohesion of the EP. Whereas in most member states the party make-up of a newly elected parliament is known within hours or at most days of the election results being announced, in the case of the 1984 Euro-election the final outcome was not clear until the EP's inaugural session on 24 July 1984, by which time most people had lost interest in the election. Less than half the 59 million voters in the UK, Ireland, Denmark and the Netherlands had gone to the polls on 14 June and a further 96 million people had voted on 17 June in France, Belgium, the FRG, Italy, Luxembourg and Greece. The first results in national terms were not announced until after the polls had closed at 10.00 p.m. on 17 June 1984. Five weeks later exactly how the national results translated themselves at the Euro-level became clear. That the final composition of the EP should have been delayed so long was due primarily to the vacillations among the parties, particularly among the ranks of those formerly not represented either at all in the EP or not in an established EP party group. While the Socialist and EPP groups were expected to be the two largest groups as before, there was a good deal of speculation over the eventual composition of the Liberal group and the EPD.

The changing make-up of national delegations from certain member states was problematic also. Some newly elected MEPs either were earmarked for national office (as in Italy and Luxembourg) or promptly resigned having served their purpose of making a given list of largely unknown candidates recognisable to the public.[11] Thus, pending the EP's inaugural session and the verification of credentials, the final composition of the EP was somewhat uncertain even though the size of the major parties was known. Furthermore, given the entry of neofascists and 'Green' MEPs, as well as the increased number of non-

TABLE 12.2 The strength of party groups relative to 1979*

Political groups	Total 1984	Bel	Dk	Ger	Fr	Gr	Irl	It	Lux	Neth	UK
Socialists	130 (+6)	7 (—)	4 (—)	33 (—2)	20 (—3)	10 (—)	—(—4)	12 (—2)	2 (+1)	9 (—)	33 (+16)*
European People's Party	110 (—7)	6 (—4)	1 (—)	41 (—1)	9 (—)	9 (+1)	6 (+2)	27 (—3)	3 (—)	8 (—2)	—
European Democrats	50 (—13)	—	4 (+2)	—	—	—	—	—	—	—	46 (—15)**
Communists	41 (—8)	—	1 (—1)	—	10 (—9)	4 (—)	—	26 (+2)	—	—	—
Liberals	31 (—7)	5 (+1)	2 (—1)	—(—4)	12 (—3)	—	1 (—)	5 (—)	1 (—1)	5 (—1)	—
European Democratic Alliance	29 (+7)	—	—(—1)	—	20 (+5)	—	8 (+3)	—	—	—	1 (—)†
Rainbow Group	20	4	4	7	—	—	—	3	—	2	—
Group of the European Right	16	—	—	—	10	1	—	5	—	—	—
Non-attached	7 (—1)	2	—	—	—	—	—(—1)	3	—	1	1††
Total:	434	24	16	81	81	24	15	81	6	25	81

*32 Labour Members and one from the Social Democratic and Labour Party (SDLP).

**45 Conservatives and one Official Ulster Unionist.

†One Scottish National Party.

††One Democratic Unionist Party Member.

*Figures in brackets denote gains and losses over the 1979 result.

SOURCE *Europe 84, 9/1984.*

affiliated ('non-attached') MEPs, greater fragmentation with a consequent loss in operational efficiency was predicted for the EP.

The election results did not radically shift the political balance in the European Parliament among the major party groups. Thus, the Socialists won 130 seats, the EPP 110, the EDG 50, the Communists 41 and the Liberals 31. Manoeuvring within and between both the national delegations and the EP party groups intensified shortly after the results had been announced, with numerous meetings taking place in Brussels. These meetings were important both for determining subsequent tactics over the election of the EP President and other officers, and the allocation of standing committee chairpersonships and seats. These in turn were crucial to the setting of the newly elected EP's policy priorities, notably on such matters as budgetary reform, the EUT and adoption of a common electoral procedure for the 1989 EP elections.[12]

Looking at the main party groups, certain changes in policy orientation were likely in view of changes in the EP intra-group balance. The Socialists, having won seats relative to 1979, no longer had any Irish MEPs but had gained 15 extra Labour MEPs. This put the SPD and Labour on a par with 33 and 32 seats respectively. The SPD's former dominance and often pro-integration influence within the Group was, thereby, immediately curbed by the entry of less than committed Europeans. The two disagreed over tactics *vis-à-vis* the election of the EP President: whereas the SPD was ready to consider backing an EPP candidate on condition that the EPP supported a Socialist candidate in two-and-a-half years time (when the first EP President would have served his term), Labour saw this as against its nature. Yet, in terms of tactical manoeuvres within the EP, this would have allowed Socialist and EPP Groups with 130 seats and 110 seats respectively to secure the Presidency for themselves as, having together the absolute majority, they might not have needed to depend on support from other party groups. The intra-group situation was further complicated by the fact that only French, Greek and Italian socialist MEPs could look to national political parties enjoying government responsibility. The rest were in opposition at the national level. Nevertheless, Labour and SPD MEPs were able to outmanoeuvre the former Belgian Socialist Group chairman Glinne to elect Rudi Arndt Group Chairman and Barbara Castle as Vice-chairman. In the EPP, while the Italian DC and the CDU/CSU together have an absolute majority within the Group, past voting and alignment patterns reflected group cleavages. The DC was allied with Socialists and the Centre-Left whereas the CDU/CSU was close to the EDG and the RPR within the EPD Group. However, such cleavages were not expected to shatter the EPP's internal unity over basic issues like the EUT and the EP presidential elections in which the French (having persuaded the EPP to back Pierre Pflimlin) highlighted divisive possibilities and inter-group bargains.

Shortly after the EP election results were announced, rumours of shifting alignments were rife. The EDG (minus 13 seats), anxious about its position relative to the centre of the hemicycle and to the Liberals, tried to get seats closer to the centre. Some ED members were rumoured to be considering splitting to join the Liberals who were keen to resume seats nearer the centre (vacated ten years ago to the European Conservatives) in between the Socialists and the EPP rather than at the extreme right. While the ED's almost uni-national composition meant that it did not face acute intra-group, nationally-based cleavages, divisions over policies, a uniform electoral procedure and the EUT persisted, especially among the 45 UK Conservatives.

Like the Socialist Group, the national balance in the EP's fourth largest party group, the Communist Group, was upset significantly by the French PCF losing nine and the PCI gaining two seats, bringing the latter's total to 26 seats (against the PCF's ten seats). The PCI has almost double the number of seats held by French, Danish and Greek Communists. The pro-integrationist PCI was expected to continue diverging from the rest of the Group on policy matters.

The make-up of the Liberal Group occasioned perhaps the most speculation partly because of the uncertain future of the EPD and partly because of the numerical strength of the French (whose Simone Veil became Group chairman) in a group traditionally seen as probably the most ideologically fragmented in the EP. The Group's composition illustrated most graphically the distortions in representation arising from the absence of either a uniform electoral procedure or, at a minimum, simply an agreement to hold EP elections according to a system of PR. Thus the Group's two Danes were elected on a 12.5% share of the vote; the five Belgians with 18%; the five Italians (including Republicans) with 6.1%; the one Luxembourger with 21.2% and the five Dutch (Freedom and Democracy) MEPs with 18.9% of the vote.

However, as in 1979, one of the EC's largest Liberal parties, electorally speaking, failed to win a single EP seat. Had PR been in force in the UK, 15 Alliance MEPs would have entered the EP. The representational distortion arising from this case is magnified when compared to the share of the vote needed in other member states to secure EP seats. For example, in France the PS won 20 EP seats with 20% of the vote. Yet in Denmark, the Social Democrats secured but three seats with 19.4% of the vote. Discrepancies arise also out of the allocation of EP seats to the member states, almost irrespective of the size of their population. France is the chief beneficiary of the 'Big Four's' quota of 81 seats each. Its electorate is nearly 37 million, compared to the FRG's and Italy's almost 45 million each and the UK's almost 42 million.

Electoral thresholds also produced discrepancies. With respectively 4.3% and 3.9% of the vote, Agalev (Flemish Ecologists) and Ecolo V (Walloon Ecologists) secured one Belgian EP seat each, whereas the FDP was excluded with 4.8% of the vote. The Greek EPEN and KKE-es MEPs were elected with 2.3 and 3.4% of the vote respectively. In Italy, lower percentages still secured seats. The cost per seat to member states and parties was thus unequal.[13]

Nor surprisingly, the Liberals and prominent EPP MEPs were quick to condemn the lack of a uniform electoral procedure. Former EC Commission President, Roy Jenkins, stressed that PR in Northern Ireland had, as in 1979, resulted in turnout being twice that of Great Britain. He pointed out at a press conference in Strasbourg on 25 July 1984 that '5.4 million voters in Britain ... elected 45 Conservatives, over 11.5 million voters in Italy only 26 Christian Democrats. Such figures distort the entire political balance ...'.[14]

The political balance in the Liberal Group was itself altered primarily by the exclusion of the four, formerly disproportionately influential, FDP MEPs. The Group's policy orientation is thus expected to be more conservative and right-wing although this is an image the Group hoped to dispel. The Liberals' shift to the right could have been magnified had the EPD split as rumoured with RPR members seeking admission to the Liberal Group and their Irish colleagues from Fianna Fail seeking entry to the Socialist Group. The EPD's future was open to debate too, given talks over a mooted name-change to make it more attractive to other MEPs disaffected from their own group or 'lacking a home'. This tactic had, after all, inspired the European Conservatives to re-name themselves European Democrats in 1979 though this did not increase the EDG's attractiveness outside British and Danish circles. In the event, the EPD, calling itself a 'rassemblement', re-named itself the European Democratic Alliance (EDA).

As the EP party groups were constituted, the greatest interest centred on the chances of new groups[15] forming around firstly the Greens and their associates, and secondly the French National Front. Not only would new party groups alter the EP's political balance and orientation, notably in the 18 standing committees decided upon at the inaugural session, but theoretically, at least, they would reduce the chances of an obstructionist group like the former Group for the Technical Co-ordination and Defence of Independent Groups and Members (TCG) impeding the EP's business. Yet the eventual constitution of new party groups confirmed the second elected EP's greater fragmentation.

The entry of extreme right-wing and 'Green' MEPs revived the debate on amending Rule 26 of the EP Rules of Procedure to increase the number of MEPs needed to form an official EP party group. The whole issue came to the fore briefly when members of the TCG met on 13 July 1984 to discuss prospects for re-constituting the TCG or forming a party group based on ideological affinity (as provided for by the Rules of Procedure). Some felt that all that should be set up was a loose co-ordination group for technical purposes.[16] Political machinations continued until the EP's first meeting after the elections when the establishment of two new party groups was announced: the Rainbow Group and the Group of the European Right. That left seven MEPs 'non-attached'.[17]

The 20-strong Rainbow Group comprises three MEPs from the European Free Alliance (Flemish People's Union and Val d'Aosta Union and Sardinian Action Party), eleven from the Green alliance, the two Belgian ecologists and the four Danish Anti-EEC Movement MEPs. It has four co-chairmen: one Dane, Belgian, Dutchman and German. The Italian Radicals were excluded partly for political reasons that accentuated the divisions within the Rainbow Group. Acute internal rifts led to contradictory statements over the Group's ambitions being issued. On the one hand, it was said that the Group was merely a technical co-ordination group that would revise its statutes to permit other parties (including the Italian Radicals) to join it; on the other hand, it was argued that the Group would draft a 'legislative agreement' valid until the next Euro-elections to help it protect minority parties' interests *vis-à-vis* the EP's major groups. The idea of protecting minorities' interests is advocated mainly by MEPs from smaller EC member states, and this theme was echoed by Luxembourg's six MEPs.[18]

Great controversy surrounded the establishment after many denials and rumours of a Group of the European Right comprising ten FN MEPs (whose leader J-M. le Pen became Group chairman), five Italian (MSI) MEPs and one Greek (EPEN) MEP. There was and continues to be much dismay that such a group should not only be large enough to gain recognition as an official EP group but that its members (notably the French) could claim a legitimacy, denied them at home, through their membership of the EP. Disapproval at their entry into the EP was marked not just by the Liberals' and the EDG's anxieties over EP seating arrangements but also by MEPs, mainly Socialists – led by Arndt whose father was killed by the Nazis – wearing white roses (the wartime symbol of resistance to fascism) at the EP's inaugural session. Jean-Pierre Cot sent a letter to his colleagues noting that while individual MEPs' rights must be respected, whatever their opinions, 'a democratic parliament [could] not allow itself to be represented by opponents of democracy'.[19] He immediately asked his Group to put to the EP Bureau a Rule amendment requiring that EP party groups subscribe to European democratic principles before assuming responsibilities associated with the EP, notably *vis-à-vis* other states, parliaments, interest groups and so on. Several MEPs remain worried over the European Right's potential participation in EP standing committees and over any role they may assume in either sensitive subcommittees, the acquisition of rapporteurships, or posts on new committees.[20]

How the constellation of political forces in the EP will affect its work and policy orientations, as well as the future of the EUT (widely seen as the first elected EP's most vital legacy to the new MEPs), remains to be seen. Yet the inaugural session hinted at the nature of the EP's priorities at least for the short-term.[21] The session was dominated by the election of the EP's President, presided over by the EP's second oldest member Jacqueline Thome Patenôtre (born 1906) as the oldest MEP Nikolaos Gazis (born 1903) was in hospital. She addressed the EP, stressing the need for a political Europe of free peoples and for prompt action towards European Union as 'we no longer have the time to wait'.[22]

Intense inter- and intra-party bargaining preceded the nomination and election of candidates for the Presidency. The election went more smoothly than in 1979. Pierre Pflimlin was elected on the second ballot.[23] The EP Vice-Presidents, who with the President constitute the EP Bureau, were elected the following day. Five Quaestors, who deal with administrative matters concerning MEPs, were also elected.

In his inaugural speech President Pflimlin called for the abandonment of Euro-pessimism in favour of positive action to make the EC competitive and to enable it to regain its lost lead, especially in research and technology. He stressed also the need for the EP to acquire co-legislative powers and to make common cause, as appropriate, with the Council.[24] This view was reiterated by the new Council President, Dr

Garret FitzGerald, by Commission President, Thorn, and by Irish Foreign Minister, Peter Barry. The latter stressed that agreement on budgetary issues was paramount, not least among member governments divided over raising extra funds for 1984 by EC regulation or inter-governmental agreement: the British contested the need for more funds and argued for savings and deferrals of expenditure until 1985.

Party groups' reactions to these speeches, and notably to the call for greater EP-Council co-operation, bode ill for the rest of the session generally and in particular for the discussion of the British and German budget refunds and for prospects for a 1984 supplementary budget. In the first Group reply to the earlier speeches and to talk at Fontainebleau about creating a citizens' Europe, Arndt insisted that people did not want a powerless EP respected by neither the Commission nor Council; but that they wanted an EP to defend their interests, even if this involved rejecting budgets and sacking the Commission. When the Ten did something about jobs, peace, the environment and human rights, he said, people would be more in favour of the EC. This was far more vital than the Euro-Council's creation of a committee to examine ways of making the EC more of a reality to EC citizens. Indeed, as Egon Klepsch (EPP) pointed out, a citizens' Europe could not exist without a strong Parliament.

The budget issues dominated other EP Groups' replies,[25] and the EP passed several resolutions against the outcome of the Fontainebleau summit.[26] These culminated in the EP expressing its dissatisfaction both at not being consulted (in its capacity as part of the EC's budgetary authority) over the financial decisions taken at Fontainebleau; and at the UK government not standing up to its earlier pledge to support a supplementary budget before receiving its budget rebate. Thus, the EP decided by 214 votes to 70 votes with three abstentions not to release the 1202 million ECUs in rebates due to the UK and FRG from their contributions to the 1983 budget. The EP agreed to consider releasing the United Kingdom refund of 750 million ECUs when a 1984 supplementary budget was submitted.

THE FUTURE

It is no accident that the second elected EP, like its predecessor, should begin by confronting the Council over still unresolved critical budgetary (and hence CAP-related) issues. But it must do more than its predecessor to force the Council not only into accommodating its position, but into making the necessary reforms without which spending on new and much needed programmes will be impossible. Financial and institutional reforms along lines advocated in the EUT are the *sine qua non* of progress. The EP resolution (adopted by 190 votes to 66 votes with 22 abstentions on 27 July 1984) requesting the Council to liaise with the EP and to use the EUT as the starting point in its deliberations in the two 'Spaak committees' must not be allowed to sink without trace. But is the EP up to challenging the member governments on these two fronts? Does it have the requisite expertise and will to do so? Or has the EP lost to national political life and other pursuits or through electoral vagaries most of the first elected EP's most experienced and active members?

There is a good deal of continuity in the EP's composition: 228 sitting-MEPs were re-elected and 50% or more were returned from each state except France, Greece, Italy and Luxembourg. Indeed, in the case of the latter, the elected MEP may well stand down by 1985. Actual turnover compared to the 1979 EP is, however, somewhat higher given the changing composition of some national contingents between 1979 and 1984. Yet the fall from 125 to 49 in the number of dual-mandated MEPs may indicate that people are developing careers within the EP itself, rather than seeing it simply as a convenient stepping-stone to more rapid advancement in national politics. Yet this

TABLE 12.3   *Composition of the new EP*

Country	MEPs	Former MEPs	Women 1984	Women 1979	Dual mandate 1984	Dual mandate 1979
Belgium	24	13	4	2	0	18
Denmark	16	11	6	5	1	6
France	81	34	17	18	6	22
Germany	81	56	16	12	1	28
Greece	24	6	2	2*	5	0
Ireland	15	7	2	2	8	13
Italy	81	35	8	11	16	21
Luxembourg	6	1	1	1	5	6
The Netherlands	25	14	7	5	0	2
United Kingdom	81	51	12	11	7	9
Total:	434	228	75	69	49	125

*Elections in Greece 1981.
Source   *European Parliament Briefing*, Strasbourg, 24–27 July 1984.

does not mean that the EP will necessarily be any more influential than its predecessor.[27] What matters is whether MEPs share a conviction that the EP has a duty to the electorate to agitate for and secure financial and institutional changes. Such changes must be valued for the impact they will have on making the EC more responsive and more effective over a range of policies rather than only for the increased power and room for manoeuvre they will afford the EP. The danger for the EP's aspirations is that what MEPs may advance in terms of democratising EC decision-making could too easily be condemned by national governments, parliaments and parties as the pursuit of self-interest.

Indeed, former EP President Dankert erred perhaps in arguing that national parliaments must be persuaded to relinquish some powers to the EP.[28] It is not national parliaments but national governments who will find EP power gains encroaching upon their autonomy. Moreover, MEPs should beware of committing themselves to further integration when they know that governments will certainly frustrate it. The second elected EP cannot afford to muddle through or to let governments, by way of the Council of Ministers and the European Council, dictate a course for procrastination and failure. MEPs accept the need for the EP to exploit fully its existing powers. Starting with the budget and its obligation to see a uniform electoral procedure in effect for 1989, the EP must demand a single seat for itself (preferably in Brussels) and so develop its legislative capacity as to alter the EC's institutional balance and render the EC effective. No amount of Euro-symbols of identity will compensate for visible and tangible reform. But it remains the task of MEPs to select and focus their political priorities to good effect. Most realise that they must influence policy outputs; exercise effective control over the Commission and Council; and act consistently, not least in agricultural matters, to rationalise and re-direct EC spending. If they cannot do so, then they cannot realistically expect either national parties or the electorate in 1989 to become sufficiently motivated to ensure a high turnout. Nor can they expect to see endorsed their vision of a European Community or a European Union in which a democratically elected Parliament plays an effective legislative role initiating, scrutinising and legitimising policy, and convincingly exercises scrutiny and control powers over the Commission and Council. If the distribution of power among EC institutions is to be altered to the benefit of the European Parliament, MEPs must now demonstrate their competence and persuade the public that only through democratic institutional reform can the EC hope to progress and meet future challenges. If MEPs cannot establish the EP as a dynamic force for policy reform and democratic change and if they and the national parties fail to make known a positive record of achievement to voters in a newly enlarged EC in the 1989 EP elections, they will only have themselves to blame for a dismal turnout.

NOTES AND REFERENCES

1. See J. Lodge, 'European Union and the First Elected European Parliament: The Spinelli Initiative', *Journal of Common Market Studies*, 22 (1984) pp. 377–402; and J. Lodge, 'European Union and Direct Elections 1984', *The Round Table*, 289 (1984) pp. 57–68.
2. See J. Lodge and V. Herman, *Direct Elections to the European Parliament: A Community Perspective* (London, 1982).
3. See the Mannheim MEP survey of 1983 and K. Reif, ed., *European Elections 1979/81 and 1984: Conclusions and Perspectives* (Berlin: Quoraum, 1984).
4. *Eurobarometer*, no. 20 (Dec. 1983) and no. 21 (Apr. 1984).
5. See Report drawn up on behalf of the Political Affairs Committee on a draft uniform electoral procedure for the election of Members of the European Parliament (Seitlinger Report, Parts A and B/C), *European Parliament Working Documents*, 1-988/81/A (10.2.82) and 1-988/81/B-C (26.2.82). See, also, J. Lodge, 'The 1984 Euro-Election Tour: The Quest for Uniformity', *The Parliamentarian*, 54 (1983) pp. 204–12; and C. Sasse *et al.*, *The European Parliament: Towards a Uniform Procedure for Direct Elections* (Luxembourg, 1981).
6. They included two MEPs who, having been ministers, were subsequently to become Commission President (Thorn and Delors), Werner, Wolter, Santer, Debatisse, Boden, Oelsen, Spautz, Colombo, Nothomb, Vanderpoorten, Fleisch, Faure, Roudy, Cresson, O'Leary, Desmond, Kavanagh, De Clercq, Tindemans, De Keersmaeker, Georgiadis, Cluskey, Schwarzenberg, Craxi, Visentini, Ruffolo and Pattison. Turnover was higher still since some of their successors in turn resigned.
7. Dekker, Josselin, Gaspard, Estier, Forni, Jalton, O'Connell, Sarre, Ansart, Oehler, Colla and Brandt.
8. Martinez and Poniridis. More than a dozen MEPs died.
9. The number of dual-mandated MEPs rose then to 18, four of whom were Members of the House of Lords. Of those elected to the House of Commons in May 1983, few also sought re-election to the EP. There was some criticism that MEPs had used service in the EP as a shortcut to a seat in the Commons.
10. *Eurobarometer*, no. 21 (1984). See *Europe* (July 1984).
11. Elected MEPs who had become ministers (in Italy and Luxembourg) were initially expected to attend the EP's July session, their names having been notified on the EP register, even though it was clear that they would have to resign their EP seats given the incompatibility, under the 1976 Act, between the exercise of ministerial duties and an MEP's mandate.

12. *Europe*, no. 3883 (4 July 1984 p. 3.
13. See J. Lodge and V. Herman, op. cit., pp. 250–1.
14. *The Week* (24–27 July 1984) p. 26.
15. *Europe* no. 3886 (7 July 1984) p. 3.
16. *Europe*, nos 3891 and 3892 (14 and 16 July 1984 respectively).
17. Two Belgians, three Italians, one Briton and one Irish MEP. The two 'non-attached' Belgians, Jos Happart and Jef Ulburghs waited to join the Socialist Group.
18. *Europe*, no. 3890 (13 July 1984). MEPs decided to table an amendment to the EP Rules of Procedure such that each member state is represented in the EP Bureau because the new Bureau lacked a Luxembourger.
19. *Europe*, ibid.
20. The fear that they may try to chair a committee responsible for human rights having responsibility for relations with South America was lessened at the July 1984 session of the EP when motions requesting the establishment of a committee on human rights and a committee on fisheries were rejected, though the former became a PAC sub-committee. As the EP's standing committees with 24–45 MEPs were set up, the Right did not win posts as chairmen or vice-chairmen. German Rainbow MEPs were more successful.
21. The inaugural session opened on 24 July 1984 in accordance with the Rule that the EP should meet on the first Tuesday to fall after expiry of an interval of one month from the time the last polling stations close.
22. *The Week* (24–27 July 1984).
23. After the first ballot, le Pen stood down and announced his support for Pflimlin whereupon Pflimlin was asked by Socialists if he would accept the Right's votes should they be needed to win him the Presidency. He noted that they were not needed. Of 413 valid votes in the first ballot, he won 165, Dankert 123, Spinelli 11, Lady Elles 44, Pajetta 37, Bloch von Blottnitz 17 and le Pen 16. Of 403 valid second ballot votes, Pflimlin won 221, Dankert 133 and Spinelli 49.
24. *Europe*, no. 3899 (26 July 1984).
25. *Europe*, no. 3899, op. cit., pp. 10–11, and *Europe*, no. 3902 (30–31 July 1984) p. 3.
26. *Europe*, no. 3910 (18 Aug. 1984) p. 2. Mr Pisoni (Italy/EPP) sent Mrs Thatcher a letter arguing that the EP was right to block the UK budget rebate as the UK government was preventing the EC from honouring commitments already made to EC farmers, and that CAP surpluses would fall if the UK respected the EC preference. A resolution tabled by the Communist Group, opposing permanent refunds to the UK as contrary to the Treaty, was adopted by 188 votes to 70 votes with 27 abstentions. Another resolution, tabled by the Socialists, stating that long-term budgetary solutions should be based on spending on programmes for combating unemployment, poverty and environmental problems, was passed by 140 votes to 99 votes with eight abstentions. The EP rejected, by 127 votes to 99 votes, Council's request that the EP consider as a matter of urgency the question of the 1984 budget shortfall. Since the Council had still to agree a proposal, it was felt inopportune to give an Opinion.

27. See J. Lodge, 'The European Parliament: in search of institutional change', *The World Today*, 38 (1982) pp. 361–8. As the average age of MEPs has dropped from 54.6 years to 50.5 years and the number of women (who in the previous elected EP proved more hard-working than their male counterparts) has risen slightly from 69 to 75 some hoped for a more vigorous EP. Women had held 20.2% of committee posts but only 16% of EP seats. Their average age in 1979 was 49. More women contested the 1984 election: but few led lists, the exceptions being Frau Focke, Colette Flesch, and three Danes (Hammerich, Boserup and Nielsen).
28. *Europe*, no. 3872 (18–19 June 1984) p. 5.

Bibliographical Note

Apart from the works cited in the notes and references at the end of each chapter, extensive bibliographies on the European Parliament and direct elections can be found in *The European Parliament: Bibliography 1970–1978* (Luxembourg: Directorate-General for Research and Documentation, European Parliament, 1979), *The European Parliament: Bibliography 1981–82* (Luxembourg: Directorate-General for Research and Documentation, European Parliament, 1983), V. Herman and J. Lodge, *The European Parliament and the European Community* (London: Macmillan, 1978), J. Lodge and V. Herman, *Direct Elections to the European Parliament: A Community Perspective* (London: Macmillan, 1982) and J. Lodge (ed.), *The European Community: Bibliographical Excursions* (London: Frances Pinter, 1983), J. Blumler (ed.), *Communicating to Voters* (London: Sage, 1983), G. and P. Pridham, *Transnational Party Cooperation and European Integration* (London: Allen & Unwin, 1981), G. Hand *et al.*, *European Electoral Systems Handbook* (London: Butterworths, 1979), C. Sasse *et al.*, *The European Parliament: Towards a Uniform Procedure for Direct Elections* (Florence: EUI, 1981) and Parlement Européen, *Une Assemblée en pleine evolution* (Luxembourg: Parlement européen, 1983).

Index